The Little Stick Figures for Emotional Self-Healing

"A magical tool! I send billions of thanks to Jacques Martel for creating it. For years, in my training and coaching sessions, with my friends and relatives, I shared the Little Stick Figures Technique. From the dynamic entrepreneur to the overwhelmed mother, from the teenager to the grandfather—everyone has found a light that has helped them. I would need a whole page to list the types of problems that the Little Stick Figures Technique has helped solve—removing conflicts, regaining self-confidence, calming stress, taking a step back to put things into perspective, looking at situations and/or people in a new light, health problems experienced more lightly, and more! Read this book and be positively surprised by the results."

—**Christine Miège,** coach, human resources consultant, and feng shui expert

"This simple, accessible, and fast technique holds an important place in my personal and professional life. When used, I immediately feel the relief of no longer wavering, and I let the 'asking for the best' phrase explained in this book take effect. I feel the conscious and unconscious bonds of attachment being pleasantly released. In my practice, I help therapists clean up and improve their professional activity by practicing these techniques daily and offering them to their own clients/patients."

—**Sarah Bonjour,** hypnotherapist and childhood educator

"A simple, intuitive, powerful technique. I've always drawn a heart with lines of light radiating as my symbol. *The Little Stick Figures Technique for Emotional Self-Healing* teaches us to understand and use visual soul language consciously for healing and transformation."

—**Julia Paulette Hollenbery,** bodyworker, therapist, healer, facilitator, and author of *The Healing Power of Pleasure*

– THE –
Little Stick Figures
TECHNIQUE FOR EMOTIONAL SELF-HEALING

Created by Jacques Martel

Lucie Bernier & Robert Lenghan

Translated by Dan Conley

Findhorn Press
One Park Street
Rochester, Vermont 05767
www.findhornpress.com

Text stock is SFI certified

Findhorn Press is a division of Inner Traditions International

Copyright © 2015 by Lucie Bernier, Robert Lenghan, and Les Éditions ATMA Internationales
English edition copyright © 2016, 2022 by Lucie Bernier and Robert Lenghan

Originally published in French in 2015 by Les Éditions ATMA Internationales, Canada, under the title *Technique des petits bonshommes allumettes*
First English edition published in 2016 by Les Éditions ATMA Internationales, Canada, under the title *The Little Stick Figures Technique*
First U.S. edition published in 2022 by Findhorn Press

All rights reserved. No part of this book may be reproduced or utilized in any form or by any means, electronic or mechanical, including photocopying, recording, or by any information storage and retrieval system, without permission in writing from the publisher.

Disclaimer
The information in this book is given in good faith and intended for information only. Neither author nor publisher can be held liable by any person for any loss or damage whatsoever which may arise from the use of this book or any of the information therein.

Cataloging-in-Publication data for this title is available from the Library of Congress

ISBN 978-1-64411-521-3 (print)
ISBN 978-1-64411-522-0 (ebook)

Printed and bound in the United States by Lake Book Manufacturing, Inc. The text stock is SFI certified. The Sustainable Forestry Initiative® program promotes sustainable forest management.

10 9 8 7 6 5 4 3 2 1

Cover design and illustration by Damian Keenan
Cover photo by leedsn @ www.dreamstime.com
Text design and layout by Josée Boucher
This book was typeset in VAG Rounded and Myriad Pro

To send correspondence to the author of this book, mail a first-class letter to the author c/o Inner Traditions • Bear & Company, One Park Street, Rochester, VT 05767, USA and we will forward the communication, or contact the author directly at **www.atma.ca**.

To all of you
who have the courage to think outside the box,
who have the open-mindedness that guides you to new possibilities,
who agree to trust yourselves and take responsibility for your lives,
who take the opportunity to heal your emotional wounds,
which allows you to experience more Love
and to be a beacon of Light for the people around you
and the world!

Contents

Thanks 9

The Birth of This Book 11

Introduction 13

Notice to Our Readers 15

Chapter 1   Interview With **Jacques Martel**, the *Technique's* Creator 17

Chapter 2   General Information Prior to Using the *Technique* 23

Chapter 3   Application of the 7 Steps of the *Technique* 35

Chapter 4   An Exercise to Detach Myself from a Person 47

Chapter 5   An Exercise to Detach Myself from a Situation 55

Chapter 6   An Exercise to Detach Myself from a Part of Myself... 61

Chapter 7   General Questions on How to Properly Apply the *Technique* 71

Chapter 8   After Applying the *Technique*: Some Issues concerning the Results Obtained........ 93

Chapter 9   The *Technique's* Many Applications and Some Questions from the Public 107

Chapter 10   A General Cleansing and Rebalancing Protocol 163

Conclusion 165

Testimonials 167

About the Co-authors 177

About Jacques Martel, the Creator of This *Technique* 179

Chapter Overview – Technique, Questions, and Applications 181

Thanks

Our thanks go to Mr. Jacques Martel, the creator of this *technique*, for his collaboration in answering all our questions throughout our research and his generosity in permitting us to widely share this priceless information to help in the well-being of the greatest possible number of persons in the world.

Our thanks also go to Mr. Denis Tremblay, Production Manager at **Éditions ATMA Internationales**, for his participation in the visual production and the copyright protection application process for this book and this *technique*.

We also wish to thank the many persons, therapists, health professionals, collaborators, several of our clients and the general public who wrote to us and shared their comments, their observations and their questions after using this *technique*. All of that precious information has made it possible to produce this book, which is intended to be a complete reference document.

Lucie Bernier and *Robert Lenghan*

The Birth of This Book

Every manuscript has its history. This one began in Québec, Canada, on a morning of April 2015 at 5:55 a.m. I suddenly woke up and received the message that the **Little Stick Figures** must become known world-wide. I immediately took a pencil and paper and began to write automatically what I was receiving as prime information about the broad outlines of this *technique*, which had been explained by Mr. Jacques Martel in two videos, already viewed by more than 500 000 persons on the Internet.

This *technique* was created in 1993 by Mr. Martel who is also the author of the best-seller **The Complete Dictionary of Ailments and Diseases**, read by more than TWO MILLION readers; a book that was produced with the collaboration of Ms. Lucie Bernier.

The message received was very clear: this *technique* must also become the subject of a book in paper version. Immediately, the scenario of the book took form, the subjects, the table of contents and the broad outlines of the messages to be conveyed to the general public in a simple and widely accessible form. The purpose of this reference book is to help the greatest possible number of persons.

The next morning around the same time, I woke up suddenly again, and this time, it was the content of the cover page that stood out more clearly, with the picture of the person best suited to collaborate as the co-author in writing this book, namely Ms. Lucie Bernier.

That is how this book came to be!

Robert Lenghan
Consultant in Change Management
and Human Resources
Québec, Canada

Introduction

A great number of people are seeking the means to improve their everyday lives. In fact, I (which means "each one of us") experience situations in my everyday life that are sometimes conflicted or in disharmony. Of course, there are many professionals who can help me (therapists, psychologists, social workers, physicians, etc.),[1] but what about those actions I can do myself at home, at work or elsewhere and that will really help me? This is where the **Little Stick Figures Technique**© comes into play.

This *technique*, which takes only a few minutes to do, enables me to free myself from my dependencies, my fears and my **conscious** or unconscious attachments. It enables me to have more detachment toward a person or a situation and to develop more unconditional **love**.

Using it on a regular basis enables me to effect positive changes in my life. These changes result from my decision and my intention to change and from the fact **that I spell out this intention in writing. In this way I act on my conscious as well as on my subconscious**. It thus becomes a powerful tool for transformation.

By showing my openness when I do the exercise, I set off a whole process where my energy level is raised, where I manifest a raising of **consciousness** and make room for changes. A little like when the wind blows on clouds and they dissipate and make room for the blue sky and the sun that can better show the **light** through its rays. The sun was shining before, but was hidden by the clouds that represent my fears, my doubts, my insecurities, my dependencies, my attachments, my judgments about myself and others.

The *technique* allows me to initiate the inner "wind of change." The more detached I am and confident in the results, the more capable I am of accurately identifying those results (changes) in my Life. There

---

[1] The *technique* offered in this book cannot replace the necessary help from a health professional (medical or psychological). It is a complement to any other form of traditional or holistic medicine.

follows a lightness, a well-being that is sometimes difficult to account for with my mind. I thus reclaim full power over my life!

What is wonderful is that, even if I don't consciously know exactly what I need to work on or integrate in relation to another person, it works! Because of my intention, which is to change, and the "letting go" that I am ready to accept↓♥ regarding the person or situation and the results, I assert, I materialize, I crystallize my intention in practical reality. And by using the *technique*, I send an order to my subconscious and it will then work for me so as to bring positive changes into my life.

This is similar to the artist concretely painting on his canvas the image in his imagination that he wants to express materially. By keeping the open attitude that **"I want what is best for myself and for the other person"**, great things can be achieved.

If I have a closed mind and too great a desire to direct or control the results, there may <u>seem</u> to be less results. I then need to work on my attitude, on my attachments to the results and ask myself questions about my real intentions, such as: why I have attracted this situation into my life. This *technique* therefore enables me to work on myself and becomes a tool for self-knowledge and personal development.

I wish you, then, enjoyable reading, good practice and great discoveries!

Lucie Bernier
Lecturer, Therapist
New Brunswick, Canada

Notice to Our Readers

The examples used to demonstrate the *technique* (also called the *method* or the *exercise*) will mostly involve the first and family names of the two authors and are used for illustrative purposes only. The examples with the figures occasionally portray a woman or a man. There is no discrimination or preference in the gender choices of the figures when they both apply in any given example.

The **"I"** is used throughout this book to enhance the direct understanding of the text (without resorting to the customary "you"). **"I"** here simply means each one of us.

The *technique* presented in this book in no way replaces any needed help from a health professional (medical or psychological). It is a complement to any medical profession, whether traditional, holistic or other.

↓♥ This symbol, which appears in the text after the word "accept", represents the energy associated with a mental image or an emotion related to a situation that I move from my head toward my heart♥. This then leads to a healing in **love** or to the reinforcing of a positive attitude.

The content of this book is authorized and approved by the creator of **The Little Stick Figures Technique**©2003,[2] Mr. Jacques Martel. All the rights are reserved. The rights to use it for personal purposes are authorized. However, all the reproduction rights of this book by any means whatsoever are strictly forbidden without a written and signed authorization by the authors. Any commercialization of the book is forbidden without an agreement duly approved and signed by the authors and the publisher of the original edition, **Les Éditions ATMA Internationales**.

---

[2] Trademark 2005 ATMA Inc.; Legal deposit ISBN: 2-9805800-9-0; Commissioner for Oaths: Gaétane Pichette 109536

Any copy, change, modification or falsification of the product in whole or in part with the intent to commercialize the product will be considered to be a serious offence concerning the protection of the authors' intellectual rights and will be actionable for damages.

CHAPTER 1

Interview with Jacques Martel, the *Technique's* Creator

The origin of this *technique*

The story of the **Little Stick Figures Technique**© began in the 1970s. At that time, I was a smoker. Beginning in January 1976, I started to become spiritually engaged and to do contemplation exercises, which among other effects resulted in elevating my vibratory level. In July 1976, I still felt like smoking, but when I did smoke a cigarette, I became nauseated. This led me to eventually stop smoking altogether.

I became **aware** of the fact that this taste for smoking would come to me mainly when I went to see one of my aunts who was also a smoker. Even if she didn't always smoke in my presence, I felt like smoking when I was with her. I therefore understood that I was attuned to her energies as a smoker and that this was affecting me.

Then I tried something new: I traced out a *circle of light* around myself and when I was shaping this *circle of light*, the urge to smoke would stop completely. I therefore concluded that the fact of surrounding myself with a *circle of light* protected me.

Later on, when I met other persons, I would sometimes imagine a *circle of light* around me and also imagine this *circle of light* around the other person. And I would further imagine a *circle of light* around both of us. That meant:

1. I want what is best for me;

2. I want what is best for the other person;

3. I want what is best for both of us.

At that time, I was only doing the exercise at the level of visualization and energy. Then I got the idea of transposing it onto paper. I began to draw **little stick figures** by drawing a *circle of light* around myself, around another person and around the situation. Besides, in the first French edition of the book **ATMA, the Power of Love**, an example is given of a young man who had to go to court with his ex-girlfriend who was suing him. The drawing began with the young man, Bernard, surrounded by a *circle of light*, his lawyer surrounded by a *circle of light*, his ex-girlfriend surrounded by a *circle of light*, the lawyer of his ex-girlfriend surrounded by a *circle of light*, the judge surrounded by a *circle of light*, and all those five persons together were also surrounded by a *circle of light*. I feel like saying that this was the first version of the *Little Stick Figures Technique*, which gave very good results.

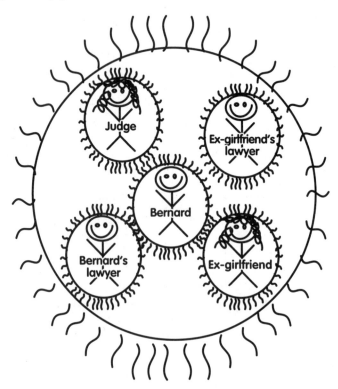

Later on, I changed the *technique* and, instead of doing it with several persons at once, I did it with only two persons, myself and another person, but adding onto it the links of **conscious** and unconscious attachment. These were the lines linking each of my own and the other person's 7 energy centers. It was from that point on that I developed this second part of the **Little Stick Figures Technique** that now makes up the 7 steps to follow in order to apply the *technique* effectively.

The functioning of the *technique* and its results

What often occurs, in fact, is that this *technique* works for some people at the subconscious level. For instance, if I don't like criticism or if I have the impression that someone is always criticizing me, I send information to others to the effect that: *"Show me that I'm right in thinking that it's not OK for me to be criticized."* Then the other person, again at the subconscious level, gets the message: *"Yes Jacques, you know how much I **love** you, I'm going to prove to you that you are right in thinking that it's not OK to be criticized... I will criticize you as much as possible."*

Therefore, when I do the **Little Stick Figures Technique**, I stop sending this information to the other person and often, the other person will change, **not because I have acted to influence her, but because the information she receives from me has changed**. Now, I no longer send this information, and so the person will change automatically. Roughly, that is how the *technique* works.

I experimented with the *technique* in my own life and it worked remarkably well. One day in June 2014, I drew the *Little Stick Figures* with some people around me in relation to a schema[3] I had been experiencing in my life over several decades. Thanks to this *technique* that I used with each of the persons involved, I was able to free myself from this schema, or pattern, that had tormented me for over 30 years!

During the last years when I gave personal development workshops, I had made a habit of making the workshop participants draw some *Little Stick Figures*. Each participant did the exercise involving themselves with me as the workshop leader. Often, the workshop leader is perceived in

---

3   **Schema**: A patterning process whereby a similar situation reproduces itself repetitively.

a workshop session as the savior who will "fix everything and answer all our questions."

There thus often exists much attachment and dependency in the participants toward the workshop leader, consciously or not. And so occasionally, when the participants were doing this exercise at the beginning of the workshop, some of them would become nauseous, felt like vomiting or became a little dizzy. All this denoted the attachment, sometimes unconscious, that they felt toward the workshop leader. It was therefore important that they detach themselves from the workshop leader and thus allow him to be freer to give the workshop in his own way.

This exercise of the *Little Stick Figures* has been very successful so far. In early 2015, we noted, on the various Internet platforms, that more than 500 000 persons had viewed both of the videos I produced that clearly explain this *technique*. This means that thousands of other persons have also experienced this exercise. We often receive comments to the effect that in the minutes following the exercise, some people get results because the subconscious registers 90% of what they write and of what they visualize. **It is therefore important to do it in writing so that our subconscious will register the information.** All this derives from the fact that, as we say, **for the subconscious everything is possible**, then what makes this *technique* effective is that it acts **automatically** at the level of the subconscious.

That is the secret of this *technique*!

The choice of authors for this book

I accepted↓♥ that Ms. *Lucie Bernier* and Mr. *Robert Lenghan* should write this book about the *technique*, because they are persons who have my trust and have themselves experienced the *technique* for several years. The book will greatly respond to the public's needs. They are people who have known me for years and who also work with this tool. Ms. Lucie Bernier has also been a close collaborator for many years. I am confident that the results of this book will prove beneficial for all those who will read it and apply its content in their own lives.

The book on the **Little Stick Figures Technique** will make it possible to answer many more questions than what is mentioned either in the two videos on the Internet explaining the *technique* or in the book **ATMA, the Power of Love** in which the *technique* is also explained in general terms.

For a few years now, questions have been e-mailed to us concerning the *technique*, which will be answered here. This book contains answers to most, if not all, of the questions that people have addressed to us. Furthermore, there are more explanations about the best conditions under which the exercise should be done for it to be most effective, and further possibilities for using it than those mentioned in the **Little Stick Figures Technique** videos or in the book **ATMA, the Power of Love**.

Legal protection of the *technique*

We already have a registered copyright on **The Little Stick Figures Technique**©,[4] in order to guarantee that there will be no changes in the *technique* or in the way it could be shown to other people. Indeed, if any changes were made to it and it were not applied properly, this could diminish its effectiveness; and afterward, some people might claim that *"Jacques Martel's* **Little Stick Figures Technique** *doesn't work very well."*

Readers may show the *technique* to those around them, friends or family. However, **it is very important to follow the 7 steps in their proper order** as the exercise has been demonstrated. One must always keep the exercise as simple as possible, at first, and avoid making personal additions to it as some people do, such as drawing the attachment links with the colors of the energy centers, doing the exercise for 21 days, adding other items of information in the ball of **light**, etc. Although some elements might be interesting, it could lead a person to assume certain CONDITIONS that are not, in fact, necessary.

---

[4] All rights are reserved (see page 15).

The book ***The Little Stick Figures Technique for Emotional Self-Healing*** was designed to answer the questions we have received on this subject in recent years, so it would be preferable that the greatest possible number of concerned people buy this book, because it was written precisely to answer just about all of the questions asked by the people who did not have the book in order to do the exercise and make it as highly effective as possible.

CHAPTER 2

General Information Prior to Using the *Technique*

Who can use the *technique*?

This *technique* was designed to be both **effective** and **simple** to apply. It reminds us of children's drawings. Which assumes that they are drawn simply, from the heart♥, without using the mind. That is how it can be used by everyone, whatever a person's age.[5] The words *"stick figures"* are used because the arms, the legs and the body are drawn with straight lines, as if I were using matchsticks.

Under what circumstances can I use the *technique*?

This *technique* can be used in any situation

A situation perceived as negative: A situation where I'm experiencing some discomfort, a conflict, a disappointment, an unresolved issue, a frustration, etc. In short, any situation where I want to develop more harmony and well-being.

A positive situation: Though I am happy in my couple's relationship, in my family, at work, etc., there is always some room for improvement. I may also be experiencing attachment and dependency with the people I **love** and the fact of doing the exercise will improve the relationship, by

---

5   See pages 83 and 85 to learn from what age one can do the *technique* and how to show it to a child.

increasing my detachment from this person and helping me to tune in to **love** rather than to my fears and my dependencies.

The 5 essential rules for using the *technique* effectively

There exist 5 rules that must be strictly followed for using the *technique* and getting the best results. All the rest is secondary. These 5 rules are:

1. I want WHAT IS BEST FOR ME AND FOR THE OTHER PERSON. (Attitude and intention)
2. Apply the *technique* GRAPHICALLY ON PAPER.
3. Do the 7 STEPS IN THE SAME SEQUENCE shown in this book.
4. I ALWAYS DRAW MYSELF FIRST, and then another person or a situation. I never do the *technique* "just for two other persons" without first including myself.
5. Make sure, when drawing the lines of attachment and dependency, THAT ALL 7 OF THEM ARE THERE.

There will be reminders of these 5 very important rules throughout this book. They are essential for obtaining maximum results and making sure that I have the right attitude while doing the exercise. Each rule will be presented in detail.

Preparation (state of mind and attitude) before doing the *technique*

As mentioned above, I want what is best, I have no special intentions. It is as though I were leaving to my subconscious and to the divine energy the power to decide what is the best that will happen for myself and for others.

It is not necessary to prepare myself in any special way before doing the exercise, but some persons do like to perform the exercise as in a ritual, by preceding it with a meditation or deep breathing in order to feel more present, focused and attuned during the exercise. When I make it a habit of doing the exercise regularly, I can develop my own ritual (mantra, prayer, meditation, incense, special music, etc.). All this is good, but not necessary for the method to work.

> **I must avoid adding any further conditions for using the *technique* other than the 5 rules mentioned on the previous page.**

Why always draw myself first, and only then another person or a situation?

If I am tempted to do the exercise for two other persons without first including myself in the exercise, in their place, out of their presence and without their permission, it is because I feel a great impulse to control these persons and the situations they are experiencing. Though my intention may seem good, I have no right to interfere in their lives. I must always be part of the exercise and must ALWAYS draw myself first, as in Figure #1.

Suppose, for instance, that I am concerned about the relationship of my daughter **Mary Bernier** with her spouse **Peter Brown**; I **cannot** do:

I must instead do the **Little Stick Figures** in the following way:

A first drawing with me and Mary Bernier:

ME (name and surname)   **Mary Bernier**

A second drawing with me and Peter Brown:

ME (name and surname)   **Peter Brown**

Then, the issue of whatever in going on between Mary and Peter is none of my business, because it concerns their life experiences and belongs only to them. However, through the exercise, I will have greatly succeeded in no longer projecting my own fears onto their relationship as a couple and will have thereby given them better chances at resolving a situation or at least becoming more **aware** of it.

> **It is forbidden for me to do the exercise
> "for two other persons",
> without first including myself.
> I also have no right to interfere in other people's lives
> without their permission.
> That is called "white magic",
> and there is a price to pay when I do that.**

White magic is a set of techniques, often ritualized, that enable the practitioner to produce phenomena intended to influence a person's destiny or behavior. However "noble" my intentions, I have no right to interfere in people's lives without their permission, because there is always a price to pay[6] when I want to interfere in the lives of others. The same holds of course for black magic, which, in its case, is motivated by a taste for vengeance and where I desire to create negative effects on others or on their situations. Each of us has experiences to live through, and if I want to control what is happening in the lives of others, I am ATTACHED to those persons, an attachment that implies one or several fears about what they are experiencing. Rather, I must accept↓♥ in my heart♥ what is happening and remain open to the life lessons I can derive from it.

It is important to develop wisdom and to be non-judgmental toward other persons. By remaining open to what is happening, even if I don't understand it and may feel saddened by what is happening for them, I can learn some life lessons from these situations that others are experiencing without having to experience those same things myself. This does not mean to be insensitive or to not care: it means to remain open, neutral and to not judge what is happening. The **Little Stick Figures** exercise will help me do this!

---

6   For example, if I want to control others, I will attract events where other people will control me in return.

> **There exists a spiritual law that states that:
> I attract, I become or I project
> what I have not accepted↓♥.**

In other words, whenever I aim a judgment, whether at a person or at a situation, sooner or later I will be forced to experience the same thing so that I can become **aware** of the fact that all situations happen so that we can become **aware** of something. That's it, period! It is neither good nor bad, it is just an experience. And the more detached I am, therefore with no fear and no judgement, the more I live in openness and unconditional **love**, which is essential for true **freedom**!

What happens if I do the exercise for a negative purpose?

The intention with which I do the *technique* and the goal pursued are very important. If I use it to do harm, if I want to influence the results of a vote for example, if I want to "play God" and direct or control other persons or situations, the law of cause and effect or of return will apply. And it does not apply only here with this *technique*, it is a spiritual law that applies to everything in life.

> **The only power I have is over myself
> and on no one else.**

If my attitude is negative, chances are that the expected results will not materialize, and it is the opposite that will probably occur. But if I am acting in good faith and truly want what is best for both of us, **"I cannot be wrong"**, and so positively, only good can ensue!

> It is better to do something
> with a good attitude
> than to do nothing at all!

Are there any contra-indications (risks) in using this method?

I would say **YES**, and this concerns strictly the **attitude** and the **purpose** with which I want to do the exercise we have just mentioned above. Sometimes, I want to control events or persons out of fear or misunderstanding. I must clearly understand that when I do this exercise, it is important that my attitude be: **I want what is best for me and for the other (or the others) according to our development**: that is what the 3 circles of **light** mean.

> I want what is best for me
> (even if I don't know what that is)
> I want what is best for the other person
> (even if I don't know what that is)
> I want what is best for both of us
> (even if I don't know what that is)

Indeed, what is best for me may be different from what I want personally. For instance, if I do the **Little Stick Figures** with a person I find attractive and with whom I would wish to develop a relationship, even my doing the exercise does not guarantee that someday we will be in a relationship together. But it does guarantee that I am making a request to the universe (Life) in a detached manner and am freeing myself from the **conscious** or unconscious attachments I have toward this person. Because if I "absolutely" want to be in a relationship as a couple with this person, it is as though I were saying: *"This person is the only one who can make me happy…"* which is untrue. I may fear that if the person says "No" to me, I will "lose" something or "miss" something. What

I don't know is that right next to my home, there may be another person who would be even better suited to me, and me to her, and whom I've still never met! And if getting closer to this person is beneficial for my development, the *technique* will help "that" to show up!

Therefore, if I want to control someone else, life will send me situations where I will be controlled and where I will lose control. This is just the law of karma[7] in action! And it operates not only when using this *technique*, but in each thought and action every day!

There is an actual case where a person promised a good friend of hers that if she did the *technique* with a friend, their friendship would be transformed into **love**… **FALSE!!!!!** First of all, no specific result can be guaranteed with this *technique*, because it would mean wanting to control the results, which is attachment and not **love**. Second, it is not a magic wand where "I just have to do the exercise and all my wishes are granted, good or bad!" **NO!!!!!** It is not the person doing the exercise who decides with their ego what is going to happen, but the divine energy, the higher self or whatever name I give to the higher power.

The attachment and the dependency that I have toward a person control me in my everyday life and guide me toward false solutions. My attachment and dependency distort my judgment without my knowing it and to my detriment. They handcuff me in my relations with people, especially with my life partner and the members of my family. I would be surprised to know the number of persons who are in a relationship as a couple because of the attachment and dependency they have with one another and not because of the true and free **love** they have for each other. That is why sometimes, certain persons have wanted to use the *technique* for the purpose of approaching another person, and the opposite is what happened. Why? Because by cutting off their previous attachment and dependency, there was nothing left to hold them together! There was not enough **love** between them both for them to be able to stay together in a way that was beneficial for both of them! <u>The fact of separating was what was best for the two persons and their development!</u>

---

7   **The law of karma**: A spiritual law that states that for each of my actions or thoughts (positive or negative), an action or a thought of the same order will return to me. This law is also called the *law of cause and effect*. This law applies to everyone, whether or not I am aware of it.

People often remain in toxic relationships because of these two elements that are attachment and dependency, but are unaware of them.

> **When I take the positive attitude of:**
> ***I want what is best for myself and for the other person,***
> **I am always guided and protected,**
> **and so is the other person.**

It is important to have trust in the exercise and in a force that acts beyond my personal will.

Why is it necessary to do the *technique* with pencil on paper?

Why physically draw on a piece of paper rather than simply visualize the figures in my head? Because:

> **My subconscious recalls 90%**
> **of what I visualize AND especially of what I WRITE.**

When I write, my thoughts transform themselves into something tangible and my request becomes clearer. I apply all my attention to what I am doing, I am in an active process of transformation. I can observe how I feel, if I have any resistances to doing the exercise, any discomfort when I cut away the links of my attachments, etc. I use all my senses, which makes it a far more powerful process.

If I need to fill my car's gas tank, can I just imagine filling it up in my head, or is it better to physically go to the gas station with my car and fill it up? Which method will give me the best results?

From experience, I have noted that whenever I decided to do the exercise "in my head," it was because I unconsciously wanted to escape from something. It was as if I knew that the exercise could be beneficial for me, but there was something I didn't want to let go of, in relation to the person or the situation involved. Attachment sometimes makes me "leech onto" persons, things or ideas, and I may want to remain in my familiar comfort zone. That is why I must do the exercise with my heart♥ open and not just with my head, because I risk wanting to control the results. I may even create a situation where the exercise will produce no apparent result, to my great satisfaction (though I won't admit it!!!).

It is all the more important to do the exercise in writing when I am doing it for the very first time. Although this *technique* is very simple, I have seen several persons doing it for themselves or showing it to other people in their own personal way or incompletely.

**It is critically important to follow the 7 steps
in the same sequence
to ensure maximum results.**

For I am working at the level of the subconscious.

**Because the brain does not tell the difference
between what is real, imaginary, virtual or symbolic,
it then takes the information as real
and makes the modifications accordingly.**

Therefore, if I send the right command to my subconscious, chances are that I will receive a better result! Exactly as the fact of finding the right radio frequency to get a clear broadcast from a specific program network.

By applying the *technique* with the 7 steps and following the 5 rules for success, I can see the results coming out in the following seconds and from ocean to ocean. Time and distance are not important, because it takes place at the subconscious level. It's as though our brains, in fact the approximately 7 billion persons that we are on Planet Earth, were interconnected. Somewhat like a radio set, we connect more especially with one or several other persons during the exercise. I resonate and amplify the radio frequency of what unites us. And I entrust to my subconscious the task of doing the necessary work to cut away the links of attachment and dependency that link us.

Once I have practiced the *technique* 10, 15 or 20 times, my mind will reliably register the steps and I will be able to do it without having to check them in the book every time. I can always refer to page 53, which gives a good visual summary of the 7 steps.

An exception: Doing the exercise in my head

I once went for an appointment with a person and, just before arriving at my place of destination, I felt the urge to do the exercise. Having neither paper nor pencil, I decided to do the exercise in my head with myself and the person I was about to meet. **And I decided that it would work!** Having already experienced it on paper, I clearly recalled the steps to follow. The interview went quite well.

I therefore first imagined myself, and then the person I was going to meet in front of me. I first put myself in a *circle of light* and then the other person too. Finally, I put a *circle of light* around both of us.

It is better to do something than to do nothing at all! But that should not become an excuse for not doing the exercise on a piece of paper with the 7 steps when conditions allow it. **Indeed, the exercise is most effective when performed on paper.**

What materials do I need to do the exercise?

1. A piece of white paper or parchment paper.

    It is important that the piece of paper be white, not lined or graph paper.[8] If I want to use colored paper, I should use a clear, pale color.

2. Preferably a lead pencil.[9] A ballpoint pen can also be used. Some persons like to use colored pencils to draw the 7 lines of attachment with the color matched to each energy center,[10] but that is <u>optional</u>.

3. A pair of scissors. If I don't have one, I will tear the page apart with my hands.

That is all! This is what shows the simplicity and the power of this exercise.

> **Almost all the work is done by my subconscious, because it is symbolic work.**
> **I just need to allow my brain**
> **and my emotions to do their job.**
> **My subconscious is working in my service!**

---

[8] The fact of having a blank page enables my subconscious to have a clear and well-defined image of what I want. Lined or graph paper only overloads the subconscious and confuses the drawing.

[9] Charcoal, another noble material, may also be used.

[10] See page 69 for the explanation.

CHAPTER 3

Application of the 7 Steps of the *Technique*

How to identify the situation and each of the figures: #1 (on the left) and #2 (on the right)

I must choose a situation where I may experience frustration, sorrow or anger for example, or other emotions experienced as negative toward a person. A situation with something wrong, that is unsatisfactory, that I would like to see improving or being positively different. **It is absolutely essential that I be involved in the situation.** Therefore, **I must always draw myself first**, and then add another person (or a situation)[11].

For instance, if I want to improve my relationship with my spouse, I will draw:

<u>Me</u> with my spouse:

Lucy Bernier

Larry Ricker

---

11 See page 55 for explanations of the exercise with myself and a situation instead of a person.

For example, if I want to improve my relationship with my father, I will draw:

Me with my father:

Lucy Bernier

Fern Bernier

For example, if I want to improve my relationship with my boss:

Me with my boss:

Lucy Bernier

Robert Lenghan

For example, if I want to sell my house:

Me with the sale of my house:

Lucy Bernier

Identify the address, the asking price, the desired moving date

Application of the 7 Steps of the Technique

For example, I want to detach myself from my pet animal who is sick:

Me with my sick pet:

Lucy Bernier

Snowy[12]

For example, if I want to harmonize a facet of my personality:

Me with a facet of my personality:

**Lucy Bernier
Filled with joy**

**Lucy Bernier
Filled with sadness**

Me and a special situation:

Lucy Bernier

My retirement

---

12 See the detailed explanation of the *technique* with an animal on page 157.

Me and a thought:

Lucy Bernier
Abundance

Lucy Bernier
Poverty

Me and a material object:

Lucy Bernier

Finding my keys

Etc....

I always first draw myself on the left side
and then another person or a situation on the right.

For example, if my two children, Monica and Victor Bernier, are always in conflict, I must not do the exercise with Monica and Victor without first including myself.

I have <u>no right</u> to interfere in their lives, even if I love them very much.

It is as though I were wanting to control their lives, which amounts to attachment, dependency, control and expectations. I could, however, do the following two exercises, one after the other:

Lucy Bernier

Monica Bernier
(1st child)

Lucy Bernier

Victor Bernier
(2nd child)

Similarly, if I have grand-children and I see a situation affecting them and their mother (my daughter), I **cannot** do the exercise with my daughter on the left and my grand-children on the right. Rather, I should draw:

Me on the left and my daughter on the right
and then
Me on the left and one of my grand-children on the right.[13]

In the next two chapters, many examples will explain to me how to choose the two elements that will be drawn (figure #1 on the left and figure #2 on the right).

---

13   I can do the 7 steps of the *technique* with each one of the grand-children concerned.

Step-by-step explanations of the *Little Stick Figures Technique*

Here are the 7 steps of this **Little Stick Figures Technique**. <u>**They must always be done in the sequence presented here.**</u>

The first 5 steps consist in positioning the 2 figures and the situation in a circle of **light**.

The last 2 steps consist in cutting the **conscious** and unconscious links of dependency or attachment.

Here is a reminder of the 5 rules to follow with the *technique*:

1. I want <u>what is best for myself and for the other person</u> (attitude and intention).
2. Perform the *technique* <u>in writing</u>.
3. Perform the 7 steps <u>in the same sequence</u> shown in this book.
4. I always draw <u>myself</u> first, with another person or a situation. Never do it "just for two other persons."
5. Make sure that there are 7 links of attachment and dependency between the energy centers of the figure on the left and those of the figure on the right (or the rectangle).

Application of the 7 Steps of the Technique

Step 1

I first draw <u>myself</u> and write my name and family name under the drawn figure.

Robert Lenghan

First of all, **I must always begin by drawing a figure that represents me**. I then write my first name and my family name under the figure, as shown in the illustration above.

If I am a woman, I can use my married name or my original family name.[14]

Step 2

I draw the figure of the <u>other</u> person and then write down his or her first name and family name under the figure.

Robert Lenghan   *Lucy Bernier*

Later on, I draw the figure of the person with whom I want to see things improving. For example, if the person's name is Lucy Bernier, I write "Lucy Bernier" under the drawn figure (the person's first name and family name).

---

14   In the 2 videos by Jacques Martel, which can be found on the internet on the site ***www.atma.ca*** and that show the *technique*, it is said that I write down the first name and the initial of the family name, but it is preferable to write down the entire family name.

Step 3

I put a *circle of light* around <u>me</u> by drawing **light** rays all around.

The **light** rays around me show that this ball of **light** is really luminous and radiates **light**. This also means that *I want what is best for myself*, even if I don't know what that is.

Step 4

I draw a *circle of light* around the <u>other</u> person.

The rays all around the other person show that this *ball of light* is really luminous and radiates **light**. This also means that *I want what is best for the other person*, even if I don't know what that is.

Step 5

I put a *circle of light* around the 2 persons by drawing the rays of **light**.

This symbolizes that "the whole situation" is put into the **light**. This also means that *I want what is best for both of us*, even if I don't know what that is.

We have now completed 5 of the 7 steps. Now we must understand this drawing. The first figure symbolizes that I am putting myself in the **light** to ensure that I will be as enlightened as possible spiritually and objectively.

Similarly, I make sure that the other person will be as spiritually enlightened as possible and more objective. Lastly, the situation is put into the **light** so that the two persons involved will experience **what is best for them** spiritually.

An exercise for detachment

What are *attachment & dependency* and why free myself from them?

The notion of *dependency* indicates a relationship in which at least one of the parties cannot exist or flourish without the other or the others. As a result, I thus give up a part of my **freedom**. Because if I experience dependency, I don't have my complete autonomy, and <u>consciously or not, I am subjugated by another person</u>.

Attachment grows from a lack of something. It mainly originates from the wounds I have inside of me, from my conscious or unconscious desires or fears. It also takes place when I am afraid of losing someone or something. Instead of being detached and loving the person with **unconditional love**, I need to exert some *control*, conscious or unconscious, over that person. Attachment and dependency often become very invasive without my being aware of it and they influence my actions and my decisions to the detriment of my well-being and my integrity.

This results in conflicts with myself or with others, because I resist the necessity for letting go and letting live, because I am afraid. It implies a lack of self-confidence and trust in the other person. Because attachment relies on a false premise, and so my *tie* to the other person distorts both the reality and the truth.

But what, then, am I afraid of?

There are 6 basic fears[15] that are at the source of all the other fears.

---

15   According to the author **Napoleon Hill** in his book ***The Laws of Success.***

Those fears are:

1. **The fear of death**
2. **The fear of poverty**
3. **The fear of receiving criticism**
4. **The fear of sickness**
5. **The fear of aging**
6. **The fear of losing someone's love**

If none of those fears were present in my life, I would experience an **unconditional love** for all the people around me and I would therefore have no **attachment** and no **dependency**. The result would be a life **without expectations** and I would be totally satisfied with all the aspects of my life and my being.

As I am human and have had all sorts of experiences that sometimes left some emotional wounds, as a result I develop protective or defence mechanisms to protect myself from being wounded again, and attachment is one of them.

Attachment, for an adult, is not true **love**. It leads me to consciously or unconsciously want to control, which curtails my **freedom** and that of others. Even if I am acting in good faith. With attachment, it's as though I were saying: *"I absolutely need you for my survival and my feeling of security."* A little like when I was a child and experiencing this attachment to my mother and my father. It is as though I believed that by being an adult, I should always experience this attachment.

If I am true to myself and look at the conflicted situations in my life, I realize that what the other person should be providing me with is actually what I should be creating for myself. If I accuse my spouse of not communicating, I must ask myself: *"Just how much am I communicating my own needs to others?"*

That is why if I do this exercise of the **Little Stick Figures** and then consciously decide to cut away, and free myself from, the links of attachment and dependency that tie me to others, the result will be a greater sense of **freedom** from the person in question, but also in my life more generally. Chances are that the person portrayed in the exercise feels likewise. It will also result in greater Wisdom in the way I am with myself and others. **Love** and **light** will manifest themselves more. Indeed, by letting go and having no expectations nor control over others, I can remain with an open heart♥, by wishing the best for everyone. More **love** opens the door to individual and collective flourishing.

CHAPTER 4

An Exercise to Detach Myself from a Person

The purpose of the following exercise is to enable me to have more detachment toward a person or a situation. I recall that in a certain sense, **attachment and dependency are not true love**. Whereas **love** is also wisdom and **freedom**, attachment places me instead in the position of wanting, consciously or unconsciously, to control someone else or a situation, thus preventing the divine energy from flowing freely for the greatest benefit to myself and to others.

To simplify, let us say that attachment originates from one of the **6 basic fears** mentioned on page 45. The **conscious or unconscious** attachment that exists between two persons can be found at the level of each energy center, each of which corresponds to a state of **consciousness**, of **awareness**.

I have within me 7 main energy centers, also called chakras.[16] They are located as follows, counting from bottom to top:

---

16 **Chakra**: A Sanskrit term meaning "wheel." It refers to the energy centers making up my **consciousness**, my physical body and my energy system. They correspond to my body's main neural plexi.

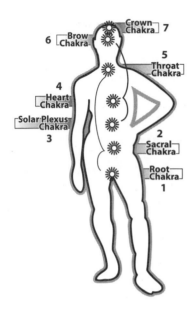

7. Above the head, called the coronal center

6. At the root of the nose between the eyebrows, called the frontal center or "third eye"

5. At the throat, called the laryngeal center

4. At the heart♥ in the middle of the thoracic cage, called the cardiac center

3. At the solar plexus, just below the sternum, called the solar center

2. At a few centimetres below the navel, called the sacral center

1. At the level of the coccyx at the base of the spine, called the coccygeal center

Each of these 7 energy centers is linked to an endocrine gland, each of which has the effect of regulating the functioning of the organs and systems in my body.

Each of these 7 energy centers also corresponds to a level of **consciousness**, namely, and in the same order:

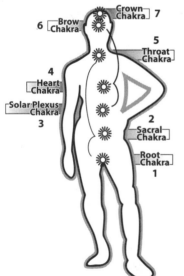

7. The divine wisdom, intuition

6. The intellect

5. Communication, self-assertion

4. **Love**

3. The emotions

2. Creativity in matter, sexuality

1. The basic needs in terms of lodging, food or basic emotional needs such as a mother's **love** for her child.

An Exercise to Detach Myself from a Person

I can experience a **conscious or unconscious** attachment with respect to any of these aspects with the persons and situations in my environment. The purpose of the following exercise is to free myself from my attachment to certain persons or situations in order to make more room for **love**.

Step 6

I draw the **conscious** or unconscious links of attachment connecting the 7 energy centers[17] of both persons.

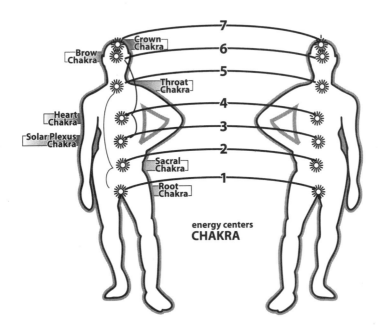

energy centers
CHAKRA

Each link represents the **conscious or unconscious** attachment that exists between the two persons at the level of each energy center, each of which corresponds to a state of **consciousness**.

---

17   These **7 energy centers** are located in the following places: 1.- At the level of the coccyx at the base of my spine; 2.-My 2nd center is located between my navel and my pubis; 3.- My solar plexus is at the base of my sternum; 4.- My cardiac center is located at the level of my heart♥; 5.- At the level of my throat; 6.- At the level of my 3rd eye, at the root of the nose, between the eyebrows; 7.- Right on top of my head.

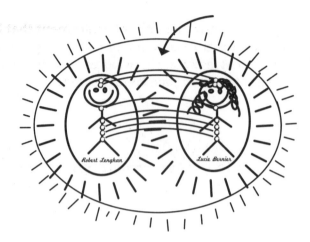

So I draw myself and another person as I did in the previous illustration. I then draw **the links of attachment that I consciously or unconsciously maintain between me and the other person**, which connects each of my energy centers to the other person's.

I don't need to know the percentage (%) of attachment I may have at any level with the other person. The work is done in any case.

Step 7

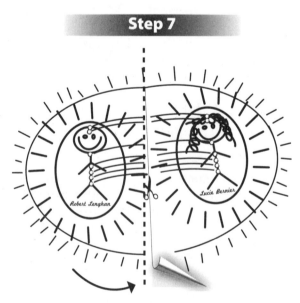

I <u>cut away</u> the conscious or unconscious links of attachment between the 2 persons. I say: **"Thanks. It's done!"**

Again, **these lines represent the links of attachment that I have or might have with the other person**. Once these links are drawn, I take a pair of scissors and cut the image in two. I can tear the page with my hands, which is acceptable and I don't need scissors.

> Sometimes, I may hesitate to cut the page with my links of attachment or dependency because I may have the impression that I am cutting myself off from this person or from love, but that is not the case!

> I am simply cutting away the links of attachment, NOT THE LOVE.
> Here, attachment is not Love.
> Attachment (or dependency) is related to my emotional wounds.

I may also be afraid of doing this exercise because that will make me freer from this person, and as a result it will make me still more responsible for my own life. Sometimes too, moving toward more happiness can also make me a little afraid because it is not familiar for me. **But it is important for me to remember that I will find myself with more Love, more Wisdom and more Freedom.**

> Through this exercise, I free myself from my inner prison where I was living and that was of my own making.

> Human beings often feel safer in what they know, their prison, than in the unknown, their freedom.

Summary of the 7 steps of the *technique* with another person

1. I first draw <u>myself</u> and write my first name and family name under the figure.

2. I draw the <u>other person</u> and write the person's first name and family name under the figure.

3. I draw a <u>circle of **light**</u> around <u>me</u> (including my first and family names) with the rays.

4. I draw a <u>circle of **light**</u> around the <u>other</u> person (including their first and family names) with the rays.

5. I draw a <u>circle of **light** around both persons</u> with the rays.

6. I <u>draw the 7 conscious or unconscious links of attachment</u> by connecting each of the 7 energy centers of the two persons.

7. I cut away <u>the 7 conscious or unconscious links of attachment</u> connecting the two persons.

I say: **"Thanks. It's done!"**

Using the *technique* with a person
THE 7 STEPS IN IMAGES

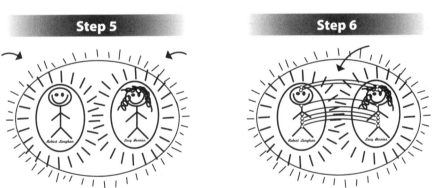

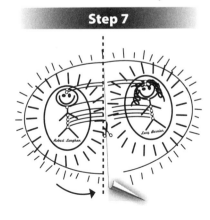

CHAPTER 5

An Exercise to Detach Myself from a Situation

Another way to do the exercise is to perform it with a situation instead of a person, for example the signing of a contract, a meeting, an encounter with a client, or any other activity. It is then a matter of first drawing myself, as previously, and then, instead of another person, simply drawing a rectangle and writing the title of the situation inside the rectangle, for example **"my contract with the Good Bread Company Inc.,"** then connecting all the conscious or unconscious links of attachment from my energy centers over to the rectangle.

Remember to draw the *circle of light* around the rectangle just as with a person. And so, a *circle of light* around me, around the rectangle containing the identification of the situation and a *circle of light* around the two elements, namely the person (me) and the rectangle representing the situation.

Here are some examples of situations that I could put in the rectangle on the right. As a general rule, I just need to **name the situation that concerns me or that I want to harmonize inside the rectangle**.

My vacation in Hawaii:

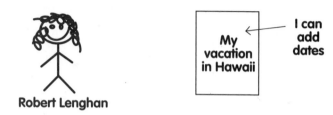

And I do the 5 other steps.

I may have **conscious** or unconscious fears about being able to gather enough money for the trip, being able to free up enough necessary time because of my job or my family obligations, the fear of not finding someone to accompany me, etc. The exercise can partly or entirely remove those fears that might prevent me from carrying out this project.

My difficulties in my current job:

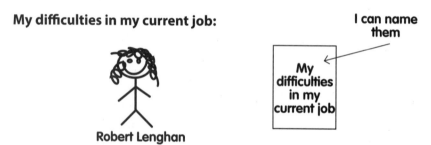

And I do the 5 other steps.

If I have issues in my current job, it is because of my conscious or unconscious inner conflicts. Cutting away the conscious or unconscious links of attachment will help me feel better in my job and will enable me to see the situation more objectively.

Obtaining a contract:

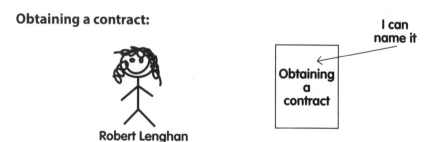

And I do the 5 other steps.

If I am afraid of not being able to get this contract that could well happen, because **for the brain, the solution to the fear of something is that the thing in question happens**. This is a brain process that tends to manifest the object of that fear so as to diminish the stress associated with it. The exercise of the **Little Stick Figures** will tend to eliminate those fears.

In the case of a situation where several persons are involved, for example before a court of justice to settle a situation involving a divorce, I begin by drawing myself, Step 1, and I will follow the 6 other steps with each of the other persons such as:

- Me and my lawyer,
- Me and my male or female partner,
- Me and the lawyer of my male or female partner,
- Me and the judge.

Then, I can do another exercise by drawing on the right side a rectangle representing the whole situation, and writing in the rectangle:

"My divorce contract with .... (the person's name)"

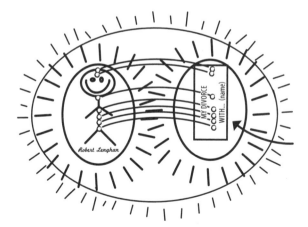

Summary of the 7 steps of the *technique* with a situation

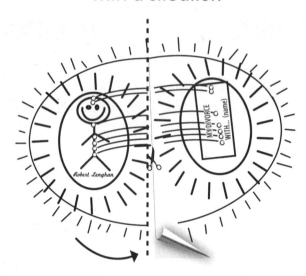

1. I first draw <u>myself</u> and write my first name and family name below the figure.

2. I draw the situation and identify it. I can add the place and the date of the event in question if this applies.

3. I draw a *circle of light* around <u>me</u> (including my first and family names) with the rays.

4. I draw a *circle of light* around the <u>situation</u> and the explanatory text with the rays.

5. I draw a *circle of light* around <u>me and the situation</u> with the rays.

6. I draw the <u>7 conscious or unconscious links of attachment</u> by connecting each of the 7 energy centers on both sides.

7. I cut away the <u>7 conscious or unconscious links of attachment</u>.

I say: **"Thanks. It's done!"**

An Exercise to Detach Myself from a Situation

Using the *technique* with a situation
THE 7 STEPS IN IMAGES

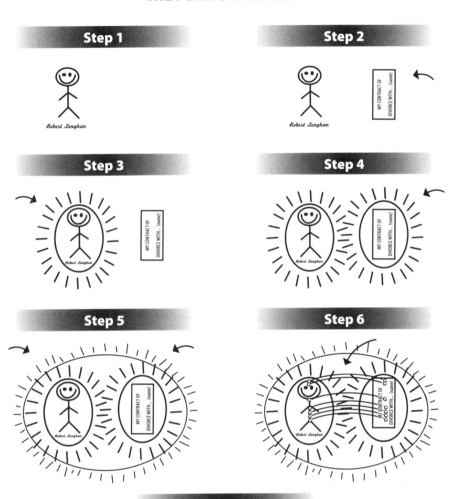

CHAPTER 6

An Exercise to Detach Myself from a Part of Myself

Me with me

We have previously seen how to do the exercise with another person or a situation where I am experiencing disharmony. But what about with myself? In fact, as all other people, I experience dualities, inner conflicts and insecurities with certain facets of myself. This *technique* will help me achieve more Inner harmony by enabling me to free myself from certain links that I have maintained with my ways of seeing myself and acting.

A very good example is to do the *technique* with my **YIN** and **YANG** sides. Every one of us, woman or man, has these two sides or these two facets inside of us. But just how comfortable am I with that? Boys are often uncomfortable with their YIN, feminine, creative, emotional side (that mostly artists have developed). Women are sometimes less comfortable with their YANG, masculine, active, rational side, because they think they will lose their femininity if they display any YANG attributes. There follows a discomfort, a duality involving one or several of these aspects. By doing the exercise with my YIN side and my YANG side, I will help enlighten these two facets of myself and become better able to fully integrate and accept↓♥ them. This will produce what follows:

Lucy Bernier **Lucy Bernier**
YIN side   **YANG side**

After doing these 2 drawings, which covers the first 2 steps, I continue the drawing by doing steps 3 to 7.

IMPORTANT: If I am a girl, I draw 2 girls with my first name and family name under them and the YIN and YANG sides.

If I am a boy, I draw 2 boys with my first name and family name under them and the YIN and YANG sides.[18]

What does this exercise enable me to do? I may experience an inner conflict because I am judging myself on the basis of one or the other of these two aspects of my personality. I may lock myself into obligations, because *"a girl is supposed to act this way"* or *"a boy doesn't do that sort of thing."* The *technique* will enable me to detach myself from the fears that are related to the manifestation of these two aspects inside of me and will allow me to fully accept↓♥ myself. What will then follow is a greater **freedom** of being and expression. I can become more detached from the judgment and the gaze of others. By ceasing to criticize myself, I will divert the criticism from others, which is a mirror of my inner criticism.

Maybe I will be more comfortable practicing sports usually reserved for the opposite sex: for example, I will dare to wear a piece of clothing without fearing the looks of others, and so on. In short, I will feel **freer** in my everyday life.

Another example that can apply to many persons is the duality that exists between my **material** and **spiritual sides**. Many people see them as opposed and have the impression that I must choose either one or the other and that both of them cannot coexist, which is false. The fact of being spiritual is not sufficient to pay for my food and my rent. Money

---

18 Some persons are tempted to draw a girl and a boy because there is talk of the feminine and masculine sides, but in this specific example, I am drawing two figures of the same sex.

is necessary. It is not money that is bad, but the **love** of money and if it is used for negative ends. Therefore, in order to help me harmonize these two aspects and cut away the links of attachment I have with either one of these aspects, I will proceed as follows:

Robert Lenghan
Material side

Robert Lenghan
Spiritual side

*After doing these 2 drawings, which covers the first 2 steps,
I continue the drawing by doing steps 3 to 7.*

Doing the exercise with the opposites enables me to position myself with respect to the two sides and possibly even to become **aware** of some of my patterns or judgments regarding what I want. The exercise will enable me to make some things clearer for me. I will thus have better chances that what I desire will manifest itself!

**Even if it makes no sense in my mind,
I do it just the same!**

I don't need to understand what I am doing for results to appear. Because the *technique* acts at the level of my subconscious. And the greater part of my life takes place at this level in any case! The subconscious takes up a place 9 times greater than the conscious in the functioning of my body and in achieving my goals. It manages the actions I perform without my having to think about them, for example: making my heart♥ beat, healing an injury, driving a car without thinking about it while listening to the radio, and so on.

Because the *technique* acts on the subconscious, it will set off some unconscious solution-seeking mechanisms, for I will **"order it to do so by applying the technique."** The subconscious will be working for me.

I am giving a reminder here
that the subconscious recalls 90% of what I write,
thus helping to manifest what I want.
My subconscious is then working for me.

There is an infinity of possible combinations
for the choice of the 2 figures
and they are all good!
Only good can come of it.
The exercise is quite safe!

There is no risk of making a *"mistake."*

A general rule:
I first draw myself on the left (with my first name
and family name)
with the positive quality or aspect.
And then
I draw myself on the right
(with my first name and family name)
with the opposite defect or negative aspect.

Here are a few examples:

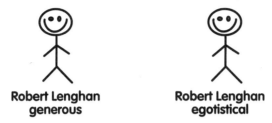

After doing these 2 drawings, which makes up the first 2 steps, I continue the drawing by doing steps 3 to 7.

In the example above, I drew two stick figures of myself with a quality of mine, **generous**, and with its opposite, **egotistical**. It may be that I experience these two attributes myself on certain occasions and to a certain percentage (%) or that I experience situations with other persons who are, for example, egotistical. Whatever the case may be, doing the exercise can enable me to see more clearly into the situation.

The more opposed or contrary the 2 words are, the more results there will be!

After doing these 2 drawings, which makes up the first 2 steps, I continue the drawing by doing steps 3 to 7.

Robert Lenghan
very joyful

Robert Lenghan
very sad

*After doing these 2 drawings, which makes up the first 2 steps,
I continue the drawing by doing steps 3 to 7.*

Lucy Bernier
very positive

Lucy Bernier
very negative

*After doing these 2 drawings, which makes up the first 2 steps,
I continue the drawing by doing steps 3 to 7.*

Lucy Bernier
very conscious and awake

Lucy Bernier
very unconscious[19]

*After doing these 2 drawings, which makes up the first 2 steps,
I continue the drawing by doing steps 3 to 7.*

---

19   I can also put the subconscious here.

I note that before each quality and defect, I added the adverb **VERY**. This has the effect of intensifying each quality and each defect, which will achieve maximum results. It is interesting to see the gains in **awareness** I make just by writing down these qualities and defects. If I react by saying to myself: *"no, this is not me at all,"* this will give me a path to work on. For if I reject an aspect, positive as well as negative that is because it belongs to me to a certain percentage (%). The fact of becoming **aware** of it and accepting↓♥ it will enable me to either further manifest it if it is a quality, or to transform it into something positive if it is a defect.

> The *technique* enables me to bring back into my
> consciousness
> some items of information
> that had remained
> so far unconscious.

The table below gives me some other examples I can use:

The figure on the left I add my first name and family name underneath:	The figure on the right I add my first name and family name underneath:
Flexible	Rigid
Generous	Egotistical
Open	Closed
Thrifty	Wasteful
Kind	Humiliating
Self-confident	Totally lacking in self-confidence
Trusting	Jealous
In perfect health	Sick[20]
Joyful	Sad
Sincere	Lying
Optimistic	Pessimistic
Patient	Impatient
Encouraged	Discouraged
Full of energy	Fatigued
Calm	Stressed
Confident	Worried
Serene	Angry

Then, I draw a series of two figures with the 7 steps for each line above.

---

20   I can write the name of the sickness I have, or that a person I know has, or that I fear I may have.

A variant: drawing the links of attachment in color (Step 6)

The 7 main chakras or energy centers mentioned above are specific points of the body through which energy exchanges take place. Their role is to receive and transmit a rhythmic vibratory energy that acts upon the organs. Each one of them is associated with a dominant color that corresponds to its vibratory frequency. The links of attachment that I draw at Step 6 connect my 7 chakras with those of the other person or the situation.

It is possible for me, if I so wish, to draw these links of attachment with the colors corresponding to these chakras. This is optional however, and not necessary for the *technique* to be effective.

Here are the colors associated with each energy center:

1. **red** for the coccyx, at the base of the spine
2. **orange** for the Hara, the sacred center (between the navel and the pubis)
3. **yellow** for the solar plexus, at the base of my sternum
4. **green** for the heart♥
5. **blue** for the throat
6. **indigo** (a sort of mauve blue) for the third eye
7. **violet** for the center above the head, the coronal

And here are the levels at which they can be found on the human body:

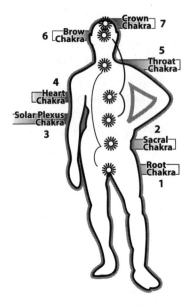

7. **violet** for the center above the head, the coronal

6. **indigo** (a sort of mauve blue) for the third eye

5. **blue** for the throat

4. **green** for the heart♥

3. **yellow** for the solar plexus

2. **orange** for the Hara (below the navel), the sacred center

1. **red** for the coccyx

CHAPTER 7

General Questions on How to Properly Apply the *Technique*

What do I do with the pieces of paper after cutting the page?

I just put them in the wastebasket! Certain persons will add an extra exercise by burning the pieces of paper in a bowl and visualizing the energy or the **light**. It is possible to do so, but it is not a requirement. Similarly, if I burn the papers and white, gray or black smoke rises from them, the work gets done in any case, whatever its color!

The page acts as carbon paper for the subconscious, as when long ago carbon sheets were used to copy text between 2 pages. What I wrote on the first page was copied onto the second. Afterward, the carbon sheet could be thrown away because it was no longer necessary. In the same way, the page on which I do the exercise is like a carbon sheet for my subconscious. That is why what I do afterward with the page is secondary, because the drawing has been registered in my subconscious.

Why put the energy centers in the rectangle that symbolizes a situation?

What do the energy centers that I draw in the rectangle that symbolizes a situation (on the right) correspond to? Any situation that I experience involves one or several persons, be they living or deceased. Therefore, the energy centers in the rectangle on the right refer to the energy centers of the persons involved in the situation, whether we know these persons or not.

For example, if I do the exercise with myself and the sale of my house, the situation involves the people living in the house, a potential buyer, a real estate agent, etc. Then the energy centers of the situation refer, by extension, to the energy centers of these persons involved in the situation. It is as though I were asking for the best to happen for all the persons more or less closely involved in the situation in question, including myself.

Another way of viewing it is as follows: I think I have some attachment to my desire to sell my house, which is related to the 6th energy center, at the mental level. I may also be emotionally attached to the house if that is where I raised my family, so it will be located more at the 3rd energy center related to the emotions. If I am attached to the financial impact of selling my house, this will rather concern my 1st energy center that concerns my basic needs and my material needs.

I don't need to worry about knowing which energy centers are most concerned, what is important is to cut away ALL the links of conscious or unconscious attachment involved in the situation.

Do I cut off the light when I cut away the links of attachment?

NO! The balls of **light** represent my will for the best to happen for me, the other person and the entire situation. This remains even after cutting away the links of attachment.

Do I cut off the love when I cut away the links of attachment?

NO!!!! That **love** exists, quite simply. **Love** is not an attachment or a link, it is a heart♥-to-heart♥ vibration. That is why cutting away the links of attachment and dependency leaves untouched the **love** already present. Because attachment or dependency, as I consider them here, are not **love**, the direct consequence is to put more **unconditional love** in the relationship with the other person or in the situation. I may even feel this **love** more after applying the *technique*.

Doing the *technique*, for example, with my spouse enables my relationship as a couple to flourish, because the links of control and power have been cut away. Our relationship will be based more on **freedom**. The same applies for any person or situation with whom I do the exercise.

Consequences:
To influence or control another person

I can ask myself: when I do the exercise with another person, when I draw them, write down their first and family names and cut away the links, do I consciously or unconsciously risk influencing them, controlling them, harming them or abusing their freedom?

The answer is **NO!** Because my attitude is: **I WANT WHAT IS BEST FOR MYSELF AND FOR THE OTHER PERSON!** This is also why I must **ALWAYS** draw myself first and why I am in the exercise with another person or a situation.

Two situations are then possible:

1. Either there is no visible effect on the other person.

2. Or that person benefits positively from the exercise, because I have freed myself from my previous attachment to them. It is as though I had previously chained the other person with my expectations, my dependencies, my attachments or fears and now, I am removing their chains! I am thus giving that person more **freedom** and **love**!

> When I draw the little stick figures
> with another person,
> I am not working "on the other person,"
> but only on my own vision of that person
> in relation to the unconscious messages
> that I can send them.

Do I have to draw the eyes, the nose, and the mouth?

Not necessarily. I suggest doing the eyes and the mouth (preferably a smile to send a positive image of myself and of the other person), but the rest is optional. The point is to keep the drawing simple. This isn't a drawing contest!

Do I draw the figures with the arms pointing up or down?

This is secondary, and both ways are good! What is important is doing the exercise!

Does the drawing have a meaning?

NO! I am aware that certain persons specialize in the analysis of drawings, especially children's drawings, which reveal their inner lives. For example, in this analysis, the left side generally refers to the past, the right side to the future, etc. As a parent, I can observe my child's drawings and learn a lot. For example, if the child uses clear and vibrant colors or dark colors with gloomy drawings such as skulls, for instance.

That is not the goal here. Therefore, the rules that normally apply to the analysis of drawings do not apply here. Similarly, whether I draw the circles toward the left or the right has no importance.

I may also raise the pencil to see how far I have progressed, and then pursue the uncompleted portion of the line. Even if there was an interruption, I just need to complete the circle with a line to connect both ends.

The sole exception: When I am drawing the 7 lines of attachment and I forget one. It is interesting to stop and see which link was forgotten. Usually, this is an indication that there is something happening at this level, which can be a blockage or a great fear tied to it. For example, if I forgot the link of attachment located at the level of the throat, it is probable that there are many things that I am holding back from saying and expressing. It is as though my mind wanted to conceal[21] this information. I may even, physically, have a cough or a sore throat, which is a sign that I need to express myself more about something, at the level of verbal or sexual communication.

If I realize that I've forgotten to draw one attachment link before cutting the page, I add it in. If I have already cut the page and then realize that there are only 6 links instead of 7, or less, I start over the exercise with the same person or situation and I take care to properly draw the 7 links of attachment. I refer you to page 48 to see the name of each energy center and what it is associated with.

---

21   To hide, omit, cancel some unwanted information.

If the person's name is unknown

I identify the person with the elements available to me. For example, if I want to find my biological parents, I do the exercise as follows:

Lucy Bernier   **my biological father**

After doing these 2 drawings, which makes up the first 2 steps, I continue the drawing by doing steps 3 to 7.

~~~~~~

Lucy Bernier   **my biological mother**

After doing these 2 drawings, which makes up the first 2 steps, I continue the drawing by doing steps 3 to 7.

~~~~~~

I can also mention their profession or the place where I met the person. For example, if I had a car accident, I can do as follows:

General Questions on How to Properly Apply the Technique

Lucy Bernier

**Driver in an accident
Paris, January 12, 2015** [22]

*After doing these 2 drawings, which makes up the first 2 steps,
I continue the drawing by doing steps 3 to 7.*

~~~~~~

Lucy Bernier

**Police officer, accident,
Paris, January 12, 2015**

*After doing these 2 drawings, which makes up the first 2 steps,
I continue the drawing by doing steps 3 to 7.*

~~~~~~

Lucy Bernier

**The helping person[23], accident,
Paris, January 12, 2015**

*After doing these 2 drawings, which makes up the first 2 steps,
I continue the drawing by doing steps 3 to 7.*

~~~~~~

---

22   Name location and date.
23   If I do not know the gender of the person, I can draw either a man or a woman.

If I am going to have a heart♥ operation:

Lucy Bernier

Heart♥ specialist
Laval Hospital, April 15, 2015

*After doing these 2 drawings, which makes up the first 2 steps,
I continue the drawing by doing steps 3 to 7.*

~~~~~~

Lucy Bernier

Nurses,
operation[24]
Laval Hospital[25]
April 15, 2015

*After doing these 2 drawings, which makes up the first 2 steps,
I continue the drawing by doing steps 3 to 7.*

~~~~~~

---

24   I draw a rectangle that represents the entire nursing personnel.
25   If several operations are planned, I can put all of them in a rectangle and write: "my operations."

General Questions on How to Properly Apply the Technique

Lucy Bernier
Heart♥ in perfect health[26]

Lucy Bernier
Heart♥ in bad condition[27]

After doing these 2 drawings, which makes up the first 2 steps, I continue the drawing by doing steps 3 to 7.

Will the exercise be more effective if I draw the links of attachment in color?

NO! Not necessarily. However, certain persons prefer to do the *technique* with the colors, and that is acceptable too.

It is important to avoid setting unnecessary conditions for doing the exercise. Many persons don't know the colors related to the chakras or do not have the necessary materials for drawing them in colors.

However, if when I do the *technique*, I have this knowledge and I want to add colors to the attachment links, I may do it.

What do I feel during the exercise?

That depends on each person. I may feel nothing. I may also experience certain emotions that rise to the surface, very lightly or very strongly during the exercise or right after it. If such is the case, I welcome what rises in me. I see if I can identify the emotion. I may feel a current of warmth going through my body or like a stitch at the level of the heart♥. This denotes only that something is going on at a certain level. It is not

---

26   Preferably, put the positive side first on the left.
27   If I don't know the gender of the person involved, it is not important; I draw a man or a woman.

necessary to know in my head everything that is going on. It is a matter of welcoming these emotions and saying **THANKS**, because a freeing and a positive change are taking place, at a level that is either physical, emotional or spiritual.

Can the exercise be done in a group?

YES! It can also be very powerful when I do it at the same time and in the presence of other persons. If a training leader teaches the *technique* in a course, it makes it possible to amplify the energy through the group's **consciousness** and more **consciousness raising** events can take place. The fact of subsequently sharing one's experience also helps to integrate the changes. I can do the *technique* with friends or with members of my family. The ensuing discussions will be very beneficial and often revelatory. It is an opportunity to open the communication channels with my children, for example.

I may also decide for example to do the exercise at home, with a friend or with my children. This becomes a good opportunity to share my feelings and emotions about a situation with the persons I **love**.

Is it important to carefully draw the rays around the 3 circles to clearly show that it is light?

YES, as best as possible, because the rays express my openness and my intention to "throw **light**" on this relationship or situation. It serves to clearly identify for my subconscious that this is indeed **light**. Otherwise, using only circles without rays, my subconscious might interpret that I am locked up inside something.

Should I do the *technique* consciously or automatically?

Both ways are appropriate. I have personally experienced the fact of doing the exercise **"consciously,"** and it was easier for me to identify my emotions about the situation or the person and to feel the changes that followed.

However, even if I do the exercise "automatically," without thinking very much about what I am doing, that is appropriate too. Even if I have the impression of just doing a simple drawing, my subconscious, through the drawing, is registering the information. It may even be beneficial for persons who are very cerebral, "in their heads," and who feel a need to understand everything. The fact of doing it like a sort of game will keep them closer to the level of the heart♥, without analyzing everything that is going on.

I can choose to use this *technique* as an active personal development tool, accessible at all times. A tool that enables me to work on my emotions on a regular basis. It results in great positive changes in my everyday life.

May I use a mantra[28] during the exercise, or use a request formula?

Is it possible to think about a special sentence while doing the exercise? The answer is **YES**, but <u>not necessary</u>. For example, while cutting with the scissors, I can say: *"I'm cutting the links of attachment with…"* (name of the person or of the situation). I can also say, for each link of attachment related to an energy center (chakra) that I am cutting: *"I am freeing this chakra from any negative emotion, attachment or dependency."*

Personally, during the exercise and especially while cutting the links, I repeat: *"THANKS, THANKS, THANKS, THANKS"* or *"I ACCEPT↓♥, I ACCEPT↓♥,*

---

28 A mantra is a condensed formula made up of one or a series of syllables repeated many times following a certain rhythm, in order to meditate or for religious purposes.

I ACCEPT↓♥," especially if it involves a situation that deeply concerns me. *"I accept↓♥"* does not mean that I agree with the situation. *"I accept↓♥"* means: **"I accept↓♥ that there is something for me to understand in this situation."** *I accept↓♥ to remain open so that the beneficial changes can take place and so that the best can happen for me and for the other person.*

And at the very end, after cutting the page with the scissors, I say: **"THANKS, IT'S DONE!"** I take it for granted that something is happening, with immediate changes, while remaining open to the different forms of manifestations of these changes.

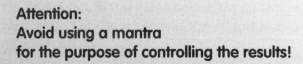

**Attention:
Avoid using a mantra
for the purpose of controlling the results!**

I could also make a written request before doing the *technique*. For example: *"I request that my attachment and my dependency involving _____ be cut away completely and replaced by a feeling of **freedom**."*

BEWARE OF WANTING TO CONTROL THE OTHER PERSON!!!

For example, it is <u>forbidden</u> for me to write: "I want _____ to **love** me;" "I want _____ to give me $1000." <u>I would thus want to control the emotions and the acts of another person!</u> My attitude must be: *"I want what is best for myself and for the other person."*

Must I do the exercise in silence?

NO, it is not necessary! The exercise works even while speaking, but I must make sure that my talking is not a way of protecting myself or a form of **escape**. In fact, doing the exercise in silence enables me to be more in contact with my emotions involving the chosen person or situation.

Because **"I become whatever I focus my attention on,"** silence enables me to be closer to the level of my heart♥. It is possible that old fears or emotions may resurface during the exercise. The fact of being silent enables me to become **aware** of them and welcome them, opening the door to a liberation. In fact, I can receive a lot of information while doing the exercise if I am listening. A healing process can even be set in motion, because I am making a written request for a situation to be resolved for the best. It is as though I were putting back some **love** into the situation, because I am letting go of my attachment and dependency involving a specific person or situation.

From what age can one do the exercise?

I can use the *technique* if I am an adult, but also if I am a child. Beginning at what age? As soon as the child is capable of drawing! Usually, this is around the age of 3. It is a matter of doing the exercise and presenting it to the child as a game.

An actual fact: A child aged 7 or 8 who had issues at school with another child (Luke) did the *technique* with him. Upon his return that evening, he exclaimed: "Mom, Mom, Luke is my friend, now."

If the child is too young to draw or is a baby, I can only do the exercise as follows:

Me (first name) and family name   **The child's / baby's first name and family name**

After doing these 2 drawings, which makes up the first 2 steps, I continue the drawing by doing steps 3 to 7.

Thus, I harmonize my relationship with the child, which gives me more detachment from her and thereby, more protection. In fact, as a parent, I want to protect my child as far as possible from her environment and sometimes, this can go too far and may prevent the child from experiencing situations that are essential for her development. By doing the exercise with my child I am consciously showing my trust in her and in life. Instead of my parental behavior being based on fears and on *"what could go wrong for her,"* I focus my attention on what could go right. This will diminish the stress level for me and my child, who will, by symbiosis, feel my greater sense of security and my openness to new experiences.

Indeed, it is important to note that children are very sensitive to their parents and manifest their parents' inner conflicts.[29] For example, if my child is hyperactive, it is because I am hyperactive myself. Maybe at 5%, 25%, 75% or 100%! Even if I give the outward appearance of an extremely calm person, it is <u>impossible</u> for me to have a hyperactive child and not have that same character trait myself, even by only a small percentage! Therefore, if I do the exercise with my hyperactive child:

Lucy Bernier

Hyperactive Baby[30] Bernier

*After doing these 2 drawings, which makes up the first 2 steps,
I continue the drawing by doing steps 3 to 7.*

It is as though I were asking to harmonize my relationship with my hyperactive baby, but also with my own hyperactivity. Then, I can do the exercise of the ***Little Stick Figures*** with:

---

29 See the video: *Les parents et la maladie de leurs enfants* (Parents and their child's illness), on: www.atma.ca
30 Here I write my child's first name.

Me (first name and family name)[31]   Me (first name and
calm and self-possessed   family name)[32] hyperactive

*After doing these 2 drawings, which makes up the first 2 steps,
I continue the drawing by doing steps 3 to 7.*

How to show a child or an adult how to do the exercise

To show a child how to do the exercise, I sit down beside her, on her left or on her right, it will make no difference. We both have in front of us a white piece of paper and a pencil. I do the exercise at the same time as the child (or the other adult), it is as though she were copying my figures on her own page. I ask her to draw exactly what I will be drawing or writing down on the page.

I must first identify the situation that the child wants to harmonize. For example, if my child is having difficulties with her math teacher, I will sit down next to my daughter, whom I shall call Nathaly.

At the same time as **Nathaly** I will draw Figure #1, on the left, and we will both write down the name **Nathaly Bernier** beneath it (my child's name). We each use our own page.

At the same time as **Nathaly** I will draw Figure #2, on the right, with the complete name of her math teacher if I know it (here, Mr. Clever Counter), or only his first name if the family name is unknown.

---

31   I write down my first name and family name.
32   I write down my first name and family name.

If **Nathaly** has forgotten it, I can write down "my math teacher" instead. We then both do as follows:

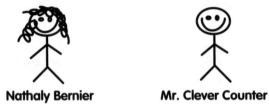

Nathaly Bernier   **Mr. Clever Counter**

After doing these 2 drawings, which makes up the first 2 steps, I continue the drawing by doing steps 3 to 7.

~~~~~~

OR

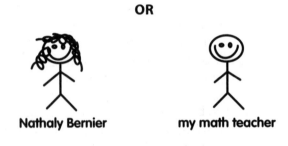

Nathaly Bernier   **my math teacher**

After doing these 2 drawings, which makes up the first 2 steps, I continue the drawing by doing steps 3 to 7.

~~~~~~

General Questions on How to Properly Apply the Technique

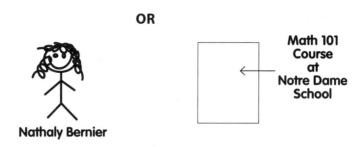

*After doing these 2 drawings, which makes up the first 2 steps,
I continue the drawing by doing steps 3 to 7.*

If my child does not know how to write or draw, I can put my hand over hers and help her by directing her hand. The child's brain will register the information in two ways. First, there is some information that passes from brain to brain, from mine to hers. Second, by the fact that the child is "writing" and performing the gesture of drawing the **Little Stick Figures**, her subconscious will also register this in any case.

Of course, the names may be somewhat illegible on her page, but that is acceptable, **the command has gone out in any case!** What is important is to keep it simple and to <u>do it as a game</u>, because the subconscious cannot tell the difference between a game and reality. By doing it as a game, there are better chances of seeing results showing up, because this greatly diminishes the resistances of the mind.

Can a blind person do the exercise?

YES!! It is a matter of proceeding as when showing it to a child, with my hand placed over hers. First of all, explain to the person the different steps to be able to "visualize" or imagine the 7 steps in her head.

Then, I hold her hand and do the exercise with them, guiding her hand while mentioning the part of the drawing I am doing. For example, by saying: "I am drawing you by forming the head, the body, the arms and legs. I am drawing the eyes, the nose, the mouth with a smile, then you write down your first name and family name underneath it." This is for Step 1. I do the same thing for each of the 6 other steps while telling her what I am drawing with her hand. At Step 7, she can cut the links of attachment with the scissors. To help her in this process, I can first fold the page inward and outward, which will provide the blind person with the "track" to follow in making the cut. It is for me to judge whether she can cut the page herself or if I should again guide her by placing my hand over hers so that the exercise can be done safely. If I am uncomfortable with the fact that the person is using scissors, she can tear the page apart with her hands.

Can a person with a physical or intellectual deficiency do the exercise?

YES! If the person can't use his arms and hands for any reason,[33] I can sit next to him and do the exercise for him, while explaining what I am doing. For a person with reduced mobility (a paraplegic for example), it is important to imagine that there is a temporary link between our two hearts♥ to be even more connected and have better results.

Therefore, for example if my nephew Alexander Martin, who can't use his hands due to an accident, experiences a situation at the day-care center, I can do the exercise in his place, <u>in his presence</u>. I explain to him simply what I am drawing.

---

33   If the person is paraplegic, cannot use their limbs following an accident, etc.

General Questions on How to Properly Apply the Technique

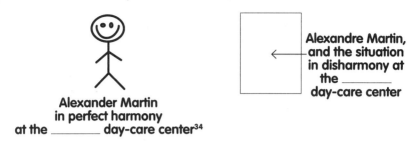

Alexander Martin
in perfect harmony
at the _____ day-care center[34]

Alexandre Martin,
and the situation
in disharmony at
the _____
day-care center

And I do the 5 other steps for him in his presence.

OR

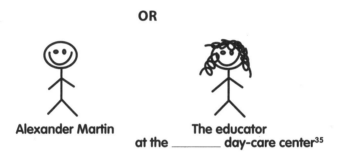

Alexander Martin

The educator
at the _____ day-care center[35]

And I do the 5 other steps for him in his presence.

OR

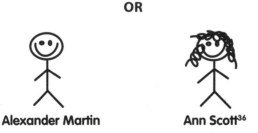

Alexander Martin

Ann Scott[36]

And I do the 5 other steps for him in his presence.

---

34 I write down the name of the day-care center.
35 I write down the name of the day-care center.
36 If I know the name of that educator.

OR

Alexander Martin

[37]

And I do the 5 other steps for him <u>in his presence</u>.

I can even do all of these possibilities! Then afterward, I can ask Alexander whether he felt something during the exercise. Children are very sensitive, and I will sometimes be surprised when I hear their comments! And if he felt nothing, that is all right too!

> **Here, clearly remember that it is false to say
> that if I feel something during the exercise,
> this means that it's working
> and if I feel nothing,
> that means that it's not working...
> NO!
> It always works in any case,
> but at different percentages (%).**

If a person is in a coma

If I know a person who is in a coma or unconscious, I cannot do the exercise in their place without their consent. Therefore, the only way to do the exercise will be for me to first place myself on the left and then this comatose person on the right:

---

37   I put in a rectangle, because there are several persons involved.
38   Again, I write down the name of the day-care center.

General Questions on How to Properly Apply the Technique

**Lucy Bernier
fully conscious**

**Josh Watson
in a coma**

*After doing these 2 drawings, which makes up the first 2 steps,
I continue the drawing by doing steps 3 to 7.*

CHAPTER 8

After Applying the *Technique*: Some Issues concerning the Results Obtained

How many times must I do the exercise?

Just once is necessary, but if it will reassure me, I can do it several times with the same situation. Some persons, who have shared their experiences over the years, say that they repeated the process of the **Little Stick Figures** as long as they still experienced emotions toward the other person or the situation. <u>In this case, I must then do all the 7 steps over again each time and in the right order.</u>

It is false to claim that the exercise must be done for 21 days for it to work.[39] The "21 days" sometimes refer, for instance, to the creation of a new habit. In this exercise, it is important to use the law of expectations regarding the results, in the sense that: I KNOW that the results are <u>immediate</u>. If I set any conditions on the time required to experience results, being skeptical or having decided in advance that it *"won't work,"* I can guess what will happen!!! Exactly what I expected! Therefore, I must keep an open mind and tune in to the fact that:

Everything is possible, here and now

---

39   In fact, some persons claim that this is necessary. Although it may be useful for some persons, **it must not become a condition** for the proper functioning of the exercise. How many "miracles" have taken place in the world with "just once"…

How many times a day can I do the *technique*?

There is no determined number of times. I must listen to myself, especially for example if I feel a certain fatigue. I can allow some time for the integration to take place before doing the exercise again. It is important to listen to my body, for it is it that dictates the pace at which I can do the exercise again! And taking some rest if I feel the need for it. My body is in perpetual change; and so by resting, I am giving it an opportunity to adjust, along with my different energetic bodies.

A very sensitive person said she could only do the exercise once a day, as it caused great inner changes every time. Others do it several times a day and feel fine.

There is no obligation to do it once a day / a week / a month or more often.

It is also possible to do the exercise with different persons or situations on the same day. The human brain is a super-powerful computer and it is false to say that *"it would get everything confused if I did the exercise more than once in the same day."*

At what point in the day should I do the *technique*?

At any time! The important thing is to do it!

After having done the exercise once, does that mean that it's done for all time?

Sometimes YES, but not necessarily so. Personally, I go with my feeling. It can take some time (minutes, days, weeks) before I can see any concrete results (although there may have been some results at a more subtle, emotional level). If I feel the need to do the exercise again, I do it over again. Especially if I still have expectations or if I still remain attached to the results.

By using the **Little Stick Figures Technique** regularly, it becomes a sort of self-therapy tool. I learn to listen more to myself when I do the exercise (my physical and emotional reactions) and to observe my reactions to the results. Personally, I have learned with this exercise to better understand, over time, what **attachment** is.[40] This *technique* also enables me to be more focused, neutral, objective, less in reaction to situations that can disturb me in my life. It helps me to trust that everything will turn out for the best, a principle that is easy to forget in the bustle of my everyday life.

This *technique* becomes a tool of personal development in order to better know myself and bring me more **wisdom, freedom** and unconditional **love**. By using this *technique* regularly, I consciously decide to undo the chains I have created involving others, these conscious or unconscious dependencies that slow me down and prevent me from enjoying the **total freedom** I deserve by divine right!

How can the *technique* be useful for a helping person (therapist, hairdresser, massage therapist, etc.)?

If I am a person providing a service where I must be close to my clients or even touch them (massages, cutting hair), this is very demanding because I am in "their energies."

The reality is that when a person consults a therapist, of whatever sort, the person is in a situation of NEED. Saying NEED is saying EMPTINESS. And EMPTINESS means it is easy to become dependent and attached, consciously or not. The needy person, even without realizing it, can "drain" a lot of energy from the other person and sees that person a little as their "savior." Again, I say this person is needy. The helping person becomes the solution, though unwittingly, to their despair, sorrow, depression or guilt. This can become very heavy to bear. Therefore, if I am the helping person or providing them with some service, my chances

---

40   Again, some people prefer to speak of **DEPENDENCY** rather than **ATTACHMENT**.

improve if the client becomes more objective and neutral toward me and the expected results. It is in fact a form of protection for me, if I am a therapist, a helping person, involved in serving clients, it makes me more objective toward my client. Similarly, if I am the client consulting, I can do the *technique* before my appointment, which improves my chances of the consultation going well for me.

By experience, I suggest doing the *technique* before each important encounter. In fact, when I see clients for REIKI[41] for example and give them an energy treatment, I always do the exercise <u>before the person arrives</u>.

Is it possible to have physical or emotional symptoms after doing the *technique*?

Occasionally, but they are not necessary for the exercise to give results. One person said that she experienced great fatigue, shivering and a sore throat after doing the *technique*. Another felt mild heart♥ palpitations. Still another was more emotional after doing the exercise. What is important is to say THANKS and remain open to detachment and to the healing process on different levels.

My inner balance (energy) adjusts itself with each situation and each person with whom I am in relation. When I cut the links, I am asking to recreate a new balance in myself. By doing the exercise, this balance adjusts itself to a new reality, a new level of detachment, therefore to a new vibration. Once the energies have stabilized, I will be more at peace with this person or situation, knowing that when a new balance is found, I will experience more serenity with these persons. More calm, detachment and objectivity will appear.

Another indicator can be found in our **dreams**. In fact, it often happens that after doing the exercise, dreams become more present and are indicative of something going on. I can write down my dreams and analyze them, because it is possible that I may discover answers to my questions through this unconscious channel of information that turns up in my **consciousness**.

---

41 REIKI is a method of energy healing by imposing of the hands using the universal neutral energy without any special intention.

My dreams may be calm or in the form of nightmares. If this is the case, it only means that there has been a liberation regarding the situation. In both cases, the work is being done, only the changes are showing up differently. I may also have more agitated sleep and dreams, depending on the level of stress I am experiencing in my personal and professional life and not only because I did the exercise.

What results can I expect after doing the exercise, and how long afterward?

The very first thing to understand is that the results are instantaneous and will take place, whether the other person lives in the same city as me or at the other end of the world.

The results depend on my level of attachment to the other person, on my openness to change, on my readiness to let go and accept↓♥ the results. I must become **aware** that certain situations with which I do the exercise have lasted for a very long time. It is possible that everything will be solved immediately, but there may also be some further work to do and that only a certain percentage will be changed.

What percentage of change will take place: 5%, 30%, 50%, 100%? That is different in each case. However, whatever the percentage, it is marvelous to do a simple exercise that takes but a few minutes and enables me to feel better! I have personally experienced this exercise about certain situations and, although the situation remained outwardly the same, on the other hand I felt better inside. I felt that, instead of being completely submerged and overwhelmed by the situation, I had gained a degree of detachment and objectivity toward it. Hence a greater feeling of **freedom** and well-being.

Sometimes, even if I want a situation to change, it may be that I still have some life lessons to learn. The situation will thus last a little longer so that I can become more adequately **aware** of it and allow myself to grow in **wisdom**. The same applies for example if I have the habit of always attracting the same sort of spouse with the same sort of defect. Even if I throw him out, I will still attract the same sort of person. Why? Because I have an inner injury that I must heal to stop the endlessly repeating pattern.

There have been many testimonials where the results appeared in the following minutes and could have been deemed "miraculous." The true miracle is accepting↓♥ to let go, to open oneself up to **unconditional love**. To accept↓♥ to let go of one's control over things and persons even if this demands great courage to do things differently than usual. To set aside my rational inclination to want to understand everything, and do this exercise with my child's heart♥.

Is it possible that no change may result?

NO! The changes may not be apparent, but they are there. Similarly, if I look at the abdomen of a woman who is only 3 or 4 weeks pregnant, can I see with my eyes the changes in her physical body? **NO!** She herself may still be unaware that she is pregnant, although important changes have been taking place in her body!

Sometimes, it is preferable that the changes take place later on or gradually. It is not for me to decide in advance what is good for me.

> **Remember that
> I want what is best for myself,
> for the other person, for both of us...**

There are cases where the person, for example Daniel who was doing the exercise, absolutely wanted to be in a relationship as a couple with another person in particular, let us call her Chantal. Daniel thus did the exercise with the sole idea that Chantal would later become his spouse. Which is not what happened. Did the exercise fail, or was it better for Daniel that he not be in a relationship as a couple with Chantal?

Often, I am protected by the fact that certain things do not happen in my life, even if I desire them. My higher self knows what is good for me more than my human **conscience**.

Is it possible that I mistakenly interpreted the situation?

NO! I can however do the exercise again, this time identifying more precisely the situation and the persons involved. For example, if I want to harmonize my work relations at the office and I first did the exercise with me and the whole group in my office, I can decide to do the exercise separately with each of my office colleagues and my boss.

Sometimes, I may think that I misidentified or did the exercise badly, because I have the <u>impression that</u> *"nothing is happening…"*

Is it possible that there was nothing to be changed?

NO! Even if I do the exercise with a person with whom I am experiencing a harmonious relationship, it is unlikely that I have 0% attachment or dependency with this person. That is why doing the exercise enables me to free myself from it. I may not see any concrete results because my relationship is already good, but there will be results at another level (emotional or spiritual).

What are the causes that can affect the results or its manifestations?

- My fears and my resistance to change
- My skepticism that closes my mind
- My expectations that may be too great
- My attachment to the results
- To not acknowledge the changes that take place

I may also fear doing this exercise because it will free me more from this person, which will have the effect of making me even more responsible for my life. **But it is important for me to remember that I will find myself with more Love, more Wisdom and more Freedom.**

It does happen sometimes that moving toward more happiness makes me a little fearful, because I am not familiar with it and I am facing something unknown. I must then trust and accept↓♥ that I am ready for more abundance in my life, at whatever level it might be! To move toward more happiness also assumes that I will be more responsible, which can indicate a hidden fear, that of being self-responsible.

I accept↓♥ abundance in all the aspects of my life here and now!

Several persons have testified that they did not get any results at first, but after a moment of reflection, they added:

"It's still the same, but we don't quarrel any more…"

"Nothing has changed, but communication is now easier…"

"He still has the same behavior, but now I feel comfortable with that, which wasn't the case before…"

So there have been results, only they are different from those I had anticipated!

Be careful before saying that there have been no results!!!!

Can the person with whom I do the *technique* have a reaction or a feeling?

First, this depends on the person's level of sensitivity. We are all mutually interrelated with each other. We have all one day experienced the fact of sensing someone at a distance, even if we lived in different cities, countries or continents. For example, someone I **love** is experiencing a difficult period and her image appears to me constantly. Often even, the telephone rings and it is this same person who is calling me and needs help. Therefore the fact of doing the *technique* may have the effect that the other person will feel something or not, somewhat like telepathy. But that is out of my control.

If the person changes her behavior after I did the exercise with her and I have the impression that she is more in reaction to me than before, she may unconsciously react to the fact that I decided to cut off the links of my attachment to her and that she finds it difficult to let go. It may have awakened in her, for example, a fear of losing me. That was already present, but the *technique* only made it more apparent so we can now be more **aware** of it. Because our relationship has already changed and the other person may find it difficult to explain what is happening. Especially so for those persons who are very much in their minds and need to control everything, if they have the impression that they have lost control over something or someone and do not even know what, this can prove destabilizing. What usually happens is that if someone in my entourage shows more reactions, I will be more in control of myself and less affected by that.

Here is an example of what Jacques Martel experienced during a sharing session in a personal development seminar in the spring of 2013 in Tahiti. A lady of more than 80 years of age had a son, as a neighbor, who did not have a good attitude toward her and was given to alcohol. After doing the **Little Stick Figures Technique** with her son, he became even more verbally violent, calling her by all sorts of names. Jacques was a little surprised at hearing that, because usually the situation calms down, and he was wondering what was positive in the fact that this lady had done the exercise. He got his answer when the lady testified that *"now, my son's behavior no longer bothers me."* She had thus achieved more autonomy and detachment from the situation with her son.

If the person who reacts is someone I **love** (family, spouse, friend, etc.), I just need to reassure them, reaffirm my **love** and explain that I am changing. If I feel an openness in the other person, I can explain the exercise and my reasons for doing it. If I have any doubts about their openness, I will refrain from speaking about it. That might only have the effect of adding to their insecurity.

Can the results be negative?

NO! I may have the <u>impression</u> that the results are <u>different</u> from those I expected and <u>judge</u> that it is negative. For example: I want to sell my house and I do the *technique* to find a buyer. I wait a few days or a few weeks, and still no buyer shows up… Has the *technique* failed? I dare say **NO**. In this case, one must ask the right questions:

1. Do I really want to sell my house?
2. Are my attachment to this house and the memories tied to it stronger than my desire or my need to sell it?
3. Do I really need to sell it, or is there some other solution that would allow me to keep it (in case of financial difficulties for example)?
4. Are there any other persons living with me who refuse to sell it, consciously or not?
5. Am I unconsciously asking a very high price for my house so as to scare buyers away?

If I remain open to examine this apparent absence of results, I will learn to know myself better and allow myself to change some things in my life so that I may not need to sell it. And if I still want to sell it, I will have worked on aspects of myself that were previously hidden, such as my fears, my attachments to this house. Maybe even also the fear of change and the fear and insecurity about my future.

Another example is a lady who was seeing her boyfriend 4 times a week and reveals that since doing the exercise, they now only see each other once or twice a week. She judges the results as negative, because she had wished to see him even more often. The question arises: do I want to control the results? Could it be that the best for both persons is that they see each other a bit less often? We don't have all the details of this situation, but sometimes, I take the other person for granted, and seeing each other less often enables me to benefit more from the present moment. **Love** can't be quantified by the amount of time spent with a person, but by the quality of the relationship. The fact of embracing the other person's freedom of choice and accepting↓♥ those choices is a sign of detachment. Sometimes, life faces me with situations that make me **aware** of this.

I repeat: I must ask for the best to happen to me and to the other person, and not want to control the other person, which is attachment and dependency!

How can I know that it is working and recognize the results if they don't stand out as obvious?

When I observe the situation for which I did the exercise, it is important to set aside my expectations about the specific results I am hoping for.

For example, if I am experiencing a conflicted relationship with my daughter and if she is often in reaction toward me, has fits of anger or stops speaking to me, I must look at the events and also see **how I am feeling**.

a. Does my daughter always have those same conflicted behaviors?

b. Do these same behaviors occur as often as before, or are they more spaced apart in time?

c. If my daughter shows the same behaviors, am I feeling differently about that?

d. Am I, MYSELF, more detached toward my daughter and the situation?

e. Whatever the results, have I asked myself any questions or made a personal effort to find out why this situation exists in my life and understand what I have to learn?

f. Has the exercise enabled me to more clearly identify what I want in my life and what I want to eliminate from my life?

All of these situations indicate that there have been some results, at one level or another.

> **Exercise:**
> I can also ask my inner voice, my intuitive side:
> "What is the percentage of change that has taken place?"
> And I will allow the answer to rise from my heart♥, without judging.
> Whatever the answer turns out to be, I say: THANKS![42]

I can then decide to do the exercise over again as many times as I want over a certain period of time if I want to increase the percentage of results.

Can I cancel the effects of the exercise?

For example, if I did the exercise with a person and am not satisfied with the results? This question came from a person who was hoping to get closer to an ex-spouse and the result was a definitive separation.

It is important to **realize** that when I want at all costs to get closer to a person, it is because there is some **affective dependency**, which is the opposite of **unconditional love**. This method enables me to get out of the patterns of **affective dependency**. As I always ask for *"the best for myself and for the other person according to our development,"* I have to accept↓♥ that in the present moment, the best thing is a separation. My

---

[42] See the "THANKS!" technique in the book **ATMA, the power of Love** or **The Power of the words... that free me!** by Jacques Martel.

sorrow may not allow me to understand why that is for the best, but I remain open to being shown why!

For this reason, I do not have to "cancel the exercise done," because it did work and gave me exactly what I needed. Because a sincere **love** will endure, whether or not I do the exercise.

> **It is only the dependency and the attachment that are cut away, NOT THE LOVE!**

How do I confirm the cutting of the links that I have already initiated?

I suggest meditating and asking to know what percentage (%) of detachment I have reached. I can do the exercise over again as many times as I feel the need for it, and I say <u>Thanks!</u> **after** doing each exercise. It is impossible to "do the *technique* too much." If the links have been totally cut away, the effect of doing the *technique* over again will be to consolidate what was changed.

I suggest doing the **great cleansing protocol** of Chapter 10 regularly or when I feel the need for it. It is a little like when I do my "spring cleaning" in my house because the dust has accumulated over the year, I can do the same thing with the great cleanup of my life by using the **Little Stick Figures**!

Conclusion about the results

> **Whatever the results turn out to be, I say THANKS!**

It is mentioned in this book that I must have a positive attitude when I do the exercise, and that:

 I want what is best for myself and for the other person.

What is best? I may have my own idea about what is best for me and have expectations. I must trust the process I engage in with this method. If my inner voice has guided me to learn this exercise of the **Little Stick Figures**, it's because I am ready to let go of the conscious or unconscious attachments in my life toward persons and situations.

CHAPTER 9

The *Technique's* Many Applications and Some Questions from the Public

Below is a list of situations where the **Little Stick Figures** can be used. It is the result of the questions from the public in recent years and from a survey among part of our clientele, as well as from situations that we have personally experienced.

These examples serve to show its multiple uses, without however being restrictive. I can do the exercise with any situation or person I wish. By reading these examples, I will better integrate the concepts of the *technique*, which will help me identify, in each case, **Figure #1** on the left and **Figure #2** on the right.

Also, some examples will be accompanied by more explanations to show the attitude to assume when I do the *technique* and the notion of **"wanting what is best for myself and for the other person."** It is important to let go and avoid wanting to control the results, which is a form of attachment.

The general principles for identifying Figure #1 and Figure #2

1. Identify the situation I want to improve, whether it is negative or positive.
2. Identify the persons who are involved in this situation.
3. Identify the emotions or the fears that I feel regarding that situation.

The sale or the purchase of my house

It is possible that I am considering moving because of a job offer in another city or another country, a marriage or a separation, to a larger house because the family is growing, etc. In this house, I have good or bad memories. If they are pleasant, for example because my children were born in it, or because it is the "family home" where I grew up, this will contribute to **my having a conscious or unconscious attachment to this house** and I may be unconsciously telling "the universe" that I don't want to separate myself from it, which will have the consequence that I will find it difficult to sell it (see p. 102).

I risk failing to sell my house because of my attachment to it. It is therefore important, when I cut away the links of attachment, to say "THANKS, THANKS, THANKS, THANKS!" for everything that happened in this house, and thereby detach myself from it, because I want what is best for myself and because I am ready to experience something different in some other place. I also want the best for the eventual buyer.

The exercise of the *Little Stick Figures* will help me cut away my conscious or unconscious attachment related to the sale of the house. I can then do the following exercise:

Lucy Bernier

After doing these 2 drawings, which makes up the first 2 steps, I continue the drawing by doing steps 3 to 7.

It is important to note that here, I want to sell my house at the right price. Because my house can be assessed at $350,000 and if someone tries to negotiate, I can lower the price to $325,000, which I consider a fair price. But I don't want to let it go at $250,000. So my attitude will be: *"I want to sell my house at a fair price and I want everything to proceed in harmony and for the best for me and the other persons involved."*

I can also do the following exercises:

ME (first name + family name)   **(first name + family name) of the real estate agent**

After doing these 2 drawings, which makes up the first 2 steps, I continue the drawing by doing steps 3 to 7.

ME (first name + family name)   **The buyer of my house**[43]

After doing these 2 drawings, which makes up the first 2 steps, I continue the drawing by doing steps 3 to 7.

An actual case: A person told us that she had her house put up for sale since a year, and was able to get a promised sale in the week following the exercise, after having done the exercise of the **Little Stick Figures** In relation to the sale of her house.

If I want to <u>buy</u> a house, I do:

Buying a house [44]

ME (first name + family name)

After doing these 2 drawings, which makes up the first 2 steps, I continue the drawing by doing steps 3 to 7.

---

43 I leave this open, with no special name, because I don't know which one is the best buyer for me.
44 I can add my specifications in the rectangle: place, price, number of rooms, etc.

The Technique's Many Applications and Some Questions from the Public

ME (first name + family name)   **Seller of the house**

After doing these 2 drawings, which makes up the first 2 steps, I continue the drawing by doing steps 3 to 7.

ME (first name + family name)   **Real estate agent (first name + family name)**

After doing these 2 drawings, which makes up the first 2 steps, I continue the drawing by doing steps 3 to 7.

If there is one particular house that interests me and I may even have made a purchase offer on it, I can do:

 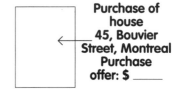

ME (first name + family name)

After doing these 2 drawings, which makes up the first 2 steps, I continue the drawing by doing steps 3 to 7.

As I am asking for what is best, it is possible that the best final result could be that my offer is refused. Why? Maybe the house has some hidden defects and I am protected by having my offer refused. I must trust and decide that what happens is the best result for me! If such is the case, by remaining open-minded, another house will turn up for me and I will discover that it is indeed better than the first one I had wanted to buy!

Sale, purchase, disposal of a material good (in general)

If I am searching, for instance, for a new car:

After doing these 2 drawings, which makes up the first 2 steps, I continue the drawing by doing steps 3 to 7.

If I have already gone to visit three car dealers and have been wondering which of the three is the best choice:

After doing these 2 drawings, which makes up the first 2 steps, I continue the drawing by doing steps 3 to 7.

The Technique's Many Applications and Some Questions from the Public

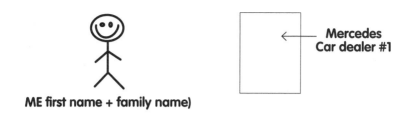

After doing these 2 drawings, which makes up the first 2 steps, I continue the drawing by doing steps 3 to 7.

~~~~~~

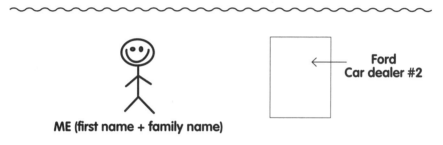

After doing these 2 drawings, which makes up the first 2 steps, I continue the drawing by doing steps 3 to 7.

~~~~~~

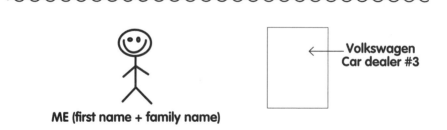

After doing these 2 drawings, which makes up the first 2 steps, I continue the drawing by doing steps 3 to 7.

~~~~~~

With my twin brother / sister

ME (first name + family name)   **Richard Bernier**

After doing these 2 drawings, which makes up the first 2 steps, I continue the drawing by doing steps 3 to 7.

If my twin brother died at birth, for instance, I can do:

ME (first name + family name)   My twin passed away[45]

After doing these 2 drawings, which makes up the first 2 steps, I continue the drawing by doing steps 3 to 7.

If I don't know whether I had a twin before my birth (Lost Twin syndrome)[46]:

---

45   Passed away means "deceased." If there was more than one, I do the exercise with each twin. They can be Twin #1, Twin #2, etc.

46   We speak of **Lost Twin syndrome** when one of the two fetuses disappears from the uterus during the pregnancy. Certain estimations by scientists indicate that approximately one person out of 8 had a twin in the mother's uterus, whereas only one out of 70 finally have a twin brother or sister at birth.

ME (first name + family name)   **My unknown twin**

After doing these 2 drawings, which makes up the first 2 steps, I continue the drawing by doing steps 3 to 7.

The relationship with my current spouse or ex-spouse

I can do the exercise with all the persons with whom I have had serious and intimate relationships in order to free myself of any expectations or attachments that might remain, especially if I have had children with the person or persons concerned. And this holds, whether these relationships are in the present or In the past.

ME (first name + family name)   **First name + family name of spouse or ex-spouse**

And I continue the drawing by doing steps 3 to 7.

When I do the *technique* with a spouse or an ex-spouse, it is doubly important to ask for **the best for both of us**. In fact, it may be tempting to use the *technique* in hopes of gaining a specific result, such as: *"I wish so much for us to get back together as a couple,"* or *"With the technique, I hope my spouse will change and become…"*

I cannot use the *technique* for the purpose of changing the other person.

A new relationship

If I enter into a new affective relationship, I can do the exercise with myself and the person with whom I am relating. It is important to ask for what is best for both of us, and not direct my attention to: *"I absolutely want this relationship to work!!"* because then I would be wanting to control the situation.

By doing the exercise, either I will get closer to the other person, or it will allow the relationship to come to an end more quickly, because that is the best thing that could happen. It is preferable to know it right away rather than wait for weeks, months or even years and end up with the *"impression that I lost my time!"*

Encountering my Soul mate (bachelorhood)[47]

The **Soul mate** is a concept that evokes a perfect compatibility in **love**, friendship and/or sexuality between two individuals. The term is used in everyday life to evoke a relationship of this type and by various New Age circles in the sense of **Souls** predestined to come together.

There is also the concept of the **Soul mate**, where I seek out the "other part of myself" so that I can achieve self-fulfillment. In fact, I already have both parts within me, but it may be that I find one partner who better reflects that "other part of myself" and, by displaying it more prominently, can enable me to achieve **self-fulfillment** more easily.

Often, if I am a bachelor over a certain period of time, it is either because the place is still taken up, consciously or not, by an ex-spouse, my job or even the children, or I have a fear of finding myself in a **love** relationship

---

[47] Although the following examples feature heterosexual couples, the principles and the *technique* apply in the same way with the search for a same-sex partner.

(fear of commitment, fear of being hurt again, fear of losing my **freedom**, etc.). It is therefore good to do the exercise with:

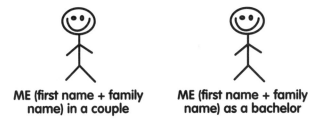

ME (first name + family name) in a couple ME (first name + family name) as a bachelor

And I continue the drawing by doing steps 3 to 7.

ME (first name + family name) My Soul mate

And I continue the drawing by doing steps 3 to 7.

It is important to do the exercise separately with each ex-spouse, because there may remain a form of attachment and dependency that is still present without my being **aware** of it. Especially if it was the other person who made the decision to terminate the relationship, I may be living, consciously or not, in the hope of resuming a relationship as a couple with this person. Especially if we had children together, I may unconsciously want to rebuild the family cell that existed in the past. It is sometimes easier to return to something familiar, even if it is uncomfortable or in disharmony, than to move forward toward the unknown.

Some stronger ties can still persist from when I was married and we have physically separated but not divorced. At the legal and energy levels, even if we have been separated for 15 years, if the divorce has not been pronounced, I am still "in a relationship as a couple" with this person at some level and "the place is taken."

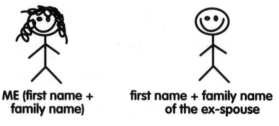

ME (first name + family name)

first name + family name of the ex-spouse

And I continue the drawing by doing steps 3 to 7.

It is also important to identify the fear I feel about the prospect of meeting this person. If it is the "fear of being hurt," I do the exercise as follows:

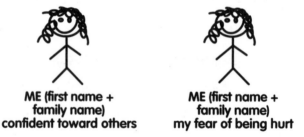

ME (first name + family name) **confident toward others**

ME (first name + family name) **my fear of being hurt**

And I continue the drawing by doing steps 3 to 7.

I may also have great expectations about the possibility of meeting someone, and this puts an unconscious pressure on me about the person I meet. Therefore I can do:

ME (first name + family name)   **ME (first name + family name) and my expectations about being in a relationship as a couple**

And I continue the drawing by doing steps 3 to 7.

After doing the exercise, I remain open to seeing the changes that will take place in me and maybe even in my ex-spouses. I must listen to my inner voice, because I can then receive clear messages, for example: initiating certain activities that will give me opportunities for meeting new persons, something I previously refused to do. By showing more openness and confidence, I increase my chances of getting results.

Separation / Divorce

The situation of a divorce was discussed on page 57. In the case of a separation, we usually think of the break-up of a couple, but there are also separations following a bereavement (our next subject), or when children leave the family home, for example. Again, I can do the exercise with myself and the person concerned and my emotions over this separation.

If it concerns me and my daughter Anne who has left the family nest and I now feel a great inner emptiness, I will do:

ME (first name + family name)   **Anne Bernier**

And I continue the drawing by doing steps 3 to 7.

ME (first name + family name) great plenitude   **ME (first name + family name) great inner emptiness**

And I continue the drawing by doing steps 3 to 7.

A deceased person (the mourning process)

When a person has passed away from this world, I may remain affected by it, sometimes even for several years. Certain persons never get over it. It is important to explain that when a person leaves their physical body, **love always remains present.** *It's my attachment to the person that hurts, not my love for them.* Applying the *technique* will help me to heal and connect myself more to this ever-present **love**. I have done this exercise myself when my father passed away. There followed a freeing of my sorrow and I now feel permanently connected to the **love** of my father. The void has been filled by his presence and his **love**.

Sometimes also, I may sense attachment, but also resentment or a feeling of abandonment following the passing away of a person dear to me. I may also remain with sadness and sorrow many years after the death of the loved person. It can be the case if it is a child who passed away at an early age.

It is therefore important to do the exercise to "clean out" those emotions. I may be amazed at the quantity of emotions I experience by doing the exercise. **This is normal and healthy!** The more I disengage myself from these sometimes deeply buried emotions, the greater the feeling of liberation and the more I can connect with the **love** that is present with the departed person. It is a beautiful gift to offer to oneself, but also to the other person who has departed this world and wants to see me be happy.

Though I sometimes have the impression that *"my mourning is totally over and everything is settled,"* it is good to still do the *technique* with the departed person to complete the process in case some unconscious attachment remains.

The **Little Stick Figures Technique** thus becomes an effective means for going through or ending a process of **bereavement**.

Doing the *technique* will help me to:

- Accept↓♥ the loss better.
- Allow my sorrow to express itself during the exercise.
- Free myself from a feeling of abandonment, for example.
- Undo some emotional attachments if, for example, I have reproaches to make or feel some hate toward the departed person.

I can do it at my own pace and as many times as I want. I can also ask a person close to me or my best friend to be present when I do the exercise to support me in my effort.[48]

---

[48] The help of a specialized therapist may also prove necessary, but the work done with the *technique* will be a step in the right direction.

ME (first name + family name)   **Fern Bernier[49]**

And I continue the drawing by doing steps 3 to 7.

───────────

An abortion / miscarriage

I can use the *technique* in the situation where I had an abortion or a miscarriage or if, as a man, I know that my wife or ex-wife experienced one of these situations.

If I am the woman who experienced the abortion:

[50]

ME (first name + family name)   **Fetus[51] passed away[52]**

And I continue the drawing by doing steps 3 to 7.

───────────

---

49   First name and family name of my father who passed away on May 15, 2014.
50   If I do not know the gender of the departed baby, I draw a boy or a girl; that is secondary.
51   If a name had already been chosen, I write down the first name.
52   Passed away = deceased.

If I am the man:

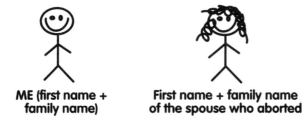

ME (first name + family name)

First name + family name of the spouse who aborted

And I continue the drawing by doing steps 3 to 7.

Birth / Adoption

For a child soon to be born or whom I intend to adopt:

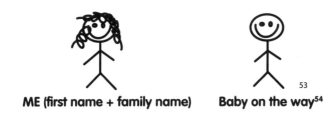

ME (first name + family name)   Baby on the way[54]

[53]

And I continue the drawing by doing steps 3 to 7.

---

53   If I do not know the gender of the departed baby, I draw a boy or a girl; that is secondary.
54   Write down the first name if it was already chosen, and then the family name.

ME (first name + family name)   Child adopted in China[56]

[55]

And I continue the drawing by doing steps 3 to 7.

My previous lives[57]

I can use the **Little Stick Figures Technique** to free myself from my previous lives. There are several possibilities here. If I am **aware** of some of those previous lives, I will do the exercise with a specific aim; for example:

Lucy Bernier today   **Lucy Bernier
a Pharaoh in Egypt**

And I continue the drawing by doing steps 3 to 7.

---

55 If I don't know the gender of the departed baby, I draw a boy or a girl; that is secondary.
56 I write down the name of the country if I have already chosen the child's country of origin.
57 For those persons who believe in this.

Lucy Bernier today

**Lucy Bernier
a High Priest in Atlantis**

And I continue the drawing by doing steps 3 to 7.

~~~~~~~~~~~~~~~~~~

If I have no information concerning my previous lives, I can use more general terms:

Lucy Bernier

**Lucy Bernier
a <u>man</u> in previous lives**

And I continue the drawing by doing steps 3 to 7.

~~~~~~~~~~~~~~~~~~

Also:

Lucy Bernier

**Lucy Bernier
a <u>woman</u> in previous lives**

And I continue the drawing by doing steps 3 to 7.

~~~~~~~~~~~~~~~~~~

Lucy Bernier

Lucy Bernier
a <u>child</u> in previous lives

And I continue the drawing by doing steps 3 to 7.

~~~~~~

Lucy Bernier

Lucy Bernier
a <u>parent</u> in previous lives

And I continue the drawing by doing steps 3 to 7.

~~~~~~

My ancestors

If I want to do the *technique* with my ancestors to free myself from my ancestral memories, I become **aware** that there are many persons involved. If I want, I can do the *technique* with myself and each ancestor whose name I know. A simpler and just as effective way is to use the two known family stocks, on my mother's side and on my father's side.

1. If I know the names of my grandparents: I can do the *technique* with myself and my four grandparents and their ancestors:

Lucy Bernier — Cecilia Dubé[58] and her ancestors

And I continue the drawing by doing steps 3 to 7.

~~~~~~~~~~~~~~~~~~~~~~~~~~~~~~~~~~

Lucy Bernier — Leo Hunter[59] and his ancestors

And I continue the drawing by doing steps 3 to 7.

~~~~~~~~~~~~~~~~~~~~~~~~~~~~~~~~~~

Lucy Bernier ← Lucy Gaudreau[60] and her ancestors

And I continue the drawing by doing steps 3 to 7.

~~~~~~~~~~~~~~~~~~~~~~~~~~~~~~~~~~

---

58   Maternal grandmother.
59   Maternal grandfather.
60   Paternal grandmother.

Lucy Bernier

Eustache Bernier[61] and his ancestors

And I continue the drawing by doing steps 3 to 7.

---

2. If I know the names of my parents but not those of my grandparents:

A simple and just as effective way is to use the two known family stocks, on my mother's side and on my father's side. For example, in my case, my mother's name is Dolores Hunter and my father's name is Fernand Bernier. I can do the *technique* as follows:

Lucy Bernier

Dolores Hunter[62] and her ancestors

And I continue the drawing by doing steps 3 to 7.

---

61   Paternal grandfather.
62   My mother's first name and original family name.

Lucy Bernier

Fern Bernier[63] **and his ancestors**

And I continue the drawing by doing steps 3 to 7.

---

3. If I don't know the names of my parents nor those of my grandparents:

Lucy Bernier

My ancestors on my father's side

And I continue the drawing by doing steps 3 to 7.

Lucy Bernier

My ancestors on my mother's side

And I continue the drawing by doing steps 3 to 7.

---

63 My father's first name and family name.

Attracting abundance in all the areas of my life

Abundance is defined as a state of affairs where available resources are in great quantities and exceed one's needs. It is important to take this definition and see what it can mean in my life, in which aspects of my life I desire to have more abundance: do I want an abundance of money, of health, of friendship, of **love**, of business opportunities, of friendly encounters, of work, etc.?

There is a principle that says it is practically impossible to *attract to myself* what I despise in others. If I am envious, jealous or scornful of the income, the house, the lifestyle, the physical tone or the quality of the **love** relationships of other people, it will be more difficult for me to attract those things to me. **My subconscious will always obey my dominant thoughts and emotions, those I most often have in mind.**

Therefore, the fact of doing this *technique* will enable me to become more **aware** of my thoughts about abundance and change my programming involving it. If I have found that the areas in which I want more abundance are money and friends, I will do:[64]

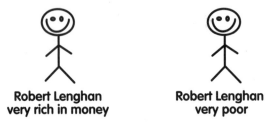

**Robert Lenghan
very rich in money**

**Robert Lenghan
very poor**

And I continue the drawing by doing steps 3 to 7.

---

64 Write down opposites.

Robert Lenghan with many good friends **Robert Lenghan friendless**

And I continue the drawing by doing steps 3 to 7.

Even if I have the impression that it makes no sense to write: "poor" and *"friendless,"* I do it just the same.

> **By doing the exercise with opposites, it enables me to position myself in relation to the two states of affairs and maybe even to become aware of certain patterns I follow or judgments I make regarding what I want.**

Am I comfortable with the idea of having a lot of money, or does it make me feel uncomfortable for fear of what others will think of me? Do I really want to have more friends or am I more the solitary type, a little reserved, preferring to do my little business by myself? Whatever the answers, the exercise will enable me to make things clearer to myself. There will thus be better chances that what I desire will show up!

Sickness or the fear of having an illness / a disability

Doing the exercise with one or several illnesses that I have enables me to be more detached from them. This will diminish my level of stress and I will thereby improve my chances of beginning to heal.

When I do the exercise with myself and an illness that I have or that I fear developing, it is important that I place myself on the left: me in perfect health[65] and me with the name of the illness on the right. The fact of using opposites will bring the greatest changes and results. It is as though I were telling my subconscious: *"Help me find a solution so that I can switch from sickness to perfect health."* I also make an affirmation, namely: *"I know that perfect health is possible for me, I need help and I want to change."* And also: *"I have perfect health in me, help me make it show."*

If I have a specific disease or disorder:

ME (first name + family name) in perfect health   **ME (first name + family name) with a gluten allergy**

And I continue the drawing by doing steps 3 to 7.

ME (first name + family name) in perfect health   **ME (first name + family name) with arthritis**

And I continue the drawing by doing steps 3 to 7.

---

65   See Chapter 6 for more information on the use of opposites.

The Technique's Many Applications and Some Questions from the Public

ME (first name + family name) in perfect health   **ME (first name + family name) with back pains**

And I continue the drawing by doing steps 3 to 7.

If I am afraid of having a disease, I risk attracting[66] it, because **I attract the object of my fears**. It is therefore important **to do the exercise with all the diseases that I fear I might have**, including the diseases called hereditary and that other members of my family have had themselves. If for example, my mother Judy Foxx[67] died of a breast cancer and I am afraid of having a breast cancer:

Lucy Bernier in perfect health   **Judy Foxx with breast cancer**

And I continue the drawing by doing steps 3 to 7.

---

66   Because fear increases stress, my brain will tend to attract this situation so as to diminish my stress.
67   Fictional name.

**Lucy Bernier
in perfect health**

**Lucy Bernier
with breast cancer**

And I continue the drawing by doing steps 3 to 7.

If I want to pursue my development, I look up the name of my disease in ***The Encyclopedia of Ailments and Diseases.***[68] I read the text concerning it and look at the emotions that can be at the root of the disease. Even if I was unable to clearly identify in my life what is involved, I do the *technique* with myself and each of those emotions.

For example, if I am **depressive**, the two major elements at the root of depression are **self-depreciation** and **guilt**. I find the quality that matches these two words, which gives:

Self-esteem ⟷ Self-depreciation
Responsibility ⟷ Guilt

I will therefore do the 3 following exercises:

**ME (first name + family
name) in perfect health**

**ME (first name + family
name) depressed**

And I continue the drawing by doing steps 3 to 7.

---

68   By Jacques Martel, published 2012/2020.

ME (first name + family name) high self-esteem   **ME (first name + family name) high self-depreciation**

And I continue the drawing by doing steps 3 to 7.

ME (first name + family name) high responsibility   **ME (first name + family name) high guilt**

And I continue the drawing by doing steps 3 to 7.

Sickness: A member of the family

Whether it is my child who is sick, a parent or any other relative, the principle remains the same: I draw myself **on the left in perfect health** and **the other person on the right with the name of the disease**:

The Little Stick Figures Technique for Emotional Self-Healing

ME (first name + family name) in perfect health

Fern Bernier asthmatic

And I continue the drawing by doing steps 3 to 7.

~~~~~~

I can also do:

ME (first name + family name) in perfect health

ME (first name + family name) asthmatic

And I continue the drawing by doing steps 3 to 7.

~~~~~~

***The fact of drawing myself with the name of an illness <u>will not have the effect of attracting that illness into my life</u>, because I bathe the drawing in **light**. The message that is sent off to the universe is:

> Show me if I need to change
> some of my behaviors, habits,
> emotions or thoughts in order to avoid
> having this disease
> and remain in full health.

With a fear

I place myself on the left with the opposite of fear and I place the fear on the right (the positive on the left, the negative on the right).

ME (first name + family name) very comfortable in water   **ME (first name + family name) very afraid of water**

And I continue the drawing by doing steps 3 to 7.

ME (first name + family name) very comfortable with heights   **ME (first name + family name) very afraid of heights**

And I continue the drawing by doing steps 3 to 7.

ME (first name + family name) in perfect health   **ME (first name + family name) with emphysema**

And I continue the drawing by doing steps 3 to 7.

An exercise with the 6 basic fears

An interesting exercise to do is to apply the *technique* with myself on the left and each of the 6 basic fears[69] (on the right), which are:

1. The fear of death
2. The fear of poverty
3. The fear of criticism
4. The fear of sickness
5. The fear of becoming old
6. The fear of losing someone's **love**

Add **"very"** before each fear to get the most results. And I see how I feel during each exercise.

ME (first name + family name) love life very much   **ME (first name + family name) very afraid of dying**

And I continue the drawing by doing steps 3 to 7.

ME (first name + family name) very rich   **ME (first name + family name) very afraid of poverty**

And I continue the drawing by doing steps 3 to 7.

---

69 From the book: ***The Law of Success,*** Napoleon Hill.

The Technique's Many Applications and Some Questions from the Public

ME (first name + family name) very much appreciated   **ME (first name + family name) very afraid of criticism**

And I continue the drawing by doing steps 3 to 7.

~~~~~~

ME (first name + family name) in perfect health   **ME (first name + family name) very afraid of sickness**

And I continue the drawing by doing steps 3 to 7.

~~~~~~

ME (first name + family name) very young   **ME (first name + family name) very afraid of ageing**

And I continue the drawing by doing steps 3 to 7.

~~~~~~

ME (first name + family name) beloved by all **ME (first name + family name) very afraid of losing someone's love**

And I continue the drawing by doing steps 3 to 7.

Dependency on alcohol, cigarettes, food, drugs, gambling, etc.

The *technique* can be done with any situation on which I have a dependency: alcohol, cigarettes, food, drugs, affective, etc.

Cigarettes

ME (first name + family name) non-smoker **ME (first name + family name) cigarette smoker**

And I continue the drawing by doing steps 3 to 7.

ME (first name + family name) in perfect health   ME (first name + family name) and my fear of lung cancer

And I continue the drawing by doing steps 3 to 7.

Alcohol

ME (first name + family name) sober   ME (first name + family name) my fear of becoming alcoholic[70]

And I continue the drawing by doing steps 3 to 7.

---

70 Specify the type of drink that I am hooked on as the case may be, for example: bourbon, gin, rhum, etc. Also, I use the most extreme adjective, even if it is more than in actual reality. The results will be greater.

ME (first name + family name) in perfect health   ME (first name + family name) my fear of liver cirrhosis

And I continue the drawing by doing steps 3 to 7.

Food

ME (first name + family name) excellent diet   ME (first name + family name) food dependency

And I continue the drawing by doing steps 3 to 7.

And so on...

Weight reduction / gain / maintenance

I can do the exercise if I am experiencing a situation involving my weight: if I perceive myself as too heavy, too thin, too fat, "I easily put on fat," etc.

The Technique's Many Applications and Some Questions from the Public

ME (first name + family name) very slim   **ME (first name + family name) very fat**

And I continue the drawing by doing steps 3 to 7.

~~~~~~

ME (first name + family name) healthy weight   **ME (first name + family name) too thin**

And I continue the drawing by doing steps 3 to 7.

~~~~~~

ME (first name + family name) maintain my weight   **ME (first name + family name) fatten easily**

And I continue the drawing by doing steps 3 to 7.

~~~~~~

Winning in a contest or at the lottery

I can do the exercise, but watch out! Is winning in a contest or at the lottery truly the best thing for me? Am I tied to the result? Do I want to control the outcome? I must adjust my attitude and do the exercise by saying: *"I want to win the contest if that is the best outcome for me and for my development."* Therefore, if I take part in a drawing where there is a car to be won, I can do the following exercises:

ME (first name + family name)

Contest
―――
(Name of the contest)

And I continue the drawing by doing steps 3 to 7.

―――

ME (first name + family name)

New car

And I continue the drawing by doing steps 3 to 7.

―――

ME (first name + family name) ME (first name + family name) Financial abundance

And I continue the drawing by doing steps 3 to 7.

When I do the exercise, I must ask **"the best for my development."** The **best** or **better** may be that I win this car. Or maybe a friend will give me one, who knows! By doing the exercise, I open myself to all the possibilities, without expecting that the car will necessarily come from any specific source. I might receive money that will enable me to buy a new car. That is why the exercise was also done with financial abundance.

My scores at school (academic results)

A situation was previously evoked of a child with her math teacher on page 85. What about if my child (or myself, if I am in a training or study program) is having difficulty with a subject and wants to improve her results? If I take the example of my course in mathematics, I will do:

Robert Lenghan

My difficulties in mathematics[71]

And I continue the drawing by doing steps 3 to 7.

---

71   I can specify the course number, for example: *Mathematics 101*.

An actual case: a 14-year-old student from France who was studying in an international school in Québec was having issues with his academic results in mathematics, which varied between 20% and 40%. He did the *technique* with himself and his math teacher. Later on, his next four examination scores were 100%, 90%, 90% and 100%!

It may be that my difficulties originate in the subject itself, or because of something it subconsciously reminds me of. As if my parents were constantly "counting" on me and this makes me feel stress at being "assigned" to perform. They might also be related to a conscious or unconscious conflict with the teacher of that subject. That is why it is preferable to do the *technique* with both situations: the difficulties in mathematics (above) and the mathematics teacher (below):

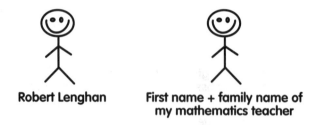

And I continue the drawing by doing steps 3 to 7.

Work (dissatisfaction with work / boss; search for a job)

If I am dissatisfied with my job or my boss, I can do the following exercise:

**Robert Lenghan
ideal work**

Title of my current job[72]

And I continue the drawing by doing steps 3 to 7.

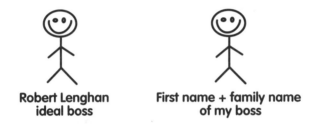

**Robert Lenghan
ideal boss**

**First name + family name
of my boss**

And I continue the drawing by doing steps 3 to 7.

I have noted that sometimes, I have the impression that I should change jobs because certain aspects of my current job don't suit me; but, as I know from experience, it is sometimes enough to become **aware** of certain facts about it for things to start getting better. The testimony on page 171 is a good example of this.

If I am in search of a job, I can do the method with myself on the left and the ideal job on the right, and then another exercise with myself on the left and my job expectations on the right.

---

72   Garage owner, technician, professor, secretary, nurse, etc.

Concerns about my car

I may have issues with my car: a breakdown, parts to change, an unusual noise, etc. An interesting fact to note is that my car symbolizes the formative vehicle of my life. Just as each part of my physical body is related to a psychosomatic[73] element, so it is too for my car.[74] For example, the wheels correspond to my legs, the motor is mainly related to my heart♥, etc. It is therefore interesting to do the exercise with myself and each malfunction that my car experiences. And even if I am skeptical about this theory, it is interesting to do the exercise with an open mind! And even if I don't know all the correspondences, my subconscious will take care of finding the appropriate matchings!

And I continue the drawing by doing steps 3 to 7.

With a person who wishes me harm

I may experience situations where I believe that other persons or groups of persons wish me harm, want to cast an evil spell on me, resent me for something I said or did: in short, that someone consciously wants to aim something negative at me.

I may use the *technique* in these situations provided that I take the proper attitude. It is imperative that I <u>not</u> use the *technique* to get

---

73 Psychological and affective disorders that manifest themselves through physical symptoms.
74 See the book by Sarah Diane Pomerleau on this subject: **Mon auto, miroir de ma vie (My car, mirror of my life).** Les Éditions ATMA Internationales, 2007.

revenge or to return something negative back to them. **I may use it however to protect myself.** There is thus no risk of reprisals.

In a first case, if I know the name of the person or persons who wish me harm, I do the exercise with myself on the left and the other person or group of persons on the right. So:

ME (first name + family name)

First name + family name of the person who wishes me harm

And I continue the drawing by doing steps 3 to 7.

ME (first name + family name) fully protected

Name of the group of persons

And I continue the drawing by doing steps 3 to 7.

The *technique* with God (positive), the devil (negative), etc.[75]

I may, if I so desire, do the exercise with myself and God, the angels, the Saints, and even the Devil! Whether I do the *technique* with a positive or

---

75   Depending on my personal beliefs.

a negative element, the result can only be positive. In fact, for example, if I decide to do the exercise with myself and God, it is as though I were asking to let go of the attachments and dependencies involved in my expectations toward Him.

And I continue the drawing by doing steps 3 to 7.

If I do the exercise with the Devil, I place both of us in a circle of **light** and I detach myself from any persons or situations that might manifest the Devil or "evil" in my life. Even if I draw a negative element, because I surround it with a circle of **light**, I am protected from this negative entity.

And I continue the drawing by doing steps 3 to 7.

I can also do the exercise with the person I detest the most, who for me represents the worst person on Earth, whether dead or alive, such as Adolf Hitler[76] for example. The exercise with him will not work only consciously, but also at the unconscious level, because it will help me detach myself from the injustices and unfair judgments I have

---

76 **Adolf Hitler** was the founder of the German Nazi Party and the man most responsible for the Holocaust in World War 2.

experienced in my life in other situations. Although my own experience was on a smaller scale, it involves the same emotions and that is what counts. Hitler is just a figurehead to work on the injustice or the tyranny I have suffered from in my own life.

Our cartoon heroes or favorite actors / actresses

What will happen if I do the *technique* with someone I admire, for example an actor, a cartoon hero or even someone who has accomplished great and beautiful things, for example Mother Theresa? Admiration fosters idealization and, depending on its intensity, I may become attached and wish to live their lives by proxy to some degree. By doing the *technique*, I gain some detachment from this person and reconnect myself to my own divine essence. I am thereby in closer contact with my inner power and I can thus myself manifest these same qualities that I admire in "my hero."

And I continue the drawing by doing steps 3 to 7.

Developing a special gift or talent[77]

I can use the *technique* if I wish to develop a special gift such as clairvoyance, magnetism, mediumship or a talent such as playing a musical instrument. I may have high expectations or be very perfectionistic and put a lot of pressure on myself in learning a gift or a talent. The method will enable me to be more in the present moment

---

77   See the testimonial on page 172 (the violin).

and let go more as far as results are concerned. The ensuing learning will be easier by letting events take place instead of wanting to provoke them.

ME (first name + family name)   **My gift of clairvoyance**

And I continue the drawing by doing steps 3 to 7.

～～～～～～～～～～～

Me and my inner child
(present and past suffering)

Most of my current suffering originates from injuries experienced in my childhood and that repeat themselves in my adult life. I can therefore use the *technique* with my inner child to help me detach myself from those sufferings. While I do the *technique*, a conscious or unconscious process of acknowledgement, forgiveness and acceptance↓♥ takes place, which is essential for healing and freeing any negative emotions.

Even if I hesitate to do the drawing because of memories surfacing, it is very beneficial to complete it to the end. I can ask my spouse, my best friend or a person I trust to be present, and I know I will experience emotions (sometimes the injuries are still very intensely fresh and just the fact of thinking about them makes strong emotions surface).

If I feel like stopping halfway through the exercise, it is important to trust and to ask to be protected and guided during the exercise and to pursue it to the end.

> **By doing this exercise, the best will happen for my development and only positive changes will happen that I am able to manage, no more.**

Lucy Bernier adult   Little abused Lucy

And I continue the drawing by doing steps 3 to 7.

If I have seen situations of suffering in other persons, for example my mother who was beaten by my father, I do the exercise not to interfere in an extreme situation but to throw **light** on my own conscious or unconscious attachments as a witness. In this situation, I can do the *technique* with myself and my Mom, and then with myself and my Dad.

ME (first name + family name)   Mom being beaten by Dad

And I continue the drawing by doing steps 3 to 7.

ME (first name + family name)   **Dad beating Mom**

And I continue the drawing by doing steps 3 to 7.

I do the two exercises because I may have experienced different emotions about what my mother and father were experiencing (two different dynamics).

With my ego / subconscious

I can do the exercise with my ego, which is my identity and is of a mental nature. The ego is like a character with whom I identify and who is born from my memories, experiences, opinions and beliefs, well-founded or not. It generates life patterns and possible conflicts with other people. It is the false representation that an individual makes of himself. This representation acts as a screen hiding my real nature as a human being.

Lucy Bernier   **Lucy Bernier**
Being   **Ego**

And I continue the drawing by doing steps 3 to 7.

With my subconscious

**Lucy Bernier
Conscious**

**Lucy Bernier
Subconscious**

And I continue the drawing by doing steps 3 to 7.

With a group of persons

It is possible to do the exercise with a group of persons, such as an association, a sports team, the members of a church, a family, etc. And also, if I know the names of certain persons in the group with whom I want to harmonize my relationship, I can do it individually with each person.

Robert Lenghan

And I continue the drawing by doing steps 3 to 7.

Robert Lenghan — The persons who are members of my church

And I continue the drawing by doing steps 3 to 7.

Robert Lenghan — The board of directors of the National Bank

And I continue the drawing by doing steps 3 to 7.

Robert Lenghan — The volunteers in my parish[78]

And I continue the drawing by doing steps 3 to 7.

---

78 Write down the name of the parish.

Robert Lenghan

And I continue the drawing by doing steps 3 to 7.

Although it is quite effective this way, it is important to also do the exercise individually with each person of this group whose names I know and with whom I more especially need to harmonize my relations.

My animal or an animal

If I want to do the exercise with my pet animal, I can draw it on the right like a person. Indeed, animals have chakras as do humans. There are 8 major energy centers in animals (see the illustration below).[79, 80]

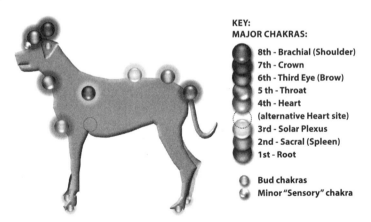

KEY:
MAJOR CHAKRAS:

8th - Brachial (Shoulder)
7th - Crown
6th - Third Eye (Brow)
5 th - Throat
4th - Heart
(alternative Heart site)
3rd - Solar Plexus
2nd - Sacral (Spleen)
1st - Root

Bud chakras
Minor "Sensory" chakra

***I can draw <u>by exception</u>, 8 chakras for me, by placing the 8th at the level of the thymus (between the throat and the heart♥) and Figure #2.

---

[79] Image reproduced by permission of Patinkas, Copyright© Patinkas 2015.
[80] Brachial Chakra Information Copyright© Magrit Coates 2015.

The Little Stick Figures Technique for Emotional Self-Healing

ME (first name + family name)

Snowy (name of the animal)

And I continue the drawing by doing steps 3 to 7.

~~~~~~

If it is sick, I can name the sickness:

ME (first name + family name)

Snowy with arthritis

And I continue the drawing by doing steps 3 to 7.

~~~~~~

If it is my child, my daughter Nathaly for example, who is affected by the sickness of my animal, I can either suggest to my daughter to do the exercise with the dog, or I can do the exercise myself as follows:

The Technique's Many Applications and Some Questions from the Public

ME (first name + family name)   **Snowy sick[81]**

And I continue the drawing by doing steps 3 to 7.

ME (first name + family name)   **Nathaly Bernier sad**

And I continue the drawing by doing steps 3 to 7.

With certain aspects of my life or causes that are important to me

I can do the exercise with causes that are close to my heart♥ or with which I have an affinity, for example the Native Peoples, the Earth, the race of dolphins, nature, bees, poverty, pollution, child beating, radiations, etc. I can be very affected by certain situations and the *technique* will help me to be more detached and objective. These elements will generally be represented by a rectangle on the right. But if I feel the need to represent it by a figure, that is all right too. It is doing the exercise that counts. The rest is secondary.

---

81   I specify the name of the disease if I know it.

ME (first name + family name)

And I continue the drawing by doing steps 3 to 7.

~~~~~~

ME (first name + family name)

And I continue the drawing by doing steps 3 to 7.

~~~~~~

Can I use the *technique* with persons or situations that are beautiful and in harmony?

The *technique* can be useful to me in relation to a person with whom I am experiencing difficulties, but **also with one or several persons with whom I feel in full harmony or for whom I feel filled with love**, whether it is my life partner, my children, my parents or my friends, and I feel like telling you to do the exercise <u>mainly with them</u>, because often, I may think that I am completely detached from a person with whom I am in harmony, whereas **there exists some unconscious zones of attachment** that risk showing up at a time when I may least expect it.

Therefore, I can draw myself with the person I share my life with and with each one of my children. I can also draw myself with my father, my mother, each of my brothers and each of my sisters, or with each of my work colleagues, my boss, each of my team leaders, etc. These persons can be in this world (living) or have left us (deceased).[82]

This can help me do some "cleaning up," somewhat like when I use an antivirus program in my computer. If I clean it out, the antivirus will eradicate the harmful computer viruses and "worms" I didn't know existed. The same goes just as well for my attachments and dependencies toward others and which are often invisible and unconscious. They act like "viruses" in my life and slow down my development, whether I am aware of it or not.

---

82   Go to page 120 for more ample explanations and examples.

CHAPTER 10

A General Cleansing and Rebalancing Protocol

By applying the **Little Stick Figures Technique**, I clean out my inner conscious and unconscious "programs" and give myself the opportunity to make space for a more detached and therefore more unconditional **love**.

If I want to carry out a big "spring cleaning" or a "rebalancing of my life," I can do the 7 steps of the *technique* with myself on the left and each of the important persons in my life, whether they are living, deceased, outside of the country, whether I mix with them or not, and whether the relationship is in harmony or not (on the right).

Here is a partial list to help me identify the figure on the right:

my current or past life partner

my mother and my father (known or not)

each of my brothers

each of my sisters

each of my children

each of my grandparents

each of my friends

my boss (present and past)

my ex-spouse(s)

each of my work colleagues

my pastor

each of my team-mates if I am in a team

each of my pet animals (present and past) (p. 157)

each of my employees

each of my therapists

each of my physicians

my job

the 6 basic fears (p. 138)

the 17 suggestions in the table on page 68

etc.

I can add to those my ancestors (see explanation p. 126) and my previous lives (page 124).

I do the exercise (the 7 steps) with each person even if the relationship seems to be very good and in harmony.

There is no minimum or maximum regarding the number of exercises to be done in a day. I just have to listen to my body: if I feel fatigue or feel more emotional, I just need to space out the time between the exercises. I can also do the *technique* over again with the same person if I feel that is what I must do. If I doubt that I am capable of properly hearing the messages from my inner voice, I can do:

Lucy Bernier   **Lucy Bernier**
Listening   **Inner voice**

And I continue the drawing by doing steps 3 to 7.

Conclusion

Done! This book has shown me innumerable ways to use the **Little Stick Figures Technique**. Now there only remains for me to experiment with it as often as possible in my everyday life. The challenge I may need to meet will be to constantly keep in mind that this *technique* can be used in my everyday life as soon as an opportunity presents itself or at any time.

It is important to refer to pages 52 and 53 that show **the 7 steps of the technique** and make sure that I am carrying out the steps in the right order. Many examples were given to ensure that the basic principles have been well integrated after having read this whole book. Thus, I can use the *technique* even with situations that are not mentioned in this book. As long as I apply **the 5 rules listed** on page 24, I am sure that I will apply the *technique* in the proper way, that I will be protected and that I will get a maximum of results.

We invite you to read the many testimonials from persons who have used the *technique* and who obtained wonderful results (page 167). Beyond skepticism or disbelief, this *technique* is a proven one and shows its results. No need to believe in it, it simply needs to be applied.

The decision was made to include some testimonials that are a little longer (those at the end), in order to clearly show some contexts in which the *technique* was used and the results obtained.

We hope that the **Little Stick Figures Technique** can help you bring more clarity, peace and calm in each of your lives, as has been the case for ourselves and for thousands of persons!

Lucie Bernier and Robert Lenghan

Testimonials

The power of writing

The *Little Stick Figures Technique* is marvelous. It enables me to cut away the ties of dependency and attachment to persons and situations without cutting away **love**, true **love**. It also enables us to become aware of the ties of attachment that we may have and that we are not aware of.

It is a *technique* that is now a part of my daily life and that I recommend to any person asking me for help. It enables us to let go. It is a great *technique* that has positively changed my life.

This is when **I realize the power of the written word and that I understand Jacques when he says that** *"the brain makes no difference between what is real, virtual, imaginary and symbolic."*

I do it for any situation and at any time (in the car, at home, on vacation…) and it helps me to "let go."

THANK YOU Jacques for this marvelous tool. *S.G.*

Letting go in love

To answer your question: **It helps me, and my clients too, to let go in love,** and also the understanding that **these events have led us to grow and we must shed some of the memories of our past in order to recover our peace of mind and our health.** *I.T.*

The power of the symbolic act

I adore this sort of simple exercise and **I believe in the power of the symbolic act. And the fact of freeing ourselves from our conscious or unconscious attachments in order to keep only the tie of love, that seems essential to me in our quest for freedom**. I waited a long time before taking the time to watch Jacques Martel's two videos because I needed a one-hour session, but I was thrilled. Thanks to Jacques Martel for offering us this gift that he teaches in his training sessions.   A.C.

A therapist

I work at home as a self-employed naturopath and massage therapist and I have found it so extraordinary that I regularly suggest it to my clients. **It is a simple, rapid *technique* and with a little letting-go, it gives extraordinary results.** I always tell my clients: *"Try it, you will see."* No pressure. **No relentless prodding, just letting do.** You only need to go and see the number of visits on your site and you will clearly find that this method is very widely used. I always tell myself that all those small gestures made can produce large results. An amusing incident: one day, I spoke to one of my sisters about the *Little Stick Figures Technique* and then, when in turn I later had to get by a little difficulty, she told me: *"Did you do the Little Stick Figures Technique?"* Just to say the effect it can have! A boomerang effect. I have only good thoughts about this method.   M. P.

An exercise that is accessible at all times

Since I saw your videos about the *Little Stick Figures Technique*, I have been doing these exercises and **it really helps me, whether it is for my energy, my health or the balance in my life**. I have truly appreciated seeing this, because I didn't have the means for consulting professionals to help me, whether it is for my state of health, my depression, my lack of energy or my chronic pains. This has given me a rebound.   L. N.

Freeing myself, growing, forgiving

I want to give you my opinion about this wonderful *Little Stick Figures Technique*… simply **marvelous for freeing, treating, finding ourselves and pursuing our lives in the right direction as Souls and physical beings**.

This *technique* helps us grow, forgive and be happy. I do it regularly with several persons, and I even pass on this *technique* to those who need it. Everyone appreciates it and experiences well-being afterward. So an enormous thank you for this great sharing. *Gigi*

Facilitating encounters or telephone calls

I have regularly used the *Little Stick Figures Technique* for years and have always been **pleasantly surprised at the positive results of those encounters and/or telephone calls that I dreaded**. Thanks for this simple *technique* accessible anywhere. *L. T.*

Sales

I congratulate you for your books and the demo of the *Little Stick Figures*, it is a *technique* that works really well. I have a company and I produce hand-painted wooden bookmarks, and also canvases and little sheep, and **since using your *technique*, our products have been selling better and better**. *J. T.*

Sadness, disappointment

I have used the *Little Stick Figures* several times. **It has helped me to free myself of emotions of sadness and disappointment.** I have practiced it in relation to my friends and relatives, my spouse, my job, etc. I have listened to the videos. Thank you. *D. P.*

Difficult situations or encounters

I use this method when I anticipate a situation that seems difficult to experience calmly, or even sometimes impossible to face. Whether it is before an exam (sore stomach, fear of forgetting, uncontrolled panic), or before communicating something important to me (**love**, positive or negative feelings or emotions). When the time has come, all goes calmly with **love** and peace and, usually, unexpectedly and unusually.

A.P.

Coach and clients using the *technique*

First of all, thanks for having had the brilliant idea of creating this *technique*. I will be brief in my testimonial, because **the best way to see its effectiveness is to try it**. For my part, I have used it many times with stupendous results. In my personal life as well as in my professional life.

As a coach and trainer, when I experience encounters turning in circles, I suggest to my clients to try it. **At first, they have a surprised attitude and they laugh; but after doing it, they are convinced of the *technique's* effectiveness.**

Thanks for this nice, very simple, but very effective tool.

G. W.

Easier discussions

I can tell you that I have tried the *Little Stick Figures*. **It enables me to not have any pressure when I meet a person and we have a discussion about certain things.** The pressure is removed and it is easier to accept↓♥ someone's stubborn opinion about how things should be done. I will do it with several persons. It's more relaxed, there's a letting go that sets in.

M. G.

Three months without any news...

Three months without any news... And then, 5 minutes after having done the Little Stick Figures, I received an SMS text message from that person! I am amazed, I can't get over it! Many thanks!   *M. C.*

Capable of saying NO

It enabled me to detach myself from events involving certain members of my family and not from the person. **I feel less guilty of saying no today.** It allows me to live more serenely while dealing with the events of my life.   *C. M.*

Well-being at work

Frankly, once I got over the fear of possibly cutting away **love** with the *Little Stick Figures Technique*, I used it several times and it has always given good results. The first time, I believed it more or less and the fear of cutting away **love** was present. So I did a test with my job. I was engaged almost body and **Soul** with my work. If someone said no to my organism, it hurt me. So I used your *technique*, without much conviction. I followed to the letter what you said to do. When I cut the links, I did it so fast that I felt physical pain in the chakra of the solar plexus. It took my breath away. But I detached myself emotionally from my job, so that when I closed the door of my office, I could leave the problems there without any guilt. **I stopped feeling an obligation to be on duty 24/7. I continued to act professionally, to do my work well, to be effective, but with detachment, therefore with a more objective eye and with no emotional involvement.** A sort of peace immediately settled inside of me.

I also used it with a person I was very close to, to the point where I took her problems upon me, I felt so responsible for her that I reacted to her problems before she did. With the *Little Stick Figures Technique*, my relationship with her changed. **I love her as much as before, I am still close to her, but I no longer feel responsible for her, and what belongs to her I now leave to her.** I have more respect for both of us, for her as much as for me. To get there however, I had to do the exercise a few more times (4 as I recall). Each time, I saw an improvement.   *N. C.*

Reclaiming my power

I met Jacques Martel during his stays in Pau and then in Ousse (France). I learned about the *Little Stick Figures Technique* by visiting the Internet site.[83] It is a *technique* that greatly helped me realize that we are not puppets under the sway of other puppets, at least in our daily lives. We can act differently from what we were taught or what was imposed upon us. **The fact of cutting the page in two enables me to concretely enact this detachment and realize that it is possible through my sole willpower.**

Thank you Jacques for having enabled me to free myself from certain influences and certain walls that I had built up around myself. Today I have an external view of things and I continue to advance. I regularly think about this *technique* when I am faced with complex situations. And I draw accordingly.   *L. F.*

Playing the violin

Dear Jacques, I went on vacation to my friend **Carole's place, whose passion is the violin. Carole likes her instrument a lot, but she had stage fright at the idea of playing in public for the end-of-year celebration at her music school.** While training at home, she asked me for my opinion about her music. I told her I appreciated the sound of the violin, but that she still had some work to do before getting to play "just so."

I know the effectiveness of the **light figures** (or matchstick figures) because I practice them daily, and so I explained to her the principle of the *technique*. **No sooner said than done: she drew herself, drew her violin, and so on.**

---

83   www.atma.ca, videos section.

During the end-of-year celebration at her music school, she had to play in a duet with another violinist. Worried and stressed, she asked me to help her if possible. I attended her last rehearsal, I sent **light** her way, but I felt this was no longer useful, I just listened to the two violinists playing. At that instant, **I saw a glorious white light descend on Carole and her violin and at the same instant, my heart♥ chakra opened wide and a powerful energy surged from my heart♥ to my friend**. All this happened very fast.

And then, Jacques, her music was no longer the same. It was magnificent, the vibrations of her music were as though divinely inspired. Her partner stopped playing and Carole continued to play alone. The performance went well, and Carole again found herself playing alone before the audience, exactly as during the last rehearsal. That evening, pleased by her performance, she again played at her home and it was magic!

I sometimes remember the beauty of those sounds and the emotion they awakened in me. As for Carole, I clearly sense that the relation she has with her violin has changed, for the greatest pleasure of everyone, and especially of my ears.

Thanks to the *Little Stick Figures*. Thank you, Jacques. L.G.

An unpleasant situation with flies

Right off upon arriving at my grandmother's in Ornans (France), I noted with little enthusiasm that this year again, it would be the *"war of the flies."* The flies were countless, excited and aggressive. They settled on me, on my plate, in my hair. Chase one away, three more appear. My grandmother and my uncle each had a fly-swatter close by at all times and at each instant, while we were talking, eating, reading or whatever else, they would interrupt themselves to try to kill one and loudly announced the verdict "missed!" or "got it!" Many dead flies were heaped on the ground, remained stuck to the swatters laid on the table and a few landed on what had been the lid of a pot of jam.

I found this situation very uncomfortable for my taste. So that very evening, I decided to do the *Little Stick Figures* with the flies and I explained the method again to my grandmother: I drew myself, I drew my grandmother, I drew my uncle, then the flies...

The next morning at breakfast, there remained but a few flies, calm and discreet, that let themselves get squashed, whereas on the previous evening they had been so lively. Then, there were no more flies until the end of my stay. The people from the village who came to my grandmother's home were astonished: *"How is it, Odette, that there are no flies at your place?!! At my place there are so many of them, I had to set up two sticky fly strips!"*

And inside the lid, instead of the dead flies, there were cherry pits.

Thank you, little matchbook figures! Thank you, Jacques!   L.G.

Healing childhood traumas

Hello Jacques,

I received from my friend Juliette a nice e-mail with which she was sending me the video about the *Little Stick Figures*. At first, I found that funny as a title, but as I am an open person, I listened to it carefully and I did the exercises at the same time as you. At first, I didn't believe very much in this method, because I had already tried all the Methods, and none of them had ever worked. *I suffered from traumas during my childhood and adolescence and over time, I had forgiven, but I was incapable of forgetting, and at the slightest incident such as a spoken word, a TV program or anything else, everything resurfaced.* I am 66 years old and still stuck with all those events of the past.

I listened to lots of videos by Bruce Lipton who explained that **it is the subconscious that runs us, not our conscious.** So when I heard you speak about that, you can imagine how I clicked, because precisely, I was telling myself that it's all very well with this subconscious business, but how can I clean up that mess? Then I told myself that I would take a whole day for healing, and I swore that I would get through all that, and that instead of repressing it, I would face it head on and I would do the *Little Stick Figures* exercises as long as the emotions surfaced.

I simply can't get over it. **It's as though I had opened up the door to my subconscious.** I did the exercise and one thing led me to another, then another, and yet another again. **Just to tell you that I spent three days and several times during the night doing the *Little Stick Figures*. I did a lot of pages, let me tell you sir.** But I went too fast and I had diarrhea for three days, but what a cleanup! **It's a true miracle, what is happening to me. I am so detached from everything I have the impression that it was a dream, and that it happened to someone else. I even have difficulty in trying to think about it, it's as though some pieces have been erased from my memory.**

Then, wild with joy, I sent the video to several of my female and male friends, but I had to stop, because several of them were coming to see me or telephoning me In tears: *"Marie-Andrée, Marie-Andrée, it's incredible, if you knew the benefits that this exercise has given me, etc., etc."* and we spent hours and hours sharing their experience.

So now, in my name and in the name of all my friends, I know that what I'm going to say to you is very small, it is just a big THANK YOU. I would give you the moon if I could, I would hug you in my arms very tight if you were close to me, what I feel for you is just too big. You are like an angel who has passed in my life. My life will be so beautiful, now that I am free of all that past that never stopped re-intruding in the present. As the saying goes: *"Lamps are not made to throw **light** on themselves"* and your **light**, your creativity have served to illuminate many people. So then, pursue your beautiful mission and I will continue spreading the good news. In everyone's name, thanks, a thousand times thanks.
Marie Andrée

ABOUT THE CO-AUTHORS

Lucie Bernier

Lucie Bernier is a therapist, speaker and personal development workshop leader. She originates from Rivière-Ouelle, a municipality of Québec (Canada) located in the Lower Saint Lawrence River region.

She completed her university training in Law and had a career as a flight attendant and a chief purser for 22 years with an international air carrier company.

In 1989 she undertook to engage in a process of working on her "Self." It was in 1993 that she became a REIKI Master (a natural healing *technique* applied by imposing the hands and using the universal neutral energy with no intention). She followed more than 2500 hours of personal and professional development workshops. She also acted as a workshop leader and/or assistant during the workshops given by Jacques Martel, mainly in Europe. She has also taught and given lectures in Québec, in New Brunswick, in Ontario and in the United States.

From 1995 to 1998, she collaborated in the production of the first French edition of the book **The Encyclopedia of Ailments and Diseases**, and also took part in working out the second edition. She now acts as the Assistant General Manager of **Éditions ATMA internationales** and, in another capacity, is a telecommunications business owner.

lucie.bernier@atma.ca

Robert Lenghan

Robert Lenghan has a vast coaching experience in the fields of change management, management, human resources management (HR), work organization, project coordination and organization, training and the organization of events, in both the private and the public sectors.

As a consultant, he has been able to use his knowledge in the service of various clienteles by providing them with effective, realistic, original, profitable solutions, in keeping with their vision, their needs and their resources.

His university training and his professional experiences have enabled him to develop a work ethic based on effectiveness, dynamism, versatility, creativity, rigor and results. He also advocates listening, harmonious communications and teamwork built on human relations.

Over the past 25 years, he worked mainly in the consultation market in Québec (Canada), as a project coordinator. He especially collaborated in implementing some important strategic mandates in organizations such as the **Commission de la santé et de la sécurité du travail** (Work Health and Safety Commission) for 12 years and with the **Régie de l'assurance maladie du Québec** (Québec Health Insurance Agency).

He has been a REIKI Master since 2008 and has followed several personal development workshops and sessions that have helped him change and further develop his exceptional qualities in communications and interpersonal relations.

robertlenghan@gmail.com

About Jacques Martel,
THE CREATOR OF THE *TECHNIQUE*

Born in Montreal (Canada) in September 1950, Jacques Martel completed his university training as an electrical engineer. An author, a trainer and an international speaker, he is the founding president of **Éditions ATMA internationales**, whose mission is oriented to health, well-being and the opening of **consciousness**. His scientific training has enabled him to combine his practical bent with his intuitive side. He is the author of many books, including **The Encyclopedia of Ailments and Diseases**, a best-seller read by more than two million readers and which has now become a reference for many professionals in health and well-being and among the general public. His personal approach and experience have already helped thousands of persons in their development. He created the *"Integration through the Heart♥" Technique*© (ITHT©). He is also a REIKI Master and a Rebirther.

Since 1990, Mr. Martel still pursues his personal and professional training, which has enabled him, over the years, to earn a solid reputation in this field. He gives speeches and takes part in health and wellness exhibitions. From 1988 to 2013, he led workshops in Canada, in Europe, on Reunion Island and in French Polynesia and on Mauritius Island. Upon request, he trains other therapists in the emotional healing *technique* (**ITHT: The Integration through the Heart♥ Technique**©) that he has developed over the years and which has given positive results to his clients.

He also occasionally gives a training session entitled: "On the road to Awakening," which helps persons who wish to achieve an inner openness to gain access to higher levels of **consciousness**, quite safely and sincerely. The interest raised among the public and among therapists by the book **The Encyclopedia of Ailments and Diseases** shows the relevance of such a title. In addition to the second edition of this book in 2007, **Jacques Martel** has published other complementary products that are highly appreciated by any person in search of healing and well-being:

The Encyclopedia of Ailments and Diseases 2020
[Le grand dictionnaire des malaises et des maladies, 1998; 2007]

ATMA, The Power of Love 2016
[ATMA, le Pouvoir de l'Amour 2005; 2013 (2nd Edition)]

The Five Steps to Achieve HEALING 2017
[Les 5 Étapes pour Parvenir à la GUÉRISON 2010; 2013]

The Power of Words... that Free Me! 2017
[Le Pouvoir des Mots… qui me Libèrent! 2011]

Conscience, Amour et Guérison (Tomes I et II) 2016
[Consciousness, Love and Healing]

La Technique d'Intégration par le Coeur© 2015
[The Integration through the Heart♥ Technique©]

Le Pouvoir de l'ENGAGEMENT… ou comment agir en GAGNANT! 2014
[The Power of COMMITMENT… or how to act by WINNING!]

Retour vers la Source *2011* [Return to the Source]

ATMA et le cercle de guérison 2008; 2013 (2nd Edition)
[ATMA and the Healing Circle]

Books co-authored with Jean-Jacques Robinet:

LE POUVOIR DU REIKI, Énergie de Vie, Énergie de Guérison 2014

ATMA, LE REIKI, Niveaux 1, 2, 3 et MAÎTRE Enseignant 2018

Jacques Martel
jacques.martel@atma.ca
www.jacquesmartel.com / www.atma.ca

Chapter Overview
Technique, Questions, and Applications

CHAPTER 1

Interview with Jacques Martel, the *Technique's* Creator 17

The origin of this *technique* 17

The functioning of the *technique* and its results 19

CHAPTER 2

General Information Prior to Using the *Technique* 23

Who can use the *technique*? 23

Under what circumstances can I use the *technique*? 23

    This technique can be used in any situation 23

    The 5 essential rules for using the *technique* effectively 24

Preparation (state of mind and attitude) before doing the *technique* 24

Why always draw myself first, and only then another person or a situation? 25

What happens if I do the exercise for a negative purpose? 28

Are there any contra-indications (risks) in using this method? 29

Why is it necessary to do the *technique*
with pencil on paper? 31

An exception: Doing the exercise in my head 33

What materials do I need to do the exercise? 34

CHAPTER 3

Application of the 7 Steps of the *Technique* 35

How to identify the situation and each of
the figures: # 1(on the left) and # 2 (on the right)......... 35

Step-by-step explanations of the
Little Stick Figures Technique 40

An exercise for detachment 44

What are *attachment* and *dependency*
and why free myself from them? 44

CHAPTER 4

An Exercise to Detach Myself from a Person 47

Summary of the 7 steps of the *technique* with
another person 52

Using the *technique* with a person (in images) 53

CHAPTER 5

An Exercise to Detach Myself from a Situation 55

Summary of the 7 steps of the *technique* with
a situation 58

Using the *technique* with a situation (in images) 59

CHAPTER 6

An Exercise to Detach Myself from a Part of Myself 61

    A variant: Drawing the links of attachment in color (Step 6) 69

CHAPTER 7

General Questions on How to Properly Apply the *Technique* 71

    What do I do with the pieces of paper after cutting the page? 71

    Why put the energy centers in the rectangle that symbolizes a situation? 71

    Do I cut off the light when I cut away the links of attachment? 72

    Do I cut off the love when I cut away the links of attachment? 72

    Consequences: To influence or control another person 73

    Do I have to draw the eyes, the nose, and the mouth? 74

    Do I draw the figures with the arms pointing up or down? 74

    Does the drawing have a meaning? 75

    If the person's name is unknown 76

    Will the exercise be more effective if I draw the links of attachment in color? 79

    What do I feel during the exercise? 79

    Can the exercise be done in a group? 80

Is it important to carefully draw the rays around
the 3 circles to clearly show that it is light? 80

Should I do the *technique* consciously or automatically? 81

May I use a mantra during the exercise,
or use a request formula? 81

Must I do the exercise in silence? 82

From what age can one do the exercise? 83

How to show a child or an adult how to do the exercise? 85

Can a blind person do the exercise? 87

Can a person with a physical or intellectual deficiency
do the exercise? 88

If a person is in a coma 90

CHAPTER 8

After Applying the *Technique*: Some Issues Concerning the Results Obtained 93

How many times must I do the exercise? 93

How many times a day can I do the *technique*? 94

At what point in the day should I do the *technique*? 94

After having done the exercise once,
does that mean that it's done for all time? 94

How can the *technique* be useful for a helping person
(therapist, hairdresser, massage therapist, etc.)? 95

Is it possible to have physical or emotional symptoms
after doing the *technique*? 96

What results can I expect after doing the exercise,
and how long afterward? 97

Is it possible that no change may result? 98

Is it possible that I mistakenly interpreted the situation? ... 99

Is it possible that there was nothing to be changed? 99

What are the causes that can affect the results
or its manifestations? 99

Can the person with whom I do the *technique*
have a reaction or a feeling? 101

Can the results be negative? 102

How can I know that it is working and recognize
the results if they don't stand out as obvious? 103

Can I cancel the effects of the exercise? 104

How do I confirm the cutting of the links
that I have already initiated? 105

Conclusion about the results 105

CHAPTER 9

The *Technique's* Many Applications and Some Questions from the Public 107

The general principles for identifying Figure #1
and Figure #2 108

The sale or the purchase of my house 108

Sale, purchase, disposal of a material good
(in general) 112

With my twin sister / brother 114

The relationship with my current spouse or ex-spouse 115

A new relationship 116

Encountering my Soul mate (bachelorhood) 116

Separation / divorce 119

A deceased person (the mourning process) 120

An abortion / miscarriage 122

Birth / adoption 123

My previous lives 124

My ancestors 126

Attracting abundance in all the areas of my life 130

Sickness or the fear of having an illness / a disability 131

Sickness: A member of the family 135

With a fear 137

An exercise with the 6 basic fears 138

Dependency on alcohol, cigarettes, food,
drugs, gambling, etc. 140

    Cigarettes 140

    Alcohol 141

    Food 142

Weight reduction / gain / maintenance 142

Winning in a contest or at the lottery 144

My scores at school (academic results) 145

Work (dissatisfaction with work / boss; search for a job) 146

Concerns about my car 148

With a person who wishes me harm 148

The *technique* with God (positive),
the devil (negative), etc. 149

Our cartoon heroes or favorite actors / actresses 151

Developing a special gift or talent 151

Me and my inner child (present and past suffering) 152

Chapter Overview – Technique, Questions and Applications

With my ego / subconscious 154

With my subconscious 155

With a group of persons 155

My animal or an animal 157

With certain aspects of my life or causes
that are important to me 159

Can I use the *technique* with persons or situations
that are beautiful and in harmony? 160

CHAPTER 10

A General Cleansing and Rebalancing Protocol 155

From Jacques Martel

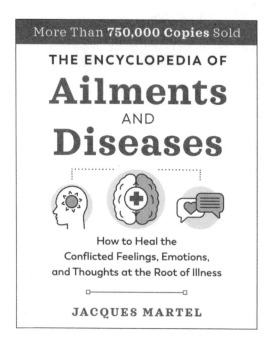

The Encyclopedia of Ailments and Diseases

In this comprehensive reference and healing tool, Jacques Martel explains how to uncover the conflicted conscious or unconscious feelings, thoughts, and emotions at the root of many illnesses and conditions. He offers healing prompts and affirmations to effect change for nearly 900 different ailments and diseases.

ISBN 9-781-64411-189-5

Also of Interest

Working with Chakras for Belief Change
The Healing Insight Method
by Nikki Gresham-Record

Detailing the Healing InSight Method for belief change, this practical full-color book explains how to transform unhelpful belief patterns and raise your vibration through a combination of chakra work, affirmations, therapeutic processes, visualization, and bodywork exercises. Includes 56 high-vibration color chakra images for therapeutic guidance, healing, and positive manifestation.

ISBN 9-781-62055-902-4

Also of Interest

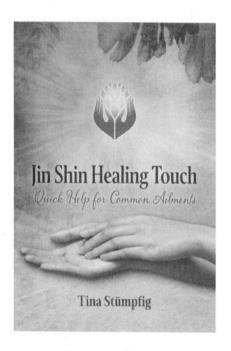

Jin Shin Healing Touch
Quick Help for Common Ailments

by Tina Stümpfig

Jin Shin Jyutsu is an ancient Japanese healing art akin to an easier form of acupressure. This full-color guide details the 52 energy points of Jin Shin Jyutsu and explains the sequence of points to hold to address specific ailments, conditions, and injuries and stimulate the body's self-healing response.

ISBN 9-781-64411-076-8

FINDHORN PRESS

Life-Changing Books

Learn more about us and our books at
www.findhornpress.com

For information on the Findhorn Foundation:
www.findhorn.org

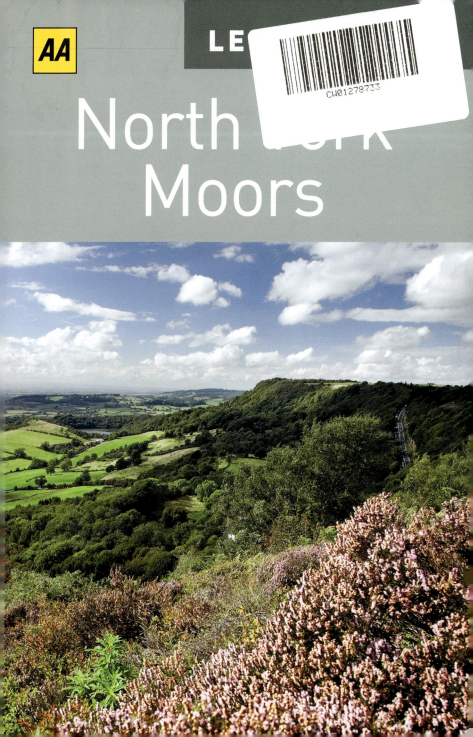

AA

LE

North York Moors

Author: John Morrison
Verifier: David Winpenny
Managing Editor: David Popey
Project Management: Bookwork Creative Associates Ltd
Designers: Liz Baldin of Bookwork Creative Associates Ltd and Andrew Milne
Picture Library Manager: Ian Little
Picture Research: Kathy Lockley and Lesley Grayson
Cartography provided by the Mapping Services Department of AA Publishing
Copy Editors: Marilynne Lanng of Bookwork and Pamela Stagg
Image manipulation and internal repro: Sarah Montgomery
Production: Rachel Davis

Produced by AA Publishing
© AA Media Limited 2007
Updated and revised 2010
Reprinted August 2011

All rights reserved. This publication or any part of it may not be copied or reproduced by any means without the prior permission of the publisher. All inquiries should be directed to the publisher.

Published by AA Publishing (a trading name of AA Media Limited, whose registered office is Fanum House, Basing View, Basingstoke, Hampshire RG21 4EA; registered number 06112600).

 This product includes mapping data licensed from the Ordnance Survey® with the permission of the Controller of Her Majesty's Stationery Office. © Crown Copyright 2011. All rights reserved. Licence number 100021153.

ISBNs: 978-0-7495-6690-6 and 978-0-7495-6703-3 (SS)

A CIP catalogue record for this book is available from the British Library.

The contents of this book are believed correct at the time of printing. Nevertheless, the publishers cannot be held responsible for any errors or omissions or for changes in the details given in this book or for the consequences of any reliance on the information it provides. This does not affect your statutory rights. We have tried to ensure accuracy in this book, but things do change and we would be grateful if readers would advise us of any inaccuracies they may encounter.

We have taken all reasonable steps to ensure that the walks and cycle rides in this book are safe and achievable by people with a realistic level of fitness. However, all outdoor activities involve a degree of risk and the publishers accept no responsibility for any injuries caused to readers while following these walks and cycle rides. For advice on walking and cycling in safety, see pages 16–17.

Some of the walks and cycle routes may appear in other AA books.

Visit AA Publishing at theAA.com/shop

Printed and bound in China by C&C

A04786

CONTENTS

INTRODUCTION ■ ESSENTIAL SIGHTS ■ WEEKEND AWAY	4
ESK DALE & NORTH ■ CAR TOUR 1 ■ WALK 1	18
WESTERN MOORS ■ WALKS 2, 3 & 4 ■ CAR TOUR 2 ■ CYCLE RIDE 1	52
CENTRAL MOORS ■ WALKS 5 & 6	88
EASTERN MOORS & COAST ■ WALKS 7, 8, 9 & 10 ■ CYCLE RIDES 2 & 3	114
INFORMATION: WALKS & CYCLE RIDES	16
USEFUL INFORMATION	154
ATLAS	155
INDEX & ACKNOWLEDGEMENTS	158

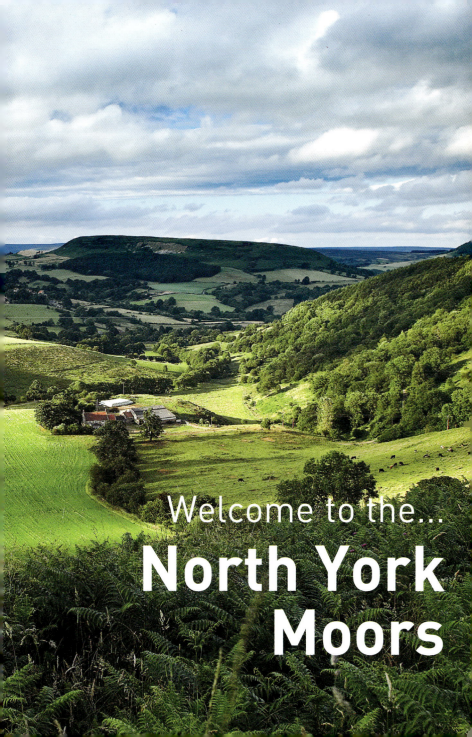

INTRODUCTION

The word 'moors' conjures up the image of a bleak, lonely and windswept landscape? Not the North York Moors. From the sharp escarpments in the west to the towering cliffs and sandy beaches on the east coast, the Moors offers a rich variety of landscapes, and attractions to please everyone.

The heart of the North York Moors – designated a National Park more than 50 years ago – is the plateau of hills that glow with a soft-purple wash of heather in the late summer. This is England's largest expanse of heather, and one of the must-see sights. You can walk for miles along old drovers' tracks that will take you past mysterious ancient earthworks and mounds and the medieval moorland crosses that are a familiar feature of the 'tops'.

Thrusting into this high land are deep and densely wooded valleys, including Bransdale, with some of the area's remote farming communities; Farndale, famous for wild daffodils; and Rosedale, with remnants of iron working in a divine setting. Many of the area's most attractive towns and villages, such as Hutton-le-Hole and Lastingham, lie in the valleys.

Southwest of the central moorland are the more gentle Howardian Hills, where picturesque abbeys – Rievaulx and Byland – and ruined castles like Helmsley rise from wooded valleys. North again around the curve of the Cleveland Hills, villages like Swainby and Great Ayton – where Captain Cook was schooled – huddle beneath the humpbacks of the hills.

Deep forests occupy much of the southeastern quarter of the area, with walks, mountain-bike trails and picnic sites set out among the trees. And strung along the glorious coast, from Staithes to Scarborough, are some of Britain's highest cliffs, coves where smugglers landed contraband, idyllic fishing villages that appear to tumble headlong into the waves, and bracing headlands. Whitby, with its abbey, quirky church, Dracula connections and memories of its whaling past, is fascinating, while Scarborough lives up to its name as 'Queen of the Coast' with everything for a traditional, seaside family holiday, from beaches to a huge castle just asking to be explored.

Whether you're an adventurer or a potterer, a walker, a cyclist or a driver, the North York Moors has something to offer. And if you're looking for peace and quiet, that is as plentiful here as fresh air, too – just as it was during the 12th century when St Aelred, Abbot of Rievaulx, wrote that it offers 'a marvellous freedom from the tumult of the world'.

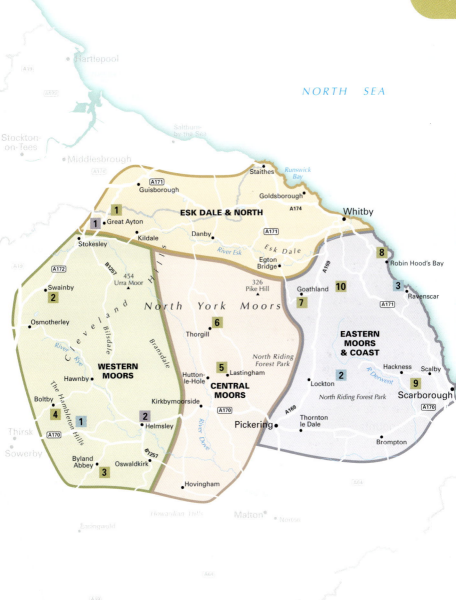

NORTH YORK MOORS

ESSENTIAL SIGHTS

Enjoy the superb views across the Vale of York from the top of Sutton Bank...walk part (or all!) of the Cleveland Way, which starts at Helmsley and ends at Filey Brigg on the coast...visit Staithes, a perfect example of an old Yorkshire fishing village...search Whitby's many antiques shops for jet or watch it being made in the craftsmens' workshops...hunt for a small carved mouse, Robert Thompson's unique trademark, on the furniture in local churches and visit the workshops at Kilburn...admire the thousands of daffodils at Farndale in springtime...linger by the extensive remains of Rievaulx Abbey...steam along the rails on the North Yorkshire Moors Railway, which runs from Pickering to Grosmont...look out for the stone crosses that litter the moors...walk along the Roman road in Wheeldale in the footsteps of Roman soldiers...take the scenic Newtondale Forest Drive through North Riding Forest.

1 Rievaulx Abbey
The magnificent ruins of Rievaulx Abbey, set in a splendid wooded valley of the River Rye.

2 Staithes
The village of Staithes is a delight to explore. Its position, wedged between steep-sided cliffs and Cowbar Beck, resulted in an attractive jumble of house building.

3 Hutton-le-Hole
Neat, flower-bedecked houses of mellow local stone, grouped around a tidy green that extends the length of the village, make Hutton-le-Hole a candidate for the title of Yorkshire's prettiest village.

4 Farndale
The remote valley of Farndale, with its maze of narrow winding lanes and patchwork of fields, is where you can experience moorland scenery at its most beautiful.

5 Egton Bridge
A tranquil corner at Egton Bridge. This pretty little village is set the lush woodland of the Esk Valley.

HOT SPOTS

6 Robin Hood's Bay
The pretty little fishing village of Robin Hood's Bay is a tumble of brightly painted cottages that seem to stagger their way along the narrow roads towards the sea.

7 Stone Crosses
Young Ralph Cross, standing tall at a junction of roads near Rosedale Head, is the symbol of the North York Moors National Park. It is just one of many ancient stones and crosses found on these moors.

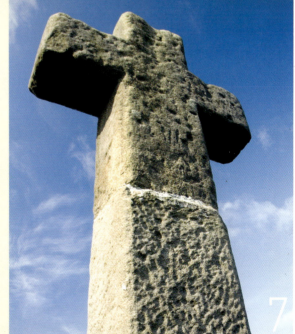

WEEKEND AWAY

DAY ONE

For many people a weekend break or a long weekend is a popular way of spending their leisure time. These four pages offer a loosely planned itinerary designed to ensure that you make the most of your time, whatever the weather, and see and enjoy the very best of the area.

Friday Night

Stay at the Feversham Arms, Helmsley. This is a charming, modernised hotel located just a few yards from the Market Square with its own swimming pool and luxurious spa. The restaurant is renowned for its good food (especially shellfish and game in season) and outstanding wine list.

Saturday Morning

Your first stop should be the local Tourist Information Centre, located in the castle, for details of any events that may be happening at the weekend.

Just a short drive north from Helmsley, on the B1257, you'll find the fascinating remains of Rievaulx Abbey to explore, one of Yorkshire's architectural gems, in a splendid setting in the valley of the River Rye.

Minor roads (make sure you have an atlas to hand) lead southwest to the fine Yorkshire village of Kilburn. Beneath the distinctive hill figure of the White Horse is the showroom of Robert Thompson's Craftsmen, whose work keeps alive the tradition and artistry of the famous 'Mouseman'. Opposite to the showroom is the visitor centre.

Saturday Lunch

Drive the short distance eastwards to the picturesque Byland Abbey where, directly opposite the ruins, you'll find the Abbey Inn. The stone-flagged floor, antique furniture and imaginative menu make this the ideal place for lunch.

Saturday Afternoon

Pass Helmsley once again and continue east along the A170 to Pickering, the terminus of the North Yorkshire Moors Railway. This preserved line offers a nostalgic return to the age of steam. A round trip to Goathland will show you some of the finest scenery in the North York Moors National Park, as well as giving you time to explore the moorland village perhaps now best known as a location for the TV series *Heartbeat*.

On your return to Pickering, drive north up the A169, passing the huge natural amphitheatre known as the Hole of Horcum, towards the port of Whitby.

Saturday Night

Three miles (4.8km) north of the town, off the A171, is Dunsley Hall Hotel, an impressive Victorian mansion in the quiet village of Dunsley where you can escape from the crowds.

DAY ONE IN NORTH YORK MOORS

ALL SAINTS CHURCH IN HELMSLEY

14 WEEKEND AWAY

RUNSWICK BAY

DANBY DALE

DAY TWO IN NORTH YORK MOORS

DAY TWO

Our second and final day starts with a visit to the bustling resort of Whitby and a nearby picturesque fishing village, before driving along the beautiful Esk Valley and across the moors, passing through a number of lovely villages, before arriving back in Helmsley.

Sunday Morning

Explore Whitby on foot. It's a fascinating town, with surprises at every turn in its winding streets. The abbey, St Mary's Church, the Captain Cook Museum and the harbour are just a few of the 'musts'.

On a different scale are the tiny fishing villages of Staithes (north of Whitby) and Robin Hood's Bay (a few miles to the south). Both are achingly picturesque; take time to explore one or the other.

Afterwards, a leisurely drive along the beautiful Esk Valley, passing the lovely villages of Grosmont, Glaisdale (look out for the Beggar's Bridge) and Lealholm will bring you to Danby. At the Moors Centre you can learn how the moorland landscape came to look the way it does, and perhaps have a coffee.

Drive south from Danby, along Blakey Ridge (this is on an unclassified road, more map reading needed). With the valley of Rosedale to your left and Farndale to your right, this is moorland scenery at its very best.

Sunday Lunch

Look out for the Lion Inn, miles from anywhere on Blakey Ridge, where travellers have long received a warm welcome. Our suggested itinerary should make this a late lunch. No problem, the Lion Inn serves its excellent meals throughout the day.

Sunday Afternoon

Continue driving along Blakey Ridge, with perhaps a moorland walk to fill the lungs with pure upland air. Look out for the guide stones on the roadside. The road brings you to Hutton-le-Hole, one of Yorkshire's picture-postcard villages and well worth exploring. Near by is the equally pretty Lastingham.

Our weekend started with one monastic gem and ends with another intriguing religious site. The church at Lastingham has a 'secret' crypt, built almost a thousand years ago.

Drive west along the A170 to arrive back in Helmsley where you can enjoy some afternoon tea before heading for home.

INFORMATION

Route facts

MINIMUM TIME The time stated for completing each route is the estimated minimum time that a reasonably fit family group of walkers or cyclists would take to complete the circuit. This does not allow for rest or refreshment stops.

OS MAP Each route is shown on a map. However, some detail is lost because of the restrictions imposed by scale, so for this reason, we recommend that you use the maps in conjunction with a more detailed Ordnance Survey map. The relevant map for each walk or cycle ride is listed.

START This indicates the start location and parking area. This is a six-figure grid reference prefixed by two letters showing which 62.5-mile (100km) square of the National Grid it refers to. You'll find more information on grid references on most Ordnance Survey maps.

CYCLE HIRE We list, within reason, the nearest cycle hire shop/centre.

❶ Here we highlight any potential difficulties or dangers along the cycle ride or walk. If a particular route is suitable for older, fitter children we say so here. Also, we give guidelines of a route's suitability for younger children, for example the symbol 8+ indicates that the route can probably be attempted by children aged 8 years and above.

Walks & Cycle Rides

Each walk and cycle ride has a panel giving information for the walker and cyclist, including the distance, terrain, nature of the paths, and where to park your car.

WALKING

All of the walks are suitable for families, but less experienced family groups, especially those with younger children, should try the shorter walks. Route finding is usually straightforward, but the maps are for guidance only and we recommend that you always take the relevant Ordnance Survey map with you.

Risks

Although each walk has been researched with a view to minimising any risks, no walk in the countryside can be considered to be completely free from risk. Walking in the outdoors will always require a degree of common sense and judgement to ensure that it is as safe as possible, especially for young children.
- Be particularly careful on cliff paths and in upland terrain, where the consequences of a slip can be serious.
- Remember to check tidal conditions before walking on the seashore.
- Some sections of route are by, or cross, busy roads. Remember traffic is a danger even on minor country lanes.
- Be careful around farmyard machinery and livestock.
- Be prepared for the consequences of changes in the weather and check the forecast before you set out.
- Ensure the whole family is properly equipped, wearing suitable clothing and a good pair of boots or sturdy walking shoes. Take waterproof clothing with you and a torch if you are walking in the winter months.
- Remember the weather can change quickly at any time of the year, and in moorland and heathland areas, mist and fog can make route-finding much harder. In summer, take account of the heat and sun by wearing a hat, sunscreen and carrying enough water.
- On walks away from centres of population you should carry a mobile phone, whistle and, if possible, a survival bag. If you do have an accident requiring emergency services, make a note of your position as accurately as possible and dial 999 (112 on a mobile).

WALKS & CYCLE RIDES

CYCLING

In devising the cycle rides in this guide, every effort has been made to use designated cycle paths, or to link them with quiet country lanes and waymarked byways and bridleways. In a few cases, some fairly busy B-roads have been used to join up with quieter routes.

Rules of the road

- Ride in single file on narrow and busy roads.
- Be alert, look and listen for traffic, especially on narrow lanes and blind bends and be extra careful when descending steep hills, as loose gravel or a poor road surface can lead to an accident.
- In wet weather make sure that you keep an appropriate distance between you and other riders.
- Make sure you indicate your intentions clearly.
- Brush up on *The Highway Code* before venturing out onto the road.

Off-road safety code of conduct

- Only ride where you know it is legal to do so. Cyclists are not allowed to cycle on public footpaths (yellow waymarks). The only 'rights of way' open to cyclists are bridleways (blue markers) and unsurfaced tracks, known as byways, which are open to all traffic and waymarked in red.
- Canal tow paths: you need a permit to cycle on some stretches of tow path (www.waterscape.com). Remember that access paths can be steep and slippery so always push your bike under low bridges and by locks.
- Always yield to walkers and horses, giving adequate warning of your approach.
- Don't expect to cycle at high speeds.
- Keep to the main trail to avoid any unnecessary erosion to the area beside the trail and to prevent skidding, especially in wet weather conditions.
- Remember to follow the Country Code.

Preparing your bicycle
Check the wheels, tyres, brakes and cables. Lubricate hubs, pedals, gear mechanisms and cables. Make sure you have a pump, a bell, a rear rack to carry panniers and a set of lights.

Equipment

- A cycling helmet provides essential protection.
- Make sure you are visible to other road users, by wearing light-coloured or luminous clothing in daylight and sashes or reflective strips in failing light and darkness.
- Take extra clothes with you, depending on the season, and a wind/waterproof jacket.
- Carry a basic tool kit, a pump, a strong lock and a first aid kit.
- Always carry enough water for your outing.

Walk Map Legend

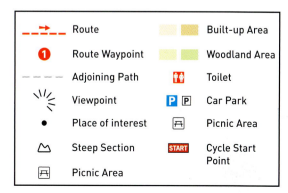

Esk Dale & North

Castleton	24
Danby	24
Egton Bridge	25
Glaisdale	27
Great Ayton	27
Grosmont	28
Guisborough	29
Kettleness & Goldsborough	30
Kildale	33
Lealholm	33
▪ CAR TOUR 1 Cleveland Hills	34
Roseberry Topping	36
Runswick Bay	36
▪ WALK 1 Roseberry Topping	38
Sandsend	41
Staithes	41
Whitby	43

INTRODUCTION

The River Esk meanders enticingly from its source on the moorlands near to Westerdale, linking a number of lovely villages before reaching the North Sea with a flourish and dividing the fascinating fishing port of Whitby into two. The National Park's Visitor Centre, which is located close to Esk, near Danby, is the perfect spot to enjoy a picnic or a riverside stroll as well as learn about the unique moorland habitats of the National Park. A little way downstream there is an arched packhorse bridge, intriguingly named Duck Bridge, over the Esk. From source to sea you will find that the River Esk holds many delights; the valley road between Stokesley and Whitby crosses and re-crosses it many times. Rail travellers follow its course more closely on the scenic line between Middlesbrough and Whitby. But the best way to see Esk Dale is on foot. The Esk Valley Walk is a waymarked route, which begins at Castleton and follows the river and the villages that lie along its banks, to the golden coast at Whitby.

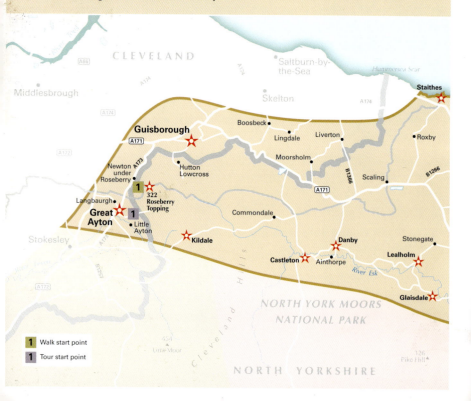

1 Walk start point
1 Tour start point

ESK DALE & NORTH 21

LEALHOLM

DANBY DALE

HOT SPOTS

Unmissable attractions

Admire the fantastic views from Roseberry Topping...explore the many twists and turns of Whitby's bustling historic streets...visit the fascinating Moors Centre near Danby and discover what makes the North York Moors such a special place...cycle along the minor roads between Castleton, Danby and Lealholm in the Esk Valley...visit Egton Bridge in August and experience the famous Gooseberry Show...drive the high road over Castleton Rigg and enjoy moorland scenery at its best...admire the gleaming old locomotives getting up steam at Grosmont station...enjoy the splendid wooded surroundings of Gisborough Hall...get some sea air at Runswick – one of the loveliest sandy bays on the Yorkshire coast.

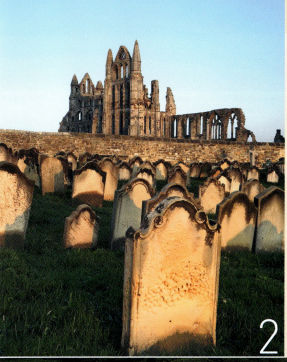

1 Roseberry Topping
The distinctive shape of Roseberry Topping, seen here looming up out of the mist, gained its distinctive profile after intensive ironstone mining caused a huge landslip in 1912.

2 Whitby Abbey
Perched high on the clifftop east of Whitby are the magnificent ruins of Whitby Abbey.

3 Sandsend
The pretty village of Sandsend is set against a backdrop of cliffs at the northern end of a long arc of sandy beach.

ESK DALE & NORTH

CASTLETON MAP REF NZ6807

The castle is long gone from Castleton; only the name and a mound to the north of the village remain – unsentimentally, a lot of the stone from the ruined castle was probably recycled and used to build Danby Castle. Castleton used to have regular markets and a goods yard on the railway; the markets have gone, but the village still has its passenger station on the Esk Valley railway line.

The River Esk, which rises at Esklets in Westerdale to the south, is joined at Castleton by a tributary, Commondale Beck. To the north of the village is an expanse of moorland, but the landscape is very different from that of the south, with a selection of minor roads, tracks and footpaths exploring a landscape of great variety. Two routes 'take the high road' over Castleton Rigg, enjoying panoramic views down into Westerdale and Danby Dale, and on to Ralph Cross (used as the National Park emblem) and the head of beautiful Rosedale. This is moorland scenery at its best; valley bottoms divided up into neat fields by drystone walls, the pattern interrupted by little copses.

Insight

MOORLAND 'INTAKES'

You'll probably notice a sudden contrast where the fields stop and open moorland begins, showing that the fields higher up the valley sides are 'intakes' – land 'taken in' from the moorland above. At the head of several moorland valleys are ruined farmsteads, which were abandoned when the living became too precarious. Here you will often see unmanaged grassy pasture reverting back to heather and bracken.

You would probably hesitate to call Commondale, northwest of Castleton on the Esk Valley line, one of the prettier villages on the moors. This scattering of houses and farms occupies a hillside overlooking Commondale Moor. The village's most striking aspect is the use of brick, as much as stone, as a building material – the diminutive brick-built Church of St Peter, in particular, stands out like the proverbial sore thumb. The reason is very simple: until the 1950s Commondale had its own brickworks here, and bricks and tiles form vital decorative elements in a number of houses throughout the village, and on the façade of the old Co-op shop.

The village name was once written as 'Colmandale'. It is said that Colman, Bishop of Lindisfarne, stopped off here on his travels to Whitby Abbey.

DANBY MAP REF NZ7008

The lovely village of Danby lies on a crossroads; blink and you've missed it. But it was to this little village that John Atkinson came, at the age of 36, as minister of the parish. He was Essex-born and until the end of his long life retained the natural curiosity of the newcomer. One of his major passions was prehistory, and the moors – with their burial mounds, standing stones and wayside crosses – provided much to excite his inquiring mind. He died in 1900, and is buried in the churchyard.

There are a number of interesting features in the immediate vicinity, and the easiest way to see them is to park at the National Park's Visitor Centre, just half a mile (800m) from the village

CASTLETON – EGTON BRIDGE

on the road to Lealholm. The Moors Centre represents the public face of the National Park. Here you can discover what makes the North York Moors so special and the unique habitats that the moors supports. The building that houses the Moors Centre was once a shooting lodge; it now hosts exhibitions and a wide variety of events, including guided walks. The evolution of the moorland landscape is explained, there's an outdoor play area and indoor climbing wall, and those whose needs extend no further than a mug of tea and a slice of cake are equally well catered for. The Moors Centre sits in 13 acres (5.2ha) of land, close to the Esk, a lovely spot to enjoy a picnic or a stroll along the riverside. A number of waymarked walks explore the immediate environs; longer walks start from the car park.

Just a little way downstream is the intriguingly named Duck Bridge. This superb late 14th-century example of an arched packhorse bridge is a tangible reminder of a time when sturdy ponies, laden down with twin pannier bags, were the main means by which goods and sundries were transported.

The packhorse trail leads towards Danby Castle, once a fortified house of distinction, though most of the medieval stonework has since been incorporated into a farmhouse; there is only limited public access. The castle, built in the 14th century, was once the home of Catherine Parr, the sixth wife of Henry VIII, who fared better than his other wives and, indeed, survived him. Past Danby Castle Farm the road goes through a minor valley; Little Fryup Dale.

■ Activity

CYCLING IN THE ESK VALLEY
The minor roads between Castleton, Danby and Lealholm in the Esk Valley are ideal for cycling as they are quiet and the valley floor level. With a little help from the OS Landranger map Sheet 94 1:50,000 it is possible to avoid most of the steep gradients on the roads out of the valley.

EGTON BRIDGE MAP REF NZ8004

Egton and Egton Bridge are two villages separated by both the River Esk and a steep descent. Egton has nothing to do with eggs; it appeared in the Domesday Book as Egetune, meaning 'the town of the oak trees'. The oaks are gone, as are the annual hiring fairs, when farmers would look to employ farm labourers for the forthcoming year. Even the weekly markets, for which the village was granted a charter by William of Orange, are no longer held in the village's broad street. But the village is important as the venue, every August, for one of the area's largest agricultural shows.

A new bridge, built in 1993, spans the River Esk at Egton Bridge. The stone arch replaces an ugly metal structure that was itself merely a replacement for the original bridge, which was swept away in floods in the 1930s.

Egton Bridge was the birthplace in 1599 of Father Nicholas Postgate, who ministered to his Catholic flock at much danger to himself. For the 'crime' of baptising a child into the Catholic faith, Father Postgate was sent for trial at York. In 1678 he was subjected – he was in his 80s – to the ultimate punishment,

EGTON BRIDGE

EGTON BRIDGE – GREAT AYTON

being hanged, drawn and quartered. In remaining staunchly Roman Catholic, Egton Bridge became known as 'the village missed by the Reformation'. The impressive Catholic Church of St Hedda contains relics of Father Postgate's ministry. Half-way up the hill to Egton is a house with a tiny chapel hidden in the roof, reached by a secret passage. The room was rediscovered 150 years after Postgate's death, since when the house has been known as the Mass House.

Every year, in August, the famous Egton Bridge Gooseberry Show is held. You will have to be a spectator rather than a competitor – at least until you are voted in as a member of the Old Gooseberry Society, founded in 1800. Size, not taste, is what matters here.

Ramblers alight at Egton Bridge, a stop on the Middlesbrough to Whitby line, and walk along the Esk Valley to Lealholm to catch the next train home.

GLAISDALE MAP REF NZ7705

Glaisdale is a straggle of little houses clinging to the hillside overlooking the River Esk. Ironstone was worked here; for a time the Angler's Arms was known as the Three Blastfurnaces. However, the Glaisdale mines were never as productive as those of nearby Rosedale.

The valley is very steep-sided here, and even with the benefit of hairpin bends motorists have to negotiate the 1-in-3 gradient of Limber Hill on their way up to Egton with care.

The area is criss-crossed with old tracks – a relic of a time when Glaisdale was an important trading centre. Through East Arncliff Wood the route is still marked by a line of causeway stones. A number of these paths converge on Beggar's Bridge, a packhorse bridge with a romantic story.

It was not easy to cross the Esk at the time when Tom Ferris was courting a local lass who lived on the opposite side of the river. If Tom was not actually a beggar, he was certainly a man of few means. He hoped to win the hand of his beloved by bettering his position, so he enlisted on a ship that was setting out from Whitby to fight against the Spanish Armada, or, as some say, as a privateer.

When he tried to say farewell to the lady, however, he was thwarted by the River Esk in spate. He sought fame and fortune, and became a very successful merchant and Lord Mayor of Hull. Yet he never forgot Glaisdale, and erected the splendid arch of Beggar's Bridge so that no other young lovers should be needlessly parted.

GREAT AYTON MAP REF NZ5610

Great Ayton is bisected by the River Leven, whose clear waters seem almost to deny that the industrial heartland of Middlesbrough is just a short drive away. Behind Great Ayton is the famous profile of Roseberry Topping (1,056 feet/322m), the conical peak, a distinctive landmark for miles around.

Great Ayton has two churches that lie almost side by side. All Saints' Church is a delightful building dating back to the 12th century, though additions have been made in every succeeding century. The original tower was demolished in 1880. The interior is quite simple, with walls of rough-hewn stone, and enough original

ESK DALE & NORTH

■ Visit

POSTGATE SCHOOL
Founded in 1704, the school in Great Ayton was designed to take eight poor boys of the town, but was soon accommodating up to 30 boys and girls. The school fees for the young James Cook were paid by the lord of the manor, Thomas Skottowe, who employed Cook's father. The school is now home to the fascinating Captain Cook Schoolroom Museum.

■ Insight

THE RAIL TRAIL
The Rail Trail extends from Grosmont to Goathland, so it can be combined with a trip along this most scenic of railway lines (the Rail Trail booklet suggests the train journey to Goathland followed by a walk back to Grosmont). The 3-mile (4.8km) footpath follows the route of the original section of line between the two villages, via Beck Hole, as laid in 1836.

■ Visit

RIVER CROSSINGS
Beggar's Bridge at Glaisdale, built in 1619, is now used by walkers; cars cross by a metal bridge, while trains on the scenic Esk Valley line pass almost overhead on a viaduct. Here, within the space of a few yards, much of the transport history of the last few centuries is represented.

fate of so many redundant churches, and is now open to the public during the summer months. James Cook's mother and five of his brothers and sisters are buried in the churchyard.

GROSMONT MAP REF NZ8305
Built largely to house those who worked on the Pickering–Whitby railway line that splits the village in two, Grosmont was originally, and unimaginatively, called 'Tunnel'. With its terraced houses and mining spoil, Grosmont presents a more industrial face to the world than the other villages of the Esk Valley. Indeed, it was while excavating the Pickering-to-Whitby line, in 1835, that the richest ironstone deposits were first discovered. Once completed, the railway was a convenient method of ironstone delivery to ships in Whitby harbour. By the middle of the 19th century, Grosmont was a major supplier of ironstone to the ironmasters' furnaces on the Rivers Tyne and Tees.

The name 'Grosmont' recalls the 13th-century Grandmontine Priory, founded here by French monks. The priory is long gone, its place taken by Priory Farm and its stonework salvaged for secular buildings.

The Pickering–Whitby line was built in 1836 after consulting with George Stephenson, who came to the project straight from the triumphant success of his Stockton–Darlington railway. The line was closed, controversially, in 1965 by Beeching's infamous axe. It was reborn eight years later, thanks to massive support by railway enthusiasts, as the North Yorkshire Moors Railway,

architectural detail to keep most lovers of old churches engrossed.

The population of Great Ayton grew to the point where the congregation could no longer squeeze into this atmospheric building. Christ Church was consecrated as the new parish church in 1877; fortunately the old church escaped the

GREAT AYTON – GUISBOROUGH

a recreational line manned by volunteers. There is nothing amateurish about the enterprise, though, for they maintain a regular timetable, come rain, shine, and even leaves on the line.

Railway buffs can spend some time admiring the gleaming old locomotives at Grosmont station, which has been convincingly restored to how it may have looked a century ago; there is also public access to the engine sheds.

Grosmont is the northern terminus of the railway, offering connections with main line services on the Esk Valley line between Middlesbrough and Whitby. It is a junction of roads and rivers, too, with the Murk Esk draining into the Esk.

GUISBOROUGH MAP REF NZ6015

Guisborough's broad main street and cobbled verges indicate that markets have been held here for centuries. The old market cross is topped by a sundial. Today the market traders put up their stalls on Thursdays and Saturdays, drawing their customers from many of the villages on the edge of the moors.

Like its close neighbour, Stokesley, the town's status has changed in recent years. Until the boundary changes of 1974, Guisborough was the capital town of the Cleveland district, which formed part of the North Riding of Yorkshire. Those reorganisations shifted the town into the county of Cleveland, but it is now back in North Yorkshire.

Beyond the main street and the market cross is the largely 15th-century Church of St Nicholas, where a cenotaph reinforces the links between the local de Bruce family and the Bruces of Scotland. Robert the Bruce's grandfather is buried near by at Gisborough Priory.

The huge east window of the ruined Augustinian priory still stands to its full height of nearly 71 feet (22m), gazing out across farmland. To wander around the evocative ruins is to escape the bustle of Guisborough's busy streets. The priory was built in the early 14th century by Robert de Brus, who was related to the Scottish king, Robert the Bruce. In their contemplation of the life to come, the monks did not neglect to lay up their treasures on earth, and by the time of the Dissolution they had become one of the richest communities in the north.

Near by you'll find Gisborough Hall, now a luxury hotel, sitting in beautiful wooded surroundings. The original hall was built by Sir Thomas Challoner, whose son began the mining of alum on the moors in about 1600. The industry proved to be vital to the moorland economy for the following three centuries. Challoner stole the secrets of alum mining and processing from the Pope, no less, who had enjoyed a near-monopoly in the alum industry. He even persuaded some of the Pope's miners to accompany him back to England to begin alum mining on the moors. For this impertinence the Challoner family was excommunicated from the Catholic Church.

Just a mile (1.6km) out of town, on the A173 in the direction of Skelton, is Tocketts Mill. The water of Tocketts Beck still turns the waterwheel of this fine old flour-mill, and on certain milling days the building is open to the public.

ESK DALE & NORTH

KETTLENESS & GOLDSBOROUGH
MAP REF NZ8414

Travellers on the A174 between Staithes and Whitby are seldom tempted to take one of the roads to the left, before they arrive in the roadside village of Lythe. The signpost indicates Goldsborough and Kettleness, a pair of hamlets whose history is by no means as tranquil as they appear today.

The handful of houses clustered together in Kettleness look as if they could fall off the cliff top at any minute. That's precisely what happened in 1829, when a landslip devastated the entire community. Fortunately, the villagers had enough warning of the impending disaster to vacate their homes and businesses and were rescued by a ship waiting for them offshore. But, you may wonder, why bother to rebuild the village on such an exposed site? The answer can be found by taking a path down on to Kettleness Point, a barren and rocky promontory. Here are the remains of productive alum mines where alum was shovelled out of the cliffs.

How precarious a living alum mining provided can be appreciated by the fact that the foundations of a large number of the mining buildings end suddenly at the cliff edge. The folk of Kettleness lost their livelihood, and their village, in the landslip of 1829; however, mining and processing of alum was fully operational again within five years. Alum was valued for its ability to fix dyes by the textile industries; other uses included several applications in leather tanning, and the manufacture of candles and parchment.

Today, Kettleness Point is a dramatic moonscape, offering nesting sites for thousands of seabirds and, to the north, a view of Runswick Bay. The promontory forms part of the Heritage Coast, a sort of linear national park, which aims to preserve undeveloped coastlines with some of the most spectacular scenery along the east coast. Special protection is now given to the 36-mile (57.6km) stretch of superb coastline that lies between Saltburn and Scalby Ness, on the outskirts of Scarborough.

Goldsborough, half a mile (800m) inland, was the site of a 4th-century Roman signal station. The Roman road commonly known as Wade's Causeway was probably built to link the settlement at Malton with the signal stations dotted at regular intervals along the coast. All that remains to be seen on the site are some grassy earthworks, sited 220 yards (200m) from the road linking Kettleness and Goldsborough. Excavations early in the 20th century produced a number of very interesting Roman finds, which suggested that the signal station might have ended its days by being suddenly ransacked. Near by you'll find a modern coastguard station.

The giant, Wade, whose moorland exploits are famous, is, according to legend, buried at Goldsborough. Two standing stones – one by Goldsborough Lane, the other adjacent to the A174 at East Barnby – are known as Wade's Stones and are said to mark the position of his head and feet. The stones are, however, more than half a mile (800m) apart, which would have made him stand out even at a giants' convention.

KETTLENESS POINT

KILDALE MAP REF NZ6009

This little moorland village has a small station on the Esk Valley line between Middlesbrough and Whitby. Completed in 1865, the Esk Valley line had to make 17 river crossings between the stations at Kildale and Grosmont. It is still a valued amenity for locals and visitors.

St Cuthbert's Church is reached via a footbridge over the railway. A hoard of Viking relics, including battleaxes and swords, was found here in 1868 when the church was renovated. These finds show that Kildale was once an ancient settlement, a notion reinforced by earthworks and other finds. A mound, cut into by the railway line, is now the only clue that Kildale once had a motte-and-bailey castle. This was one of the many strongholds owned by the Percy family, whose name is kept alive by names such as Percy Cross and Percy Rigg, high on the moors.

The Cleveland Way drops down briefly from the moors, to pass through Kildale. If you walk the route going north you will arrive on the breezy heights of Easby Moor where a monument, built in 1827, commemorates the life and exploits of Captain James Cook. From here you can enjoy panoramic views down over Great Ayton, where the young James Cook spent his formative years.

Kildale's rights of way were taken from an old map that marked only three, so there are few of the field paths that typify nearby villages. The road between Kildale and Westerdale offers splendid moorland scenery, and the watersplash over Baysdale Beck is a popular spot for a picnic on a summer's day.

LEALHOLM MAP REF NZ7607

The lovely River Esk runs through the narrow, wooded confines of Crunkly Gill, one of the many ancient gorges carved by Ice Age meltwaters, before flowing through Lealholm's grassy banks. This attractive little village, which sits astride a bend in the river, acts as a magnet for visitors. Lealholm was a favourite place, too, for Canon Atkinson, Danby's vicar, who wrote lyrically about the village in his book, called *Forty Years in a Moorland Parish*, 'Elsewhere you must go in search of beautiful views; here they offer themselves to be looked at.'

The river is spanned by a fine, well-proportioned bridge of peach-coloured stone; just a few yards away is a line of ancient stepping stones that seem to have an irresistible attraction for small children. Beyond the bridge is the Board Inn, offering refreshment and another vantage point from which to gaze down over the Esk.

Lealholm boasts no grand buildings of great note; visitors come here largely because the green is common land where they can roam at will and spread a picnic rug. On a sunny summer's day the river bank is a relaxing spot; greedy mallard ducks will eagerly dispose of any leftover sandwiches. Tea rooms and craft shops complete the picture. The National Park Authority has bowed to visitor pressure by providing a car park.

Lealholm can be grouped with other beauty spots, such as Goathland, Hutton-le-Hole and Thornton-le-Dale, as places best avoided on sunny Bank Holidays, unless you love crowds. Apart from that caveat, it's a delightful place.

ESK DALE & NORTH

Around the Cleveland Hills and Esk Dale

This route skirts the Cleveland Hills, passes high cliffs and fishing villages, before exploring the more intimate landscape of the delightful Esk Valley. Staithes, Whitby and the string of villages along the Esk Valley are well worth exploring, and Lealholm, towards the end of the drive, makes an ideal place to stop for a picnic.

Route Directions

The drive starts and ends at Great Ayton, a handsome town where Captain James Cook spent much of his boyhood. Houses overlook the River Leven, and rearing up behind them is Roseberry Topping.

1 Leave Great Ayton along the A173, signposted 'Whitby and Guisborough'. Roseberry Topping is the hill with a 'bite' taken out of its summit due to ironstone mining. Turn right at a roundabout heading towards Whitby on the A171. Keep straight ahead at the roundabout, on the outskirts of Guisborough, but turn left at the next roundabout, on to the A173, signposted 'Redcar and Saltburn'. Go across another roundabout, almost immediately, and then pass restored Tocketts Mill. Turn left at traffic lights in Skelton (signposted 'Whitby'), soon to go right at a roundabout on the A174, signed 'Brotton & Whitby'. Cross over four more roundabouts, bear right at the fifth, signposted 'Whitby', and go through Carlin How, to get your first sight of the sea. Follow Whitby signs (A174), down hairpin bends near Skinningrove, where the Cleveland Ironstone Mining Museum can be found.

The mining museum at Skinningrove, located on the site of the Loftus Mine, is based on the collections of enthusiast Tom Leonard who collected mining artefacts.

CAR TOUR 1 60 miles (96.5km)

2 Go through Loftus, still following the A174. Sea views open out as the fishing village of Staithes appears on the horizon. Pass the unsightly bulk of Boulby Potash Mine, and then Staithes.
To visit the delights of the old part of the village leave your car at the top of the village, and explore Staithes and its harbour on foot.

3 Continue on the A174 through rolling farmland past Lythe and its church.
Whitby Abbey can be seen on the horizon as you drop down steeply into Sandsend. Take great care on Lythe Bank; there have been a number of runaways here. After passing Whitby golf club you approach the town itself.

4 At a mini-roundabout, turn right, following signposts for the A171 Scarborough and Pickering. Turn right again at a T-junction near a garage. Take the left-hand fork soon after, turn left at another roundabout to arrive at traffic lights. Turn right here, still following the signs for the A171 Scarborough and Robin Hood's Bay.
Immediately over the bridge there is a road to your left. This is your route if you want to see the church and abbey at close quarters. Otherwise your road is to the right, just opposite, and signed, rather unpromisingly, 'Larpool Lane Industrial Estate'. This unclassified road takes you to Ruswarp village and the River Esk. From here, keep close to the river for most of the way back to Great Ayton.

5 Turn right to cross over Ruswarp's river bridge and adjacent railway line, then turn immediately left on the B1410 to Sleights. Follow the River Esk and then go left at a T-junction on to the A169, signposted 'Pickering'. When you are almost through the village of Sleights, look out for a road on the right, signed 'Grosmont and Egton'.
There are fine views into the delightful Esk Dale before dropping down into Grosmont, where the North Yorkshire Moors Railway connects with the Middlesbrough–Whitby branch line services.

6 Carry on to Egton and follow the signs, left, 'Egton Bridge', turning left again at a T-junction. Turn right just after the church, signposted 'Glaisdale'. Climb steeply to a T-junction; turn left here and negotiate the precipitous 1-in-3 (33%) Limber Hill.
The hill heads down to the ancient stone arch of Beggar's Bridge that once carried trains of packhorse ponies and over the River Esk.

7 Climb through the straggle of houses in Glaisdale; the signs are now for Lealholm. Keep ahead on the main road, eventually to turn right at a T-junction to descend into Lealholm village.
With its fine arched Beggar's Bridge, stepping stones and grassy riverbanks, this is one of the prettiest villages along the Esk Valley.

8 Cross the bridge over the River Esk, and then turn left immediately, signposted 'Danby'. Pass graceful Duck Bridge and the National Park's Moors Centre, where it's worth stopping if you have time, but otherwise bear left to Danby village. Keep ahead at the crossroads, signposted 'Castleton'. In Castleton village, turn right halfway up the hill, signed 'Guisborough'. Cross the River Esk once again, to climb up on to lovely open moorland. At the first junction by the White Cross base go left on a road signed 'Commondale and Stokesley'. Pass through Commondale, as fine moorland views open up. Continue through Kildale and then take two right turns following the signposts back to Great Ayton and the start of the tour.

ROSEBERRY TOPPING
MAP REF NZ5813

Roseberry Topping, which lies just to the north of Great Ayton, is Cleveland's very own 'Matterhorn'. Its height, just 1,056 feet (322m), hardly qualifies it as a major peak, yet it is a prominent landmark for miles around, standing aloof from the surrounding Cleveland Hills.

To see Roseberry Topping as nature intended, as an almost symmetrical cone, you will have to look at old prints. As soon as its mineral wealth was realised, it was exploited for its alum, iron ore, jet and roadstone. So heavily was it mined and quarried that a great chunk of the hill fell away in a landslip, making the residents of the nearby village of Newton under Roseberry fear for their lives.

This landslip created the distinctive profile we see today. Climb to the top, and to the northwest is the industrial heartland of Middlesbrough, its urban sprawl creeping inexorably outwards; to the south are views across the moors.

Roseberry Topping's prominence has made it an important landmark for more than a millennium. There is some evidence that it was even an object of veneration. 'Roseberry' is a corruption of the old Viking name, 'Othenesberg' (Odin's Hill), indicating it was probably sacred to the Danish god of creation. 'Topping', also of Scandinavian origin, means a peak. Several 17th-century references have it as 'Osbury Toppyne', at a time when it was one of the many beacon hills on which fires were built – to be set alight if the Spanish Armada were sighted at sea.

RUNSWICK BAY MAP REF NZ8016

A long arc of sandy beach extends south from the houses of Runswick, to form one of the loveliest bays on the Yorkshire coast. There is plenty of shelter from blustery winds and high seas; over the centuries many a ship's captain has been relieved to find safe harbour here.

The cliffs that protect the bay take a battering each winter; whole chunks can disappear in a storm. Since medieval times the coastline continues to change dramatically, with villages creeping ever closer to the shore, and many coastal villages sliding into the sea. You only have to look at old maps to realise that the 'lost' villages of Yorkshire's coast can be counted in scores.

The village of Runswick fell into the sea in 1682. Fortunately no lives were lost as all the villagers were evacuated in time. Today, Runswick comprises a pleasing collection of small red-roofed cottages, clinging limpet-like to the cliff and connected by a series of steps and alleyways. The sheltering bay, good soil and southerly aspect make Runswick a suntrap; in spring and summer the little terraced gardens make a pretty scene. The attractive whitewashed house on the headland was the coastguard's cottage.

A few fishing cobles are still lined up above the high watermark, though today your neighbour is more likely to be a holiday-maker than a fisherman. The lifeboat is always at the ready, however; ships can still be caught out by sudden changes in the weather. In 1901 a storm blew up while most of the fishing boats were at sea. The village women launched the lifeboat and saved many lives.

Roseberry Topping and Captain Cook Country

Climb Roseberry Topping, once mined for ironstone, for views of the countryside. After the descent from the summit, and the climb again to the woodland, the track descends over Great Ayton Moor. Ahead, the Captain Cook Monument, a stone obelisk 52ft (15.5m) high, dominates the view. The great explorer was born in 1728 within sight of Roseberry Topping at Marton (then a village, but now a suburb of Middlesbrough) and went to school at nearby Great Ayton. Just after you have gone through the gate during Point 5, the dips and hollows in the ground to the left are the remains of an ironstone mine, Ayton Banks. Further on the route you'll pass by Gribdale Terrace, a row of cottages built to house the iron miners and their families.

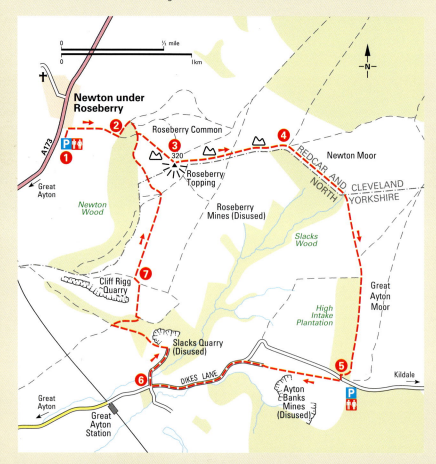

WALK 1

Route Directions

1 Take the rough lane beside the car park towards Roseberry Topping. The path goes through a gateway then rises to a second gate at the beginning of the woodland.

2 Go through the gate into National Trust Land and turn left. There is a well-worn, mostly-paved, path to the summit. It is a stiff climb to the trig point on the top of the hill.

3 From the summit, walk east from the trig point, past two iron poles set into rock, and straight on along the paved way. Go steeply downhill. At the bottom, bear right to go up a track that bends right around the corner of woodland to a gate.

4 Go through the gate and take the path alongside the wood, following yellow waymarkers. Continue on the path until it eventually follows a wall and descends the hillside to reach a road.

5 Turn right, cross the cattle grid and bear left between two benches, then go right, along the fence line, at first parallel with the road. Go down the field, through a gate and then over a stile and out into a lane. Walk past the cottages to reach a road, where you go straight ahead.

6 At a crossroads go right, down Aireyholme Lane. Follow the lane as it winds past houses, then take a signed footpath left over a stile. Follow the fence to two gates into woodland. After 0.5 mile (800m), go right at a National Trust sign, up a path ascending through the woods to a signposted stile. Over it, turn left to another stile, then after it, go right along the edge of the woodland. Bend left to a gate near a house.

7 Walk across two fields to a stile, then continue uphill to the tower. Beyond it, take a grassy path left down a gully, to a gate into woodland. Follow the path downhill through the woods to return to the gate at the top of the lane leading back to the car park.

Route facts

DISTANCE/TIME 5.5 miles (8.8km) 2h30

MAP OS Explorer OL26 North York Moors – Western

START Car park at Newton under Roseberry, grid ref: NZ 570128

TRACKS Hillside climb, then tracks and field paths, 5 stiles

GETTING TO THE START From Middlesborough, take the A272 towards Stokesley, take a left turn on the B1292 and follow signs to Newton under Roseberry.

THE PUB The Royal Oak Hotel, Great Ayton. Tel: 01642 724047; www.royaloak-hotel.co.uk

❶ It is a stiff climb to the top of the hill. Please note that Roseberry Topping is in danger from erosion due to the high number of visitors it attracts each year. You may find that some parts are cordoned off, and access is limited to other areas. Visitors can help conserve the area by ensuring that they stay on the tracks and obey any warning signs.

STAITHES

SANDSEND – STAITHES

SANDSEND MAP REF NZ6812

The approach to the lovely Sandsend along the A174 is steeply downhill from Lythe; views open up of a long sandy beach and, in the distance, Whitby Abbey dominates the horizon. Here is a place name that, for once, doesn't require interpretation. Sandsend marks the northern end of a sandy beach, one of the best on Yorkshire's coast, stretching down as far as Whitby harbour.

The village has been an industrious hive of activity for centuries; the Romans had a cement works here. More recently the bare outcrop of Sandsend Ness was mined for alum and it is still bare today, because of the heaps of mining waste. Remarkably, these mines were worked steadily for 250 years. When Yorkshire's coastal area had its railway, Sandsend was overlooked by a long viaduct, raised high above the red-tiled rooftops on tall pillars. Both the railway and the viaduct disappeared in the 1960s: more's the pity, many may think.

Today, Sandsend is a more peaceful spot, sheltered from the from the rough battering of north winds and fiercesome seas by Sandsend Ness. Mickleby Beck and East Row Beck reach to the sea at Sandsend a mere 97 feet (30m) apart; instead of staring out to sea most of the cottages are neatly clustered either side of their banks. Several paths accompany both of these valleys into lovely Mulgrave Woods, which you'll find is a traditional broadleaved woodland.

On the narrow ridge between these valleys is Mulgrave Castle, which is a splendid Georgian pile. Guests at the castle included William Wordsworth and Charles Dickens; both wrote glowingly about the fine views to be enjoyed from here. In the grounds are the evocative, ivy-clad ruins of a much earlier castle, dating from the 13th century.

■ Visit

LEWIS CARROLL
It was while strolling along the fine, sandy beach at Sandsend that Lewis Carroll first had the idea for his surreal poem about the Walrus and the Carpenter. If you fancy it, you can follow in his footsteps; at low tide it is a lovely walk of about 2.5 miles (4km) along the beach to Whitby.

STAITHES MAP REF NZ7818

It is easy to miss the Staithes turning off the main A174 coast road. Nor is the first sight of the village very promising. You have to drive half a mile (800m), park in the pay-and-display car park and proceed on foot if you want to see why Staithes is so special.

This perfectly preserved Yorkshire fishing villages is divided into two by Cowbar Beck and the steep-sided gorge through which it runs. For centuries the people of Staithes have had to cope with the twin problems of an inhospitable site and the ravages of the North Sea. They have made their living from the sea, while always taking care to respect its awesome power.

The Staithes we see today is a village that would be immediately familiar to the young James Cook, who spent an impatient 18 months working at the counter of a draper's shop in the village before realising his ambition to go to

ESK DALE & NORTH

sea. The whitewashed houses, pantiled roofs, fishing cobles and lobster pots would make him feel at home.

It may seem that time has stood still here, but the battering from the sea has been relentless. Despite the shelter given by its steep cliffs, Staithes has lost many buildings to its stormy seas. The little draper's shop was washed away; a house near the Cod and Lobster pub bears a commemorative plaque but has been rebuilt since James Cook lived and worked here. The pub itself backs on to the harbour wall and has suffered more than its fair share of storm damage, having been rebuilt three times – the last occasion being as recently as 1953.

■ Activity

VIEWPOINTS ABOVE STAITHES
A walk of less than an hour from the village of Staithes will offer a variety of viewpoints, looking down on the random patchwork of red-tiled roofs from the cliff tops – known as Cowbar Nab and Old Nab – on either side of the gorge, connected by the arch of a footbridge.

■ Insight

A MAJOR FISHING PORT
Sleepy Staithes has known busier days. During the first half of the 19th century as many as 300 men went to sea in the distinctive fishing cobles, to net mostly cod, haddock and mackerel. These small craft, with a crew of three, were often accompanied by larger yawls. Fish were moved from the cobles into larger vessels for easier transport back to harbour. Fish was dispatched from Staithes all over the country; packhorses were maintained to do nothing more than to carry some of each day's catch to the market at York.

On a sunny summer's day it is hard to imagine such destruction. You would have to make your visit in winter, when a strong northeasterly gale is blowing, and the waves are hammering against the harbour wall, to understand why the people of Staithes have earned a reputation for self-reliance. To have maintained a viable community here, despite the drawbacks, is remarkable.

Fishing has long provided a living, albeit a precarious one, for the men of Staithes. The little harbour, and the mouth of Cowbar Beck, are still full of the traditional fishing cobles – whose slightly upturned prows betray their Nordic origins. But today they go to sea mainly for crabs and lobsters; you can buy them freshly caught in the village.

Painters and photographers are attracted in droves to the village. There are echoes of some of the picturesque fishing villages of Cornwall, but few communities in the country can boast a more extraordinary setting than Staithes. The village used to have a railway station; both station and line are gone, leaving just the trackbed and the stanchions of the old viaduct over the gorge as reminders of the scenic line from Saltburn to Scarborough.

To the north of Staithes are Boulby Cliffs. At more than 656 feet (200m) they are the highest, if not the most dramatic, on England's east coast and offer excellent views. Close by is the Boulby Potash Mine, the deepest mine in Europe. The extent of the mining operation here can be gauged by the fact that tunnels extend almost 3 miles (4.8km) out under the sea.

STAITHES – WHITBY

WHITBY MAP REF NZ8910

Those who take a leisurely stroll along the pleasant harbour front may be forgiven for thinking of Whitby as just another resort devoted to the arcane delights of bingo, amusement arcades, candyfloss and 'Kiss Me Quick' hats. But Whitby has a great deal more to offer, enough to keep the most demanding visitor interested for some time. For it has a long, illustrious and genuine history as one of the country's most important seaports, and the town can claim associations with a remarkable variety of historical figures.

Whitby's setting itself is dramatic, with houses clinging on to the steep slopes on either side of the River Esk. A good overview of the town can be enjoyed from the elevated bridge that now carries through traffic on the A171 at a convenient distance from the town's narrow streets. From this vantage point you can see the Esk broaden into a large marina full of yachts. Beyond the swing bridge is the harbour, overlooked spectacularly on the southern flank by St Mary's Church and the ruined abbey – a landmark for miles around.

The scene is always one of bustle and activity. Whitby has thrived when other fishing towns and villages have declined, and new building projects emphasise that the town is looking to the future as well as the past.

Whitby has always gazed out to sea. For centuries the town was isolated from the rest of the county by poor roads and the wild expanse of moorland that surround it on three sides. Yet by the 18th century it had risen to the status of a major port, with shipbuilding, fishing and whaling contributing to a maritime prosperity that lasted until well into the early years of the 20th century. The fine Georgian houses at the west end of the town, built by wealthy shipbuilders and fleet owners, attest to this success.

Elsewhere, more traditional cottages, whitewashed and with red-tiled roofs, housed the fishermen. Space was at a premium, so their houses were built in close proximity, mostly up the steep inclines on the eastern side of the Esk. They are linked by ginnels and steps, which beg to be explored. Be sure to leave your car in one of the long-stay

■ Insight

FRANK MEADOW SUTCLIFFE

Photographer Frank Meadow Sutcliffe's bread-and-butter work was portraiture. But his passion was Whitby itself. He used a huge and cumbersome camera, which precluded any modern notion of candid photography, to photograph the town. He stage-managed his compositions (even paying some of his subjects to ensure co-operation) to produce lustrous images of gnarled old fishermen, street traders and grubby street urchins – with the tall-masted sailing ships and Whitby harbour as picturesque backdrops. It isn't merely the patina of age that makes Sutcliffe's pictures so beguiling. All the characters he photographed may be long gone, but many of the locations can still be seen today. Despite the cars, the cafés and the candyfloss, there is a continuing thread that links the Whitby of today to the Whitby that Sutcliffe knew so well. At the Sutcliffe Gallery you can find framed prints of his evocative photographs, all taken from the original negatives.

ESK DALE & NORTH

Insight

WHITBY JET

Used to make jewellery since the Bronze Age, Whitby jet was popularised by Queen Victoria, who wore it during her many years of mourning for Prince Albert. Jet is fossilised wood, which turns from its natural brown colour to the deepest black ('jet-black', as we say) once it is polished, and Whitby proved a particularly fruitful site. This craft trade expanded as women took the royal lead and took to wearing jet ornaments. But their tastes were too fickle for the business to last, and by the time of Victoria's death the demand for Whitby jet was much reduced. Today you can find original pieces of jewellery displayed in Whitby's Pannett Park Museum, and for sale in the town's antiques shops. Some new jet jewellery is being made too.

car parks near the marina; Whitby's narrow streets were definitely not built with motor traffic in mind.

The town's large harbour is still at the heart of the town, though today there are more pleasure craft passing the breakwaters than fishing cobles. Whitby traditionally offered the only safe harbour between the rivers Tyne and Humber. The North Yorkshire coast is notoriously prone to storms, and many ships have been wrecked, unable to find sanctuary in time.

The town was prosperous during the 17th and 18th centuries with the mining and refining of alum – a vital ingredient in the dyeing of wool. Coal was brought here to fire the cauldrons that separated alum from rock, and stone was needed for building; this increase in trade required the building of a better harbour. In 1753 a company was set up in the town to undertake whaling expeditions, using the sturdy ships already being built here. The ships spent many weeks at sea in the distant, inhospitable waters of the Arctic. The trade was lucrative for those who survived; some ships, sadly, never returned. Records reveal that almost 3,000 whales were brought back to Whitby up to 1833. Seals, walruses and polar bears also featured in these hauls, and even unicorns, if the records are to be believed. They were more likely to have been narwhals, whose single 'horn' probably started the unicorn myth in the first place.

The whale blubber was rendered down on the quayside to make oil; the stench, by all accounts, was vile. Even the streetlamps of the town were lit with gas refined from whale oil. An arch formed from the jawbone of a whale looks down upon the harbour today.

Smaller boats sailed out of Whitby to net herring, and the fish market was one of the busiest. The men still fish, but on a much reduced scale; many of the boats that slip anchor today are carrying sea anglers and other visitors.

The town has a special place in ecclesiastical history. In the year AD 655 King Oswy of Northumbria celebrated a heady victory in battle by promising his daughter as a bride of Christ. He founded a monastery on Whitby's eastern cliff, overlooking the town, much where the later abbey's ruins still stand today. The first abbess was Hilda, who presided over a community of nuns and monks. Her goodness and piety passed into legend, and she was recognised as a saint. In AD 664 the Synod of Whitby convened in the town to decide whether Northumbria should follow the Catholic or Celtic Christianity. In the event the Catholic Church triumphed.

The most notable member of this community was a monk, Caedmon, who is also known as the 'Father of English poetry'. A shy man, he preferred to keep his own company as a cowherd instead of singing with the choir. Caedmon had a dream in which an angel asked him to sing. When he awoke, he found that he was possessed of a beautiful voice. His poem, called *The Song of Creation*, is the earliest known poem written in English. A sandstone cross, which stands by St Mary's Church commemorates the life of Caedmon and carved panels illustrate some of the incidents in his life.

St Hilda's original abbey was destroyed by Viking raiders. The abbey that replaced it was begun in the 11th century and was rebuilt on several occasions, notably in the 13th and 14th centuries; this is what we can see today, starkly silhouetted against the sky. This building, too, suffered damage, when in 1914 two German battleships shelled the town and inadvertently hit the west front of Whitby Abbey.

Sharing the abbey's windswept site is St Mary's Church. It was built to cater to the spiritual needs of the village that grew up around the abbey. St Mary's still serves the congregations, although its parishioners have to tackle the famous 199 steps up to the church. Parts of the building date back to the 12th century; fortunately the fabric of the church suffered none of the indignities meted out to the abbey. Make sure to take a look inside St Mary's; the interior was fitted out during the 18th century with wooden galleries, high-sided box-pews and a splendid three-decker pulpit. The effect is quite startling, with a distinctly nautical feeling as the craftsmen were more accustomed to fitting out ships.

At the bottom of Church Steps is the oldest part of town. Little fishermen's cottages huddle together as if to keep out the bitter weather. Narrow alleyways lead off from the tiny market square, and if those 199 steps have taken their toll enjoy a drink in one of the harbour-side pubs and watch the fishing boats and pleasure craft.

On Grape Lane, by the harbour, you will find the home of ship owner and Quaker, Captain John Walker, to whom the young James Cook was apprenticed in 1746, before enlisting in the Royal Navy. Today the building houses the Captain Cook Memorial Museum, with fascinating room sets and interesting exhibits about his life.

Insight

DRACULA
Few graveyards enjoy a more panoramic view than the one surrounding St Mary's Church. But if the wind is whipping around the gravestones, and the full moon is shrouded by clouds, it can have a rather more menacing atmosphere. Bram Stoker realised its potential and avid readers of his horror novel, *Dracula*, will recognise some of the settings from Whitby. Look out for the skull and crossbones gravestones near the topmost gate. These are said to have inspired the novel.

ESK DALE & NORTH

■ TOURIST INFORMATION CENTRES

Danby
The Moors Centre.
Tel: 01439 772737

Great Ayton
High Green Car Park.
Tel: 01642 722835
(seasonal).

Guisborough
Priory Grounds,
Church Street.
Tel: 01287 633801

Whitby
Langborne Road.
Tel: 01723 383637

■ PLACES OF INTEREST

Captain Cook and Staithes Heritage Centre
High Street,
Staithes.
Tel: 01947 841454; www.captaincookstaithes.co.uk

Captain Cook Memorial Museum
Grape Lane, Whitby.
Tel: 01947 601900; www.cookmuseumwhitby.co.uk

Captain Cook Schoolroom Museum
Great Ayton.
Tel: 01642 724296;
www.captaincookschoolroommuseum.co.uk

The Dracula Experience
9 Marine Parade,
Whitby.
Tel: 01947 601923; www.draculaexperience.co.uk

Gisborough Priory
Guisborough.
Tel: 01287 633801; www.english-heritage.org.uk

Lifeboat Museum
Pier Road, Whitby.
Tel: 01947 602001;
www.rnli.org.uk

The Moors Centre
Lodge Lane, Danby.
Tel: 01439 772737;
www.northyorkmoors.org.uk
Free.

Tocketts Watermill
On A173, 1 mile (1.6km) east of Guisborough.

Tom Leonard Mining Museum
Skinningrove.
Tel: 01287 642877;
www.ironstonemuseum.co.uk

Whitby Abbey
East Cliff, Whitby.
Tel: 01947 603568;
www.english-heritage.org.uk

Whitby Museum and Art Gallery
Pannett Park, Whitby.
Tel: 01947 602908;
www.whitbymuseum.org.uk

■ SHOPPING

Guisborough
Open-air market,
Thu and Sat.

Whitby
Open-air market,
Tue and Sat.

LOCAL SPECIALITIES

Ceramics, Sculpture and Jewellery
Montage Studio Gallery,
12 Church Street, Castleton.
Tel: 01287 660159

Enamel
The Enamel Workshop,
128 Church Street, Whitby.
Tel: 01947 606216

Glass
Whitby Glass Ltd,
9 Sandgate, Whitby.
Tel: 01947 603553

Paintings and Prints
John Freeman Studios,
9 Market Place, Whitby.
Tel: 01947 602799;
www.johnfreemanstudio.co.uk

Grosmont Gallery
Grosmont.
Tel: 01947 895007;
www.grosmontgallery.com

Whitby Jet
Watsons Jet Workshop,
Church Street, Whitby.
Tel: 01947 605320

Whitby Jet Heritage Centre,
Church Street, Whitby.
Tel: 01947 821530;
www.whitbyjet.co.uk
Shop free; fee for workshop.

■ PERFORMING ARTS

Glaisdale
Esk Valley Summer Theatre,
The Robinson Institute
(seasonal).
Tel: 01947 897587

INFORMATION

Whitby Pavilion Theatre
West Cliff, Whitby.
Tel: 01947 604855 or 820625;
www.discoveryorkshirecoast.com

■ SPORTS & ACTIVITIES
ANGLING
Sea
Staithes and Whitby
Enquire at the harbour,
or contact the local TIC.
Fly
River Esk
Information on licences and permits from main post offices. Fishing locations from the Environment Agency, Phoenix House, Global Avenue, Millshaw, Beeston Ring Road, Leeds.
Tel: 08708 506506; www.environmentagency.gov.uk
Scaling Dam Reservoir
Fishing lodge:
Tel: 01287 640540
BEACHES
Runswick Bay has a sandy beach with easy access; a sandy beach stretches from Whitby to Sandsend with car parks and access points.
BOAT TRIPS
Whitby
Trips round the bay leave from the West Pier.
CYCLE HIRE
Hawsker (Whitby to Scarborough rail trail)
Trailways Cycle Hire,
The Old Railway Station,
Hawsker, near Whitby.
Tel: 01947 820207;
www.trailways.info
HORSE RIDING
Lealholm
Hollin Hall Riding Centre,
Great Fryup Dale.
Tel: 01947 897470;
www.hollinequest.co.uk
Borrowby
Borrowby Equestrian Centre,
High Farm, Borrowby.
Tel: 01947 840134;
www.borrowbyequestriancentre.co.uk
LONG-DISTANCE FOOTPATHS AND TRAILS
The Cleveland Way
A 110-mile (176km) walk from Helmsley to Filey Brigg.
www.nationaltrail.co.uk
The Esk Valley Walk
Begins at Castleton and follows the River Esk to Whitby.
WATER SPORTS
Scaling Dam Reservoir
Sailing, windsurfing.
Tel: 01287 640214

■ ANNUAL EVENTS & CUSTOMS
Castleton
Castleton Show, Sep.
Danby
Agricultural Show, mid-Aug.
Egton
Egton Show, late Aug.
Egton Bridge
Gooseberry Show, early Aug.
Kildale
Kildale Show, early Sep.
Lealholm
Lealholm Show, early Sep.
Whitby
Planting of the Penny Hedge, Ascension Eve, May.
Morris Dance Festival, Jun.
Blessing of Boats, mid-Jul.
Whitby Angling Festival, Jul.
Whitby Folk Festival, Aug.
Whitby Regatta, mid-Aug.

TEA ROOMS & PUBS

Tea Rooms

Danby
Stonehouse Bakery
& Tea Shop,
3 Briar Hill, Danby YO21 2LZ
Tel: 01287 660006
In the centre of Danby, this traditional bakery produces fabulous bread, including sun-dried tomato and olive breads and ciabatta. They are used to make the range of delicious sandwiches that available in the adjoining tea shop. Cakes, too, come from the bakery's ovens, and their scones are perfect with jam and cream in a traditional cream tea. Closed Sunday.

Guisborough
Macdonald Gisborough Hall,
Whitby Lane, Guisborough
TS14 6PT
Tel: 0870 400 8191;
www.macdonaldhotels.co.uk/gisborough
For a taste of luxury, in elegant surroundings, treat yourself at Gisborough Hall. As well as the traditional scones with jam and cream, there's the Traditional Full Afternoon Tea, with sandwiches and cake, as well as the scones, or the Celebration Tea, where your scones and fruitcake are accompanied by a glass of sparkling wine. Tea is served from midday to 6pm.

Lealholm
Beck View Tea Room,
Lealholm YO21 2AQ
Tel: 01947 897310
There are tables inside the cosy tea room and outside on the beck's bank. As well as good-value cream teas, regular visitors enjoy a good variety of home-made cakes, including the particularly scrumptious nut slice.

Whitby
Elizabeth Botham & Sons
35-39 Skinner Street, Whitby
YO21 3AH. Tel: 01947 602823;
www.botham.co.uk
The tradition of fine baking, begun in 1865, is still going strong in this superior first-floor café on Whitby's West Cliff. Your problem will be what to choose – gingerbread with Wensleydale cheese, lemon buns, Yorkshire tea brack loaf, the cream tea, or the salads, the sandwiches or baked potatoes.

Pubs

Danby
Duke of Wellington Inn
Danby YO21 2LY
Tel: 01287 660351; www.danby-dukeofwellington.co.uk
An attractive inn, in the scattered village of Danby, with wide views of the village in its moorland setting. Inside, the décor is warm, welcoming and traditional, with local beers and a good selection of whiskies. The evening menu might include dishes such as venison pie or braised lamb shank.

Egton
The Wheatsheaf Inn,
Egton YO21 1TZ
Tel: 01947 895271
There's a plentiful supply of Yorkshire ales in the Wheatsheaf, including Black Sheep from Masham. The pub's exterior is unassuming, but inside, the main bar has low beams, dark walls and comfortable settles. There is much good pub food on offer, using local fish and other produce – the fish stew is recommended.

Great Ayton
The Royal Oak Hotel
125 High Street,
Great Ayton TS9 6BW.
Tel: 01642 722361
www.royaloak-hotel.co.uk
Located in the heart of the tranquil village of Great Ayton, you'll find the Royal Oak to be a traditional, relaxed pub. The beamed bar provides good local beer and hearty bar snacks, while the restaurant serves simple, robust and well-cooked food with a range of puddings.

Western Moors

Ampleforth	58
Bilsdale	58
Bransdale	59
Christian Crosses & Monks	60
Cleveland Way	63
Coxwold	63
Hawnby	64
■ WALK 2 Swainby to Whorlton	66
Helmsley	68
Kilburn	69
Osmotherley	70
■ WALK 3 Byland Abbey	72
■ CAR TOUR 2 The Western Moors	74
Oswaldkirk, Rievaulx Abbey	76
Stokesley	78
Sutton Bank	79
■ CYCLE RIDE 1 The Hambleton Hills	80
■ WALK 4 Boltby and Thirlby Bank	82

INTRODUCTION

The Western Moors include Helmsley, a handsome little market town and the administrative centre of the National Park. Near by you'll find the ruins of Rievaulx and Byland abbeys and the White Horse of Kilburn. The rolling Hambleton Hills and the bleaker Cleveland Hills provide a landscape of heather moorland and pastoral dales, dotted with farmhouses and villages of red-tiled stone houses.

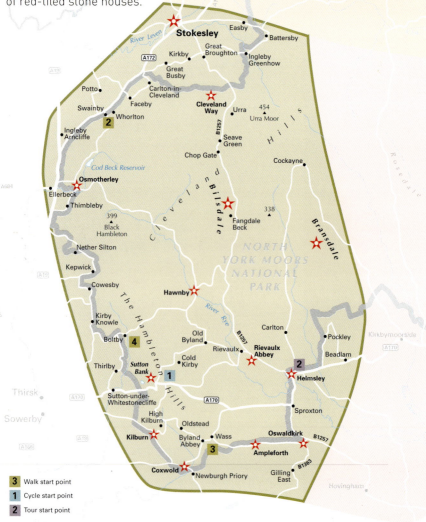

3 Walk start point
1 Cycle start point
2 Tour start point

WESTERN MOORS 55

HELMSLEY

EASTERSIDE HILL

HOT SPOTS

Unmissable attractions

There's no lack of things to enjoy here and Helmsley is a good base from which to explore the Western Moors...take a picnic to Chop Gate for fine views...walk the drove road called Westside Track near Cockayne...stroll on Rievaulx Terrace and view the fine abbey below...walk northwards from the car park at Sutton Bank along part of (or all) of the Cleveland Way for magnificent views...see the craftsmen carvers hard at work at the Mouseman Visitor Centre in Kilburn...follow the Mosaic Trail from Boltby...explore the ruins of Helmsley Castle...contemplate a monk's life in a cell at Mount Grace Priory...catch a concert in a remote country church during the Ryedale Festival...see Coxwold's octagonal church tower from the gardens of Shandy Hall.

1 Rievaulx Abbey
The atmospheric and evocative ruins of 13th-century Rievaulx Abbey, one of the great monastic houses of the north, are set in the tranquil wooded valley of the River Rye.

2 Hemlsley Castle
Little remains of Helmsley Castle's great East Tower, built in the 12th century by Robert de Roos. The castle was destroyed by Parliamentarians after a three-month siege in 1644; the story is told in the visitor centre.

3 Sutton Bank
The wonderful views from the vantage point of Sutton Bank, on the edge of the Hambleton Hills, take in the prominent landmark of Roulston Scar, wooded Hood Hill and the Vale of York.

WESTERN MOORS

AMPLEFORTH MAP REF SE5878

Best known for its public school and Benedictine monastery, Ampleforth is a linear village of handsome houses overlooking the Howardian Hills.

French monks, fleeing persecution in their homeland in 1793 during the course of the French Revolution, found spiritual sanctuary in England and patronage from the prominent Fairfax family, settling at Ampleforth in 1802. As theirs had been a teaching order, they built a school within the monastery. The oldest surviving school buildings date from 1861, while the monastery dates from 1894–98. But both establishments have been extended almost continuously up to the present day.

After the end of the First World War, headmaster Father Paul Nevill, who was also the parish priest, commissioned Robert Thompson of Kilburn to make a wooden cross for the churchyard in the village. Father Nevill was so impressed by the woodcarver's craftsmanship that Thompson was asked to make furniture for the school. The library remains one of Robert Thompson's most ambitious commissions. The present abbey church is a new addition, built between 1922 and 1961 to a design by Sir Giles Gilbert Scott; it too contains several very fine examples of woodwork and carvings by Robert Thompson.

Just southeast of Ampleforth is Gilling East, which has a 14th-century fortified tower house. Since early in the 20th century the building has been owned by Ampleforth College, and used as the college's preparatory school.

BILSDALE

The long valley of Bilsdale extends all the way along the B1257, from Helmsley in the south towards Stokesley in the north. The broad valley is farmed up to the moorland tops, as it was centuries ago by the monks of Rievaulx Abbey. The monastic connection is recalled by names such as Crossholme and Low Crosses Farm. Scattered farmsteads punctuate the valley, but today the only village is tiny Chop Gate. Pronounce it 'Chop Yat' to sound like a local.

■ Visit

PICNIC SITES

Five miles (8km) north of Helmsley on the B1257, just before you enter Bilsdale, is Newgate Bank, a fine vantage point with a picnic site, from where you can enjoy views of Bilsdale and the Hambleton Hills. A footpath returns to Helmsley via Riccal Bank. At the northern end of Bilsdale is the village of Chop Gate, which also has a picnic site and a car park.

■ Visit

BRIDESTONES

On top of Hasty Bank, the northern escarpment of the Cleveland Hills, are the Wainstones, the largest outcrop of rocks in the National Park, and a favourite with climbers. Another set of rocks can be found on Nab End Moor, in Bilsdale. These are just one of a number of rock formations on the moors that are known as the Bridestones. Others, the remains of ancient stone circles, can be found near Grosmont. The best-known Bridestones are in the hands of the National Trust on Bridestones Moor, and are most easily approached from the Dalby Forest Drive. Weathered into strange shapes, these ricks make a surreal moorland landmark.

AMPLEFORTH – BRANSDALE

The River Seph is ever-present in the valley bottom; the B1257 accompanies it almost from its source to where it joins the River Rye to the north of Rievaulx. On the roadside about 8 miles (12.9km) north of Helmsley is the Sun Inn. Just yards away from the pub is a much earlier thatched building, of cruck-frame construction, that dates back to the 16th century. This was the original Sun Inn – also known as Spout House – which dispensed ale from first receiving its licence in 1714 until 1914.

When the licence transferred to the new Sun Inn, the older building fell into disrepair. The National Park Authority rescued and renovated this delightful example of vernacular architecture. Now it is considered to be the finest example of a cruck-framed house in the National Park (not counting those in Ryedale Folk Museum) and one of the oldest. Visitors can take a look inside.

The interior has been restored to how it might have looked more than three centuries ago. A witch post still stands near the inglenook fireplace, to ward off the 'evil eye'. Up narrow stairs are tiny rooms, open to the thatch and fitted out with wooden box beds. Downstairs are the diminutive bar and snugs of the original pub layout, and the beer cellar.

BRANSDALE

The unspoiled valley of Bransdale drives deep into the moors, but most visitors pass it by. Motorists leaving Helmsley along the A170 towards Kirkbymoorside should look out on the left for a signpost to Carlton (and Helmsley Youth Hostel). The road loops around Bransdale and

Visit

THE GILLAMOOR SUNDIAL
Gillamoor boasts a sundial of novel design in front of Dial House Farm; it was erected by public subscription in 1800. A central column is mounted on top of a stepped base. On top is a stone globe mounted on an inscribed cube, with a dial face on four of its sides.

Activity

A CYCLE TOUR THROUGH BRANSDALE
The unclassified road which leaves the A170 at Helmsley and curves round in a loop through Bransdale before rejoining the A170 again at Kirkbymoorside is an ideal route for cyclists. Passing through the villages of Carlton, Cockayne and Gillamoor, the 12-mile (19km) tour offers wonderful moorland views with lonely farms and tumbling streams.

then returns to the A170 about 5 miles (8km) further east at Kirkbymoorside. This is a delightful drive.

Beyond the houses that comprise the village of Carlton, the views open up dramatically. To the left is unenclosed heather moorland; to the right the valley bottom is divided up by neat drystone walls either side of Hodge Beck. This pattern is punctuated by a handful of scattered farmsteads. The moors, with barely a tree to be seen, echo to the evocative calls of the curlew, red grouse and lapwing; sheep graze the grassy verges and wander idly across the road. Unenclosed for most of the way, the road heads north; look out on the left for examples of inscribed milestones.

WESTERN MOORS

The Church of St Nicholas sits on a hillock overlooking the valley. Though dating only from 1886, the building replaces a much earlier church. It is a typical moorland church, tiny and rather undemonstrative, but with a real sense of spirituality that grander churches so often lack. Inside, the barrelled roof is worth a look.

Flour was ground for centuries at Bransdale Mill (National Trust, but not open to the public), accessible, on foot only, from either side of the valley head. The present building, dating from 1811, was built by William Strickland and his son, Emmanuel, the vicar of Ingleby Greenhow. Stones inset into the mill walls are inscribed with 'improving' texts in Hebrew, Latin and Greek; evidence of the vicar's classical education.

The road then makes a broad sweep to the right, before continuing the circuit of Bransdale. Here sturdy farmsteads with fanciful names – Cow Sike, Toad Hole and Spout House – gaze down into the bottom of the valley. Before arriving in Kirkbymoorside, you have a chance to visit Gillamoor and Fadmoor, a pair of typical moorland villages barely half a mile (800m) apart.

The houses of both these pretty and unspoiled villages are grouped around their village greens, but Gillamoor has an extra surprise in store for the visitor. St Aidan's Church stands on its own at the end of the village; you are almost upon it before you see that it is sited on the edge of a steep precipice which commands breathtaking views across lower Farndale, the River Dove and on to the purple heather moors beyond.

CHRISTIAN CROSSES & MONKS

The life and landscape of the North York Moors have been shaped by a number of influences, but few have had a longer or more profound effect than the Christian faith. The moorland monasteries may be evocative ruins today, but in days gone by the influence of these communities extended far beyond the silence of their cloisters. For example, by the start of the 16th century about a third of the land within what is now the Peak District National Park was under the direct control of various monasteries.

The monks combined their religious devotions with remarkably successful forays into more secular activities. They may have chosen isolated sites on which to build their communities and churches, but they were not averse to comfort – even luxury. The religious buildings of the moors trace their origins back many centuries. A number of extant churches and abbeys pre-date the Norman invasion. Many more recent edifices are built on the foundations of much earlier buildings. The link with the past is everywhere to be seen.

At the dawning of the 7th century, these moors formed part of the Northumbrian Kingdom of Deira. King Edwin of Northumbria was saved from assassination by the intervention of Lilla, one of his ministers. Edwin marked Lilla's grave on Fylingdales Moor with a stone cross – the oldest of the moorland crosses. In AD 627 Edwin was converted to Christianity by Paulinus, a Roman missionary. The first Christian communities in the area

LILLA CROSS

WESTERN MOORS

Insight

ANCIENT WAYMARKERS
More than 30 moorland stone crosses still survive today; at one time there were many more. One of their functions was to define the far-flung boundaries of the sheep-grazing moors of the monasteries. But their religious symbolism is obvious, and many a lost and lonely traveller would have had his spirits lifted by the sight of a cross on the horizon. Crosses were often sited along old roads and many doubled as waymarkers. An interesting custom was for well-heeled travellers to leave coins on top of the crosses (many had a recess for this purpose) for the benefit of their needier brethren.

Insight

ENTREPRENEURIAL MONKS
The various monastic communities of the North York Moors owned outlying farms – known as granges, which were often located many miles from the monasteries. The monks (their numbers augmented by lay brothers) devoted their talents to arable farming, animal husbandry and exploiting the uplands for their mineral wealth. The monks' entrepreneurial skills created international markets for their wares and, in many cases, immense wealth and power for the monasteries.

Activity

THE MISSING LINK
An extra section of the Cleveland Way, known as the Missing Link, has been developed to take walkers in a complete loop from Scarborough back to Helmsley. This circular walk is about 180 miles (288km) long, and means that walkers can now start and finish at any convenient point on the route.

covered by this book were in Whitby (at that time known as Streanaeshalch) and Lastingham. In AD 654 St Cedd was given land at Lastingham on which to build a monastery. Just three years later Whitby Abbey was founded by Abbess Hilda, who presided over male and female devotees on this exposed cliff-top site.

Although the monasteries of Whitby and Lastingham were sacked by the Vikings, the seeds of Christianity proved to have been sown in fertile ground. By the end of the 10th century the Danish and Norwegian settlers had mostly been converted to the faith. St Gregory's Minster at Kirkdale is a fascinating pre-Norman church.

It was only after the Norman invasion, however, that the great monastic houses on the moors were founded. Benedictine monks returned to the site of St Hilda's monastery in Whitby and established another five communities in the area. The Cistercian Order was created by French monks. Finding the Benedictine regime too ready to succumb to earthly temptations, they vowed to emphasise once again the virtues of hard work and austerity. In 1131 a band of monks from France crossed the Channel and were endowed with land in Ryedale on which to build a monastery. The monks gave a French twist to the valley's name and called their community Rievaulx.

From small beginnings the Cistercian community prospered. By the time of the third abbot, St Aelred, the number of ordained monks – about 150 – was swelled by more than 600 lay brethren. Outlying farms, known as 'granges', were set up – often at some distance

CHRISTIAN CROSSES & MONKS – COXWOLD

from the mother church. Contemplation and prayer played a great part in the monks' lives, but they worked hard too.

The monks of Rievaulx developed the mining of ironstone that, many centuries on, would help to create the industrial wealth around the Tees and the Tyne. The upland moors provided grazing for huge flocks of sheep. The land (a gift from a local landowner) may have been poor for agriculture, but the monks successfully exploited it as grazing land. Wool from Rievaulx became renowned throughout Europe for its excellence.

The monks cleared forests to provide fuel for the iron furnaces. They drained land, built roads and spanned the River Rye and other rivers with sturdy bridges. They even built a system of canals to facilitate the transport of iron and stone. All this activity was in addition to the huge task, undertaken over a period of 60 years, of building Rievaulx Abbey; the impressive remains of the high church and monastic buildings still lift the spirits of visitors today.

The Carthusian Order was another to have had its origins in France. Mount Grace Priory, near Osmotherley, was founded in 1398; the ruins are believed to be the finest example of Carthusian building in the country.

Franciscan friars, who followed the strict teachings of St Francis, came to Scarborough. Their doctrine of absolute poverty provided a stark contrast to the business-like ethos and prosperity of the Carthusians. The Augustinian Canons built the splendid Gisborough Priory; visitors to the site can see the great arch of the east window that still stands.

Between 1536 and 1540, after his break with Rome, Henry VIII ordered the closure of the abbeys and monasteries, bringing to an end their huge and wide-ranging influence.

CLEVELAND WAY

When it was inaugurated in 1969 the Cleveland Way was only the second national trail in the country – coming just four years after Tom Stephenson's pioneering work in creating the Pennine Way. The name of the walk derives from the Cleveland Hills and is a little ambiguous, since for most of its 110-mile (176km) length it lies inside the North York Moors National Park.

The walk, a roughly horseshoe-shaped route, breaks into two distinct sections. From the starting point at Helmsley, the route meanders through the moorland scenery of the Hambleton and Cleveland Hills. Walkers reach the highest point within the National Park when they traverse Urra Moor. Once the North Sea is sighted, at Saltburn, walkers follow the coastal path down to the finishing point at Filey Brigg. The walk can be divided up into sections that offer a single day's hike, with each section ending at a point where budget accommodation is available.

COXWOLD MAP REF SE5377

Coxwold, about 3 miles (5km) south of Kilburn, has a 15th-century village church, with a distinctive eight-sided tower, overlooking the handsome houses lining the broad main street, which include almshouses dating back to the reign of Charles II.

Fifteenth-century Shandy Hall, lies opposite to the church, and was once the home of Laurence Sterne (1713–68). As a writer Sterne was a relatively late developer, not picking up his quill until the ripe age of 46. The publication of his picaresque novel, *The Life and Opinions of Tristram Shandy, Gentleman*, coincided with his becoming the vicar of Coxwold. Literary success was immediate, and Sterne was able to indulge his taste for high living. He contracted pleurisy and died in 1768. His skull is buried in Coxwold churchyard. Dilapidated Shandy Hall was renovated in the 1960s and filled with manuscripts and first editions and opened to the public.

To the south of Coxwold is Newburgh Priory, which was designed and built as an Augustinian house in 1145. After the Dissolution of Monasteries, Henry VIII rewarded his chaplain, Anthony Bellasis, by giving him the building. He, and the owners who followed him, transformed the priory into a fine country house.

The beautiful setting of Byland Abbey (English Heritage) wasn't the first site chosen by the band of Cistercian monks who came here from France. They had settled briefly near Old Byland, but it was reckoned to be unsuitable because the monks were confused by hearing the bells of nearby Rievaulx Abbey. Finally, in 1177, work began on Byland Abbey. Not as complete now as either Rievaulx or Fountains Abbeys, its church was nevertheless larger than either. The dramatic west façade, with its 26-foot (8m) diameter window, still stands to its full height, and gives an impression of just how huge the nave used to be.

HAWNBY MAP REF SE5489

The remote village of Hawnby is best approached from the south. A long view opens up, with the red-roofed houses of the village appearing to cling to a ledge on the flank of Hawnby Hill. This sunny situation encourages residents to create colourful terraced gardens. To the right are the equally rounded contours of Easterside Hill. The environs of Hawnby comprise one of the loveliest landscapes in the National Park and it is well worth leaving the car and exploring on foot.

Winding roads and tracks offer superb views at every turn. This gently undulating moorland landscape left an impression on John Wesley, the founder of Methodist Church, who came here to preach in 1757: 'I rode through one of the pleasantest parts of England to Hawnby'. Wesley's inspirational sermons in Hawnby gained it a reputation as a stronghold of Methodism.

He had come from Osmotherley, across the expanse of Snilesworth Moor, so it would have been a relief to arrive in the sheltered, wooded valley of the River Rye. The road between Hawnby and Osmotherley has a rather better surface than in Wesley's day, but it still twists and turns through beautiful countryside.

The little Church of All Saints, in a riverside setting near the bridge, has features which date to the 12th century. Beyond the church is Arden Hall (not open), almost hidden in the woods. It was built on the site of a 12th-century Benedictine nunnery, the hall is the seat of the Earls of Mexborough. Mary, Queen of Scots, stayed here on her long road to the executioner's axe.

THE WHITE HORSE, KILBURN

WESTERN MOORS

A Loop from Swainby to Whorlton

From the once-industrial village of Swainby, this walks takes in fine views from the northern edge of the North York Moors plateau. The route then passes through Whorlton village, deserted since it was devastated by the plague in the 14th century.

Route Directions

1 With the church on your left, walk down Swainby's village street to the right of the stream. Continue walking past a sign 'Unsuitable for Buses and Coaches' and go straight ahead uphill. As the road bends to the right, follow the bridleway sign to Scugdale, up the track that lies ahead.

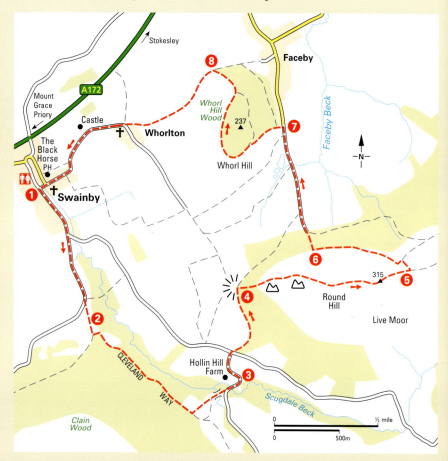

WALK 2

2 Go through a gate and turn left to join the waymarks for the Cleveland Way National Trail. Walk through the woodland, turning left, just after a seat, down to a gate. The footpath goes half right, towards blue-topped posts and downhill to another gate. Cross the stream on the footbridge to reach a lane, with another footbridge, over Scugdale Beck. Turn left.

3 Follow the lane past Hollin Hill Farm to a T-junction with telephone and post boxes. Cross the lane and go through a Cleveland Way signed gate. Walk up the path beside woodland to a gate (there's a view of the valley from this ridge).

4 The path beyond bends right to a stile and goes on to a paved track in the wood. Go straight ahead at a crossing track to another gate, and continue to follow the paved path up to the heather moorland, passing a cairn. After the first summit, the path descends beyond a large and a small cairn into a dip. Just before the paved path ends, look out for a narrow path off to the left, down through the heather.

5 After about 100yds (91m) you will reach a concrete post. Bear left and follow the narrow path down the gully to a fence beside a wood. Turn left to a signpost. Go straight on, eventually going over a spoil heap to reach a gate on your right.

6 Through the gate, go straight down the hill through woodland. At the bottom, bear right, then left to cross a stile by a gate and go down the lane. Just after the first house on the left, take a footpath over two stiles.

7 Walk up through the woodland on to a grassy track. Turn left, and left again at another track. At a T-junction, turn left again and follow the track downhill to a stile. Turn left to go over another stile. Go straight ahead along the signed track.

8 Go over a stile beside a gate and follow the track along the hillside. Over a stile with steps beyond, turn left at the bottom and follow the field-edge. Go through a gateway beside a paddock to another gateway on to a metalled lane. Follow the lane past Whorlton church and castle back to Swainby village.

Route facts

DISTANCE/TIME
6 miles (9.7km) 3h

MAP OS Explorer OL26 North York Moors – Western

START Roadside parking in Swainby village, grid ref: NZ 477020

TRACKS Tracks and moorland paths, lots of bracken, 6 stiles

GETTING TO THE START
Swainby lies just off the busy A172 Teesside road 5 miles (8km) beyond the junction with the A19 and 12 miles (19.3km) due south of Middlesbrough. Turn south down the village street alongside the stream and park by the church. The Blacksmith's Arms lies on the corner at the north end of this street.

THE PUB The Black Horse, Swainby. Tel: 01642 700436; www.blackhorseswainby.co.uk

❶ Route finding could be difficult when the mists come down over the moors – it's best to save this route for settled weather.

WESTERN MOORS

HELMSLEY MAP REF SE6183

The handsome market town of Helmsley is where the National Park Authority has its administrative headquarters. Here too is a well-stocked Tourist Information Centre, in the castle, where visitors can browse for books, brochures and maps.

It may be only the size of a large village, but Helmsley has the purposeful, bustling, reassuring air of a county town. It is especially busy on Friday, which is market day. The old market cross on its stepped base is still in place, though the square is dominated by a more elaborate monument, designed by Sir Gilbert Scott to commemorate the second Lord Feversham.

A number of roads converge here; at one time this was an important halt on stagecoach routes. A regular service ran to London from the Black Swan Inn, which still has a large wooden swan in place of an inn sign.

These days more adventurous souls arrive with walking boots, cagoule and rucksack, for Helmsley is the starting point of the Cleveland Way, a 110-mile (176km) national trail that takes off across the moors before following the coastal path down to Filey. Cleveland wayfarers should follow the 'acorn' signs up Castlegate, to get an excellent view of the castle standing 'head and shoulders' above the little town, before descending into Rye Dale and the atmospheric ruins of Rievaulx Abbey.

As is the case with many other North Yorkshire towns, behind Helmsley's prosperity is a castle and a prominent family. Of Walter l'Espec's first castle no traces now remain; the fortification we see today dates back to the 12th century. Robert de Roos was rewarded for his part in the Norman invasion by being given the manor of Helmsley. The de Roos family owned the castle until it was sold to Sir Charles Duncombe. Now it is in the care of English Heritage.

The castle was built for defence rather than show, yet it didn't witness any military action until the Civil War. It was here that the troops of Colonel Jordan Crossland, a loyal supporter of Charles I, were besieged by the Parliamentarian army of Sir Thomas Fairfax, which numbered a thousand troops. The siege, against what was regarded as one of the country's most impregnable fortresses, lasted three months. It might have lasted longer, but Royalist reinforcements were intercepted, and provisions confiscated. Crossland, forced to surrender, marched out of the castle on 22 November 1644, 'with colours flying and drums beating'.

While the Parliamentarian forces accepted this amicable surrender, they dismantled enough of the castle to ensure that it could never again be used

Insight

DAYS GONE BY

Helmsley was a major stopping point on stagecoach routes in days gone by and it is easy to imagine weary passengers emerging gratefully from badly sprung coaches to avail themselves of victuals and refreshment at one of the many coaching inns that lined the Market Square. Some of these public houses are still giving hospitality to travellers – though today most of them arrive by car or motorcycle.

by any side in a conflict. But they failed in their attempts to blow up the Norman castle keep, and the eastern wall still stands to its full height of 97 feet (30m), giving an idea of what an impressive fortification it had been.

The years have looked more kindly to Duncombe Park, just 1 mile (1.6km) southwest of Helmsley off the A170. Pride of place in these 600 tranquil acres (242ha) goes to the fine 200-room mansion designed by William Wakefield in 1713 as a fine family home for the Duncombe family and their descendants, the Fevershams. For 60 years the building was used as a girls' school, but in 1985 the present Lord and Lady Feversham took on the mammoth task of restoring the house and making it a family home once again. Now there is public access to both the house and the landscaped parkland, which boasts a delightful terrace walk, with Ionic and Tuscan temples to lend an air of romance. The temples and terrace were to have been linked by a coach drive, never completed, to the complementary Rievaulx Temple Terrace, also built by the Duncombe family.

KILBURN MAP REF SE5179

The village of Kilburn has two claims to fame, both of an artistic nature – the White Horse of Kilburn and woodcarver Robert Thompson.

The White Horse, a figure cut into the turf that gazes down from Roulston Scar, and a landmark for miles around, was created by teacher John Hodgson and his pupils in 1857. It is maintained by the Kilburn White Horse Association.

■ Insight
A FASTIDIOUS VICAR
Charles Norris Gray was vicar of Helmsley from 1872 to 1913, and had a reputation as a doughty fighter for his chosen causes, which included the state of the drains, the dangers of wearing tight corsets and the lack of cleanliness among the lower orders. Who knows the state to which Helmsley might have degenerated without such a strong hand on the tiller? The vicarage was one of the many buildings whose restoration Gray supervised; today the building is the administrative centre of the National Park.

Visitors to Kilburn should not miss the workshops and showrooms of Robert Thompson, a woodcarver and cabinet-maker whose fame has travelled far and wide. Thompson was a self-taught craftsman whose skill remained largely unappreciated until he was commissioned to make some furniture for the local church. Encouraged by the results, Thompson began to specialise in ecclesiastical furniture. You will find that many Yorkshire churches have pews, pulpits and other fixtures made by him. One of the many pleasures of visiting them is to search for examples of the craftsman's trademark: a little carved mouse that stands proud from its surroundings. Many examples can be found in Kilburn's church, where a chapel was dedicated to the 'Mouseman' shortly before his death in 1958.

You can find Thompson's handiwork further afield – including York Minster and Westminster Abbey. Even without the mouse motif, you can recognise it by the

WESTERN MOORS

Insight

THE 'MOUSEMAN'
Robert Thompson's signature, a carved mouse, can be found on all his pieces of furniture. But why a mouse? Thompson revealed in a letter that the idea came to him while working on a church screen. In conversation with another woodcarver he had mentioned that he was as poor as a church mouse. It seemed such an appropriate symbol that Thompson immediately adopted it for all his work.

Insight

THE INVITING MOORS
About 40 per cent of the National Park is heather moorland, comprising the largest expanse in England. To see the moors at their colourful best, a sea of purple, make your visit in the late summer months when the heather is in bloom. The hardy, black-faced Swaledale sheep are at home on the tops, and are brought down in to the valleys only at lambing times. Take care as you drive along the moorland ridge and roads, as the sheep have only the most rudimentary road sense and will dash into your path without warning.

heavy designs, the dark tones of the oak wood and the rippled effect left by the adze (a heavy hand tool with an arched cutting blade set at a right-angle to the handle). This furniture made to last not just a lifetime, but many lifetimes.

As the business quickly expanded, Thompson's own half-timbered house became a showroom. Behind the building are more recent workshops, in which a new generation of woodworkers follows in his footsteps. Those who can't afford one of the substantial pieces of furniture can find smaller wooden items for sale, all featuring Thompson's famous mouse. You can see stacks of neatly piled oak planks outside the workshop, being seasoned before they are used. The outbuildings house an interesting small museum and exhibition centre.

A stream meanders through Kilburn, supplying part of its name: unusual, because here a stream is known as a beck rather than a burn. The 'burn' suffix is a clue that the origins of the village are Anglo-Saxon not Viking.

OSMOTHERLEY MAP REF SE4596

This handsome village, on the junction of roads old and new, is the starting point of a 42-mile (67km) route march across the moors to Ravenscar, known as the Lyke Wake Walk. Every weekend walkers decant from their cars, don boots and cagoules, and head for the high ground. The less energetic can stroll around the village; those who manage to work up an appetite will find excellent food on offer in the pubs that surround the old market place.

Northwest of Osmotherley is Mount Grace Priory (now in the care of the National Trust), though motorists need to make a rather inconvenient loop on the A19 dual carriageway to reach it. No matter – this is the best preserved of the nine Carthusian priories that were built in England. Typically, in most European monasteries the monks lived and worked together. The Carthusian Order was particularly strict, however; the monks not only shunned the outside world, they even avoided contact with each other.

KILBURN – OSMOTHERLEY

Each monk (there were 24, including the prior) had a two-storey cell and walled garden to the back of it. Serving hatches adjacent to each cell door were ingeniously angled so that meals could be passed anonymously to the monks inside. The cells are grouped around the Great Cloister. While many of them rise no higher today than their foundations, one cell was reconstructed and furnished at the turn of the last century to show visitors how the monks would have lived their solitary lives.

The Carthusian Order was founded in 1048 by St Bruno of Reims, who took Christ's sojourn in the desert as the highest example for his monks to follow. They lived like hermits to avoid worldly distractions, with most of their day given over to prayer, study and contemplation. This harsh regime included a service in the middle of the night. Despite these privations, the Carthusian Order grew rapidly. As late as 1530 there was a waiting list for men who wished to join the Mount Grace community.

Mount Grace Priory was founded in 1398 by Thomas de Holland, with the agreement of Richard II. The monks were given land, which they rented out to tenant farmers. At the height of their wealth the income generated by the monks of Mount Grace was even greater than that of their Cistercian neighbours at Rievaulx Abbey. Yet the very success of the Carthusian communities contributed to their downfall. Henry VIII ordered them to be disbanded, and in 1539 the keys to Mount Grace Priory were handed to his representatives by John Wilson, the last prior.

Visitors now enter the priory through a manor house, built in 1654 on the site of an earlier gatehouse. It houses good exhibitions about the priory and the lives of its monks. The best preserved part of the priory is the old church, whose tower still stands to its original height. Compared with other monasteries, the church is small and simple.

■ Activity

A CHALLENGING WALK

The Lyke Wake Walk takes its inspiration from the old 'corpse roads', that crossed the moors, along which the deceased were carried to – often distant – burial grounds. Lyke refers to a corpse, as in a church lychgate; wake is the party after a funeral. This fine high-level walk, that lies between Osmotherley and Ravenscar, was begun in 1955 as a challenge walk – the challenge being to complete the 42 miles (67km) within 24 hours. However, the route has suffered erosion due to the pounding of too many walking boots.

■ Insight

THE HAMBLETON DROVE ROAD

The Hambleton Drove Road is a reminder of the days when drovers brought their cattle down from Scotland to sell at the English markets of York, Malton and beyond. This ancient ridgeway, as ruler-straight as a Roman road for much of its length, kept slow-moving cattle away from local herds and its wide verges offered free grazing. Just as importantly, the drovers were able to avoid the tolls charged for using the turnpike roads. Many sections of the Hambleton Drove Road have been incorporated into our modern road system. The Cleveland Way uses a section of the drove road, and is easily accessed from Osmotherley.

WESTERN MOORS

Byland Abbey and Olstead Observatory

Walk from the romantic ruins of Byland Abbey through lovely woodland to an old observatory at the highest point of the walk. The lumps and bumps of the final field you cross are the remains of the monks' ponds, some used for breeding fish.

Route Directions

1 Visit the abbey, then leave beside the ticket office and turn right along the abbey's north side. Opposite a public footpath sign, go left through a gateway and after 10yds (9m) right, over a stile. Cross the field to a second stile, then bear half left uphill to a waymarked gate behind a bench. Go through two more gates and on to a metalled lane.

2 Turn left. At the top of the lane go through a gate signed 'Cam Farm, Observatory'. The path climbs then leaves the wood edge to rise to a terrace. After a stile, take the left-hand path, following Cam

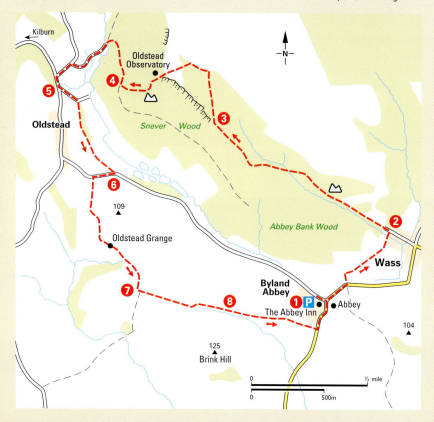

WALK 3

Farm. Go straight on at two junctions, uphill, to reach a large open space.

3 Turn right and, just before a waymarked metal gate, turn left along the wood edge. Follow the path to Oldstead Observatory, bearing left through the wood. Pass to the left of the Observatory, go down a slope and follow the path running steeply downhill to reach a signpost.

4 Turn right on the track, signed 'Oldstead'. Follow the track as it curves left to become a metalled lane. Turn left at the T-junction, and left again on to the road by a seat. Just before the road narrows sign, turn left.

5 Go through some gateposts and over a cattle grid. Then, as the avenue of trees ends, take a signposted footpath to the right, uphill. Climb up to a stile, bending around to the left beside the woodland to a gate. After the next gate, go straight ahead, through two more gates and on to a metalled road.

6 Turn right then, just beyond the road sign which indicates a bend, take a track to the left by the Oldstead Grange sign. Pass the house and go between barns and through a gateway. Bear right downhill on the track, bending right on a track to a gateway with a waymarked tree.

7 Immediately after the gateway, turn left and go through the wood to a Byland Abbey signpost. Follow the path ahead as it bends left by another sign, go over a stile and down the field with the hedge on your left, bending left then right at the end to another signpost. Go through an opening beside a metal gate and along the field with a hedge on your right.

8 Go over two stiles then bear slightly left to another stile. Go across the field to a signpost in the hedge by a metal gate. Follow the fence, then go on to the road by a wooden stile. Turn left back to the car park opposite the abbey.

Route facts

DISTANCE/TIME
5 miles (8km) 2h30

MAP OS Explorer OL26 North York Moors – Western

START Car park behind Abbey Inn in Byland Abbey for abbey visitors, grid ref: SE 548789

TRACKS Woodland tracks, field paths, 8 stiles

GETTING TO THE START Byland Abbey is located 2 miles (3.2km) south of the A170 road halfway between Thirsk and Helmsley. It is best reached by turning south off the A170 3 miles (4.8km) east of Sutton Bank. In the village turn right by the inn to access the signed car park.

THE PUB The Abbey Inn, Byland Abbey.
Tel: 01347 868678;
www.bylandabbeyinn.com

❶ In summer some paths may be choked with nettles and giant hogweed, so this walk may be unsuitable for small children.

WESTERN MOORS

Discover the Western Moors

A car tour from Helmsley through the western moors and dales, around the superb Cleveland and Hambleton Hills and taking in Rievaulx Abbey, Byland Abbey, Coxwold and Helmsley along the way. The best walking is around Chop Gate in Bilsdale, and Sutton Bank. A section of the tour is on narrow roads; please drive with care.

Route Directions

1 Begin the tour in Helmsley along the B1257, taking a left turning from the top of the square and a right turning by the church, signposted 'Stokesley'. After 1.5 miles (2.4km), turn left down an unclassified road, signed 'Old Byland'. Immediately before a little bridge, turn right over the River Rye, to see the impressive ruins of Rievaulx Abbey ahead, in a delightful setting. Drive past the abbey, through Rievaulx village and sharply uphill to rejoin the B1257. Turn left, signed 'Stokesley'.

As you pass a conifer forest on your right, beautiful views open up of Bilsdale ahead. After the scattered houses of Chop Gate climb Hasty Bank with its viewpoint; look out on the right for the distinctive profile of Roseberry Topping.

2 At a mini-roundabout in Great Broughton turn left, signed 'Kirkby' and 'Carlton', with the escarpment of the Cleveland Hills rearing up on your left. Go through Kirby and Rusby, right at the T-junction, then left, on to the main A172 in the direction of Thirsk. After 2.5 miles (4km) turn left, signed 'Swainby'. Turn right over the bridge in the middle of Swainby, a pleasant village sitting astride a beck, and immediately left. Climb gradually uphill on to Scarth Wood Moor. Pass Cod Beck Reservoir and continue on into Osmotherley. Bear right, in the centre of the village, by the market cross, 'Northallerton and Thirsk'. Next to the stepped market cross is a curious stone table; market wares were probably displayed here. John Wesley certainly put it to good use as an open-air pulpit on the many occasions he preached in the town.

3 Turn right at the T-junction and on to the A19, signposted 'Thirsk,' to join the dual carriageway southbound. Leave at the second turning on the left, signed 'Over Silton'. For the next few miles you are on very narrow roads, so drive with care. Drive through Over Silton. At a T-junction a mile (1.6km) beyond, go left, signed 'Kepwick and Cowesby'. Drive uphill to a T-junction adjacent to the gatehouse of Kepwick Hall; go right here, through the pleasant little village of Kepwick. Take the next turning on the left, signed 'Cowesby'. Drive through Cowesby (there is a sharp right bend in the village centre) to Kirby Knowle. Pass the parish church and turn left towards Felixkirk. Take the next two left turns, both signed 'Boltby'.

Descend into Boltby, a happy arrangement of cottages in the honey-coloured stone so typical of this area.

4 Climb steeply out of the village and continue steeply again through Boltby Forest; at the top, turn right, signed 'Old Byland and Cold Kirby'. Follow this ruler-straight section of the route, part of the old Hambleton Drove Road – as you turn right you can see the old, unmetalled track continuing to the left. At the end of the road turn right

CAR TOUR 2 60 miles (96.5km)

at a T-junction, signed 'Thirsk and Sutton Bank'. Pass the car park at the top of Sutton Bank.
If you need to take a break and stretch your legs, this is the ideal spot – a waymarked path along the top of the bank offers easy walking and breathtaking views across the Vale of York and beyond.

5 Go left at a T-junction by the car park, on to the A170, signed 'Scarborough'. Take the first turning on the right, signed 'Yorkshire Flying Club, White Horse'. Drive downhill through woodland to the White Horse car park.
A short walk from here allows a closer investigation of the white horse, carved into the steep hillside in 1857 – though this landmark that looks better from a distance.

6 Continue on down to a T-junction; turn right to drive into the village of Kilburn.
Look out for a half-timbered building: this is the furniture-making workshops and showroom founded by craftsman Robert Thompson.

7 Drive through the village; after 2 miles (3.2km) go left at a T-junction to arrive in the main street of Coxwold. Turn left at the crossroads at the bottom of the village, signed

'Byland Abbey Ampleforth and Helmsley'.
Laurence Sterne (author of *Tristram Shandy*) was once the vicar of Coxwold. Opposite the church is his home Shandy Hall, which is now a museum devoted to his life and work.

8 Pass the evocative ruins of Byland Abbey, drive through Wass and on to Ampleforth then pass Ampleforth Abbey with its famous Catholic public school. Oswaldkirk is next; once at the end of the village bear left, going steeply uphill, signed 'Helmsley'. At the top of the hill turn left, along the B1257 and right at the Trafalgar Arch at Sproxton, and you will soon return to Helmsley and the start of the tour.

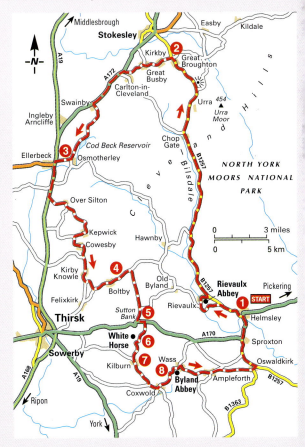

WESTERN MOORS

OSWALDKIRK MAP REF SE6278

The village of Oswaldkirk is strung out along the road beneath the steep and well-wooded Oswaldkirk Bank, and looks out across the Ampleforth Valley. The community takes its name from St Oswald's parish church. St Oswald became King of Northumbria at the age of 30 in AD 634, and has a special place in the history of the Christian Church. What we know about St Oswald comes largely from the *Ecclesiastical History of the English People* written by the Venerable Bede in AD 731.

Oswald was deeply impressed by the monastic community on Iona, founded by St Columba. Once a Christian convert, he grafted the new faith on to familiar customs – for example, building Christian churches on sites of pagan worship. It was Oswald who gave the island of Lindisfarne to St Aidan and the monks of Iona as another sanctuary from which to spread Christianity.

One Easter, while Oswald and Aidan were about to share a meal, Oswald learned that there was not enough food to feed the poor at the gate. The king gave them his own food, still on its silver platter. Aidan was so moved by this act that he took the king's right hand and said 'May this hand never perish'.

Unfortunately, Oswald's faith could not save him from defeat in battle. He died in AD 642 while fighting the heathen King Penda of Mercia. Victorious Penda had Oswald's body dismembered and the pieces stuck on stakes. But, as prophesied, Oswald's right hand did not wither, and it was taken to Lindisfarne by Oswald's brother, Oswy, as a venerated relic. Thus began a cult, with Oswald being elevated to sainthood, and many tales of miraculous cures being associated with Oswald's bones.

The nave of St Oswald's church is largely Norman; cross fragments confirm that Oswaldkirk was already settled in Anglo-Saxon times. A couple of 'mother and child' sculptures in the porch offer an evocative contrast – one is modern, the other is Anglo-Saxon. Unusually, most of the rectors of Oswaldkirk are known by name; this practice started at the beginning of the 14th century and continues today.

RIEVAULX ABBEY
MAP REF SE5785

A short drive (or pleasant stroll) from Helmsley is one of Yorkshire's finest treasures. Today the setting of Rievaulx Abbey (English Heritage) is sheltered and inviting, but when Walter l' Espec dispatched a group of French monks to find a suitable site on which to build a new community it was reported to be fit only for 'wild beasts and robbers'. At that time there were no roads in the area; instead of neat copses and lush meadows there were only impenetrable thickets. To the devoutly ascetic Cistercian monks this part of the Rye Valley represented the sort of challenge on which they thrived.

In 1131, the monks began to build the mother church of the Cistercian Order in England. Many people today consider Rievaulx to be the pre-eminent Cistercian abbey in the country. The nave is Norman, while the rest of the abbey was built in the Early English style.

WESTERN MOORS

■ Insight

THE VILLAGE
The delightful little village of Rievaulx, with its thatched cottages of honey-coloured stone, grew up only after the Reformation. It is rather ironic that many of the houses were built from stone salvaged from the ruins of the abbey.

Enough remains of all the buildings to give visitors a very clear impression of what monastic life was like all those centuries ago.

The monks may have started out with a strictly ascetic attitude towards wealth and lifestyle; indeed the establishment of the Cistercian Order was partly due to what they considered to be the wicked corruption of the Benedictines orders. But the 140 monks and nearly 600 lay brothers of Rievaulx Abbey succeeded in creating wealth and influence.

The monks farmed sheep, cultivated vegetables, ground corn and smelted iron, a process that required the felling of perhaps 40 trees to make a hundred-weight of metal. They even built canals to enable the iron to be transported. Stone for the buildings was brought to the site from local quarries by the same method. By 1538, when Henry VIII destroyed their way of life for ever with the Dissolution of the Monasteries, the monks had become very wealthy indeed.

Cut into the hillside above the abbey is Rievaulx Terrace (National Trust), a curved grassy promenade that is more than a match for the landscaped terrace at nearby Duncombe Park. The terrace at Rievaulx was designed in 1758. It offers strollers tantalising glimpses of the abbey between the groups of trees, with fantastic views of the Rye Valley and Hambleton Hills. There are temples, one in the Ionic style, with a fine sumptuous interior, the other Tuscan, to mark both ends of the terrace.

STOKESLEY MAP REF NZ5208

Now bypassed by the A172, Stokesley maintains the unhurried character of a market town. The broad verges of West Green create a little space between the Georgian façades of the houses and the main street that winds through the town. Stokesley still has regular markets, held every Friday on the cobbled edges of the main street. There are also monthly farmers' markets and, each September, the market town is the site of one of the largest agricultural shows in the area.

The big open spaces include College Square and the market square. Behind them is Levenside, where the River Leven, little more than a stream at this point, follows its tranquil winding course between grassy banks and underneath a succession of little bridges. The oldest of these is the handsome arch of a fine old packhorse bridge; near by is a ford.

With the re-drawing of the county boundaries in 1974, Stokesley slipped into the county of Cleveland, though it has now been brought back into North Yorkshire. The National Park boundary makes a detour to exclude the town and neighbouring Great Ayton. While many of Stokesley's inhabitants commute to industrial Teesdale immediately to the north, Stokesley has, nevertheless, kept its own identity.

RIEVAULX ABBEY – SUTTON BANK

The Cleveland Hills form a backdrop to the south as you drive northeasterly direction along the A172 between Osmotherley and Stokesley. Once used by drovers, packhorse men, pedlars and monks visiting their outlying granges, the paths of the Cleveland Hills are now used by weekend walkers.

SUTTON BANK MAP REF SE5183

The view from the top of Sutton Bank is one of the finest in Yorkshire. Below you, spread out like a vast picnic blanket, is the flat plain of the Vale of York. It would be hard to imagine a sharper division between the rich, arable farmland that lies to the south and the heather moors of the Hambleton Hills immediately to the north. On a clear day, armed with a pair of binoculars, you can see York Minster and the Three Peaks of the Yorkshire Dales. Gormire Lake, directly below and almost hidden by trees, was once imagined to be bottomless.

The A170 marks the midway point between the market towns of Thirsk and Helmsley by making a long 1-in-4 climb to the top of Sutton Bank. You can watch cars and lorries labouring up what is one of the steepest stretches of road in the country. For those who want to stretch their legs and enjoy the view, or for those whose engines overheat, there is a car park (and information centre) conveniently sited at the top.

From here there is a splendid, and undemanding, walk along the edge of Sutton Bank. The Yorkshire Gliding Club operates from the top of the bank, and on summer weekends the sky will be filled with slim, silent planes exploiting the thermals rising up the scar. Powered planes tow the gliders over the edge – a moment that will moisten the palms of all but the most nonchalant of flyers. With the addition of microlight aircraft, hang-gliders and, of course, soaring birds, the skies beyond Sutton Bank can get very busy indeed.

The walk continues along the top of Roulston Scar, offering beautiful views all the way, to Kilburn's White Horse – a landmark which looks best from a distance. Thomas Taylor, a Kilburn man who made good in London, was so taken by the famous White Horse cut into the chalk downs near Uffington that he decided to create his own. He persuaded John Hodgson, a teacher from Kilburn School, to involve his pupils in the cutting of the figure. The main problem was that his chosen hillside, while suitably steep, was not chalk-based. Hodgson commandeered his pupils to help create the outline of a gigantic horse, and used gallons of whitewash to make the design stand out.

The White Horse of Kilburn is almost 325 feet (99m) from head to tail, and 227 feet (69m) high. Finished in 1857, it is now the only major landscape figure in the north of England. Whitewash fades in time, so these days chalk chippings are used. A White Horse Fund has been set up for the purpose of maintaining the horse, which is a very distinctive and much-loved landmark for miles around. There is another car park, directly beneath the White Horse, for those who don't want to walk too far. However you get to the horse, be careful not to damage the figure by walking on it.

WESTERN MOORS

The Hambleton Hills

Enjoy some of the north of England's best views and experience a bit of adventure with a ride along the edge of the escarpment. The long tarred lane that takes you north from Sutton Bank seems unremarkable, but there's a history dating back to the Iron Age tribes who settle here around 400 BC. They would have used the route long before the Romans followed in their footsteps.

Route Directions

1 Before you leave Sutton Bank Visitor Centre, take a look at the panoramas to the south and west. From here you can see for miles across the flat fields of the vales of Mowbray and York. Alf Wight, alias the fictional vet James Herriot, believed this view to be the finest in England. Apparently, both York Minster and Lincoln Cathedral are discernible on a clear day. From the visitor centre car park, turn left up the lane signed to Cold Kirby and Old Byland. Then take the left fork past Dialstone Farm and its tall communications mast, before heading north on an ever-so-straight lane through cornfields and pastures.

2 The lane comes to a T-junction by a triangular wood, called the Snack Yate Plantation. This is a popular

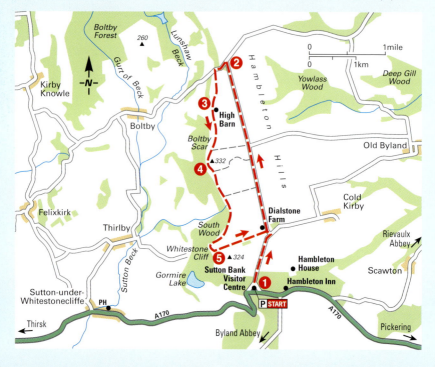

CYCLE RIDE 1

starting point for serious mountain bikers who will swoop down on rough tracks through Boltby Forest. Your route turns left down the lane. It's a gentle downhill ride for a short distance. Just before the road dives off the edge, turn left through a gate on to a grassy bridleway to cycle along the escarpment's edge. You are now riding on the Hambleton Hills. The first stretch is slightly uphill, but the track is firm and the views wide-sweeping. You'll see a small reservoir surrounded by forestry and the little village of Boltby huddled beneath a pastured hill.

3 The bridleway climbs to the top of the hill at High Barn, an old stone ruin shaded by a fine stand of sycamore. The going eases and the cliffs of an old quarry appear ahead. Here the bridleway goes through a gate on to a walled track for a short way. Ignore the bridleway on the left, which goes back to the Hambleton Road, and stay with the edge path to the hill above the rocks of Boltby Scar. This is the highest point of the ride. Note the wind-warped larch trees around here – they add to the views across the Vale of Mowbray.

4 The trees of the Boltby Forest now cover the west slopes, almost to the summit. Beyond the next offshoot bridleway, which you should ignore, the path becomes much narrower with a few embedded rocks in places. The difficulties are short-lived, but the younger and less experienced riders might prefer to dismount. The riding gets easier again as the bridleway arcs right above South Wood. At the end of this arc you turn left to a sign that tells you that the continuing edge path is for walkers only. This is a fine spot to linger and admire the views. To the south the half-moon-shaped Gormire Lake lies in a nest of broad-leaved woodland and beneath the sandy-coloured Whitestone Cliff.

5 When you've rested for a while, turn left on a bridleway to Dialstone Farm. This heads east across large prairie-like fields. Beyond a wood, the High Quarry Plantation, you will see the hurdles of the equestrian centre. Past the large farm, turn right along the tarred lane, then right again, back to the visitor centre car park.

Route facts

DISTANCE/TIME 7.4 miles (12km) 2h

MAP OS Explorer OL26 North York Moors – Western

START Sutton Bank Visitor Centre, grid ref: SE 516831

TRACKS Good level lanes followed by undulating bridleways on the edge of the escarpment

GETTING TO THE START Sutton Bank is situated 6 miles (9.7km) east of Thirsk. Take the A170 Scarborough turn-off from the A19 at Thirsk. This climbs the difficult road to Sutton Bank (caravans prohibited). The centre and car park are on the left at the top.

THE PUB The Hambleton Inn, Sutton Bank.
Tel: 01845 597202;
www.hambletoninn.co.uk

❶ A short section near Point 5 becomes narrower and with a few rocks in places. Inexperienced cyclists should dismount.

WESTERN MOORS

Out on the Tiles at Boltby and Thirlby Bank

The western boundary of the North York Moors National Park passes just outside Boltby. It is a delightful, small-scale place, with a tiny 19th-century chapel and stone-built houses, typical of the area. At the start of the walk you'll see a glittering mosaic of a kingfisher on a wall beside the Gurtof Beck. This is one of 23 that mark points on the Hambleton Hillside Mosaic Walk. Our route passes Tang Hall and Southwoods Hall before passing through Midge Holme Gate and into woodland. This is pheasant country, and you are likely to flush out one or two of these noisy birds during the walk. On the top of Boltby Scar, just as you begin the descent from the Cleveland Way you'll pass the scant remains of a Bronze Age hill-fort.

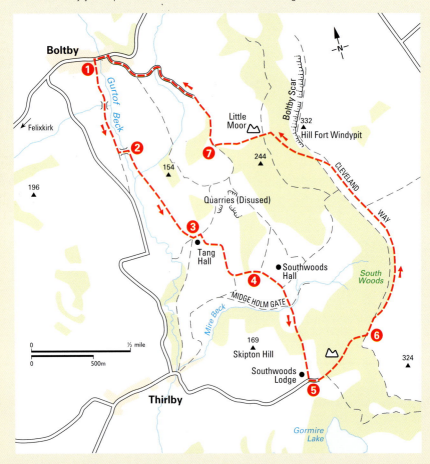

WALK 4

Route Directions

1 From the humpback bridge in the centre of Boltby village, follow the signed public footpath along the stream to a gate, and through three more gates to pass over a small footbridge to a stile. Continue following the stream; cross a gated footbridge, go over a stile and through a gate, then bear left over the stream and right to a gated stone footbridge.

2 Cross the bridge and continue over two stiles, then go straight on, beside the hedge, to go through two gates on to a metalled track at Tang Hall.

3 Turn left and, at the end of the farm buildings, turn right by a sign to Southwoods and through a gate to go diagonally left across the field; the route is marked by stones. At the end of the field, go through two gates then continue with a wire fence on your right. The path veers left and descends to a gate.

4 Continue along the track to a handgate. Go straight ahead on a track, confusingly named Midge Holm Gate. Follow the track to reach another gate beside a cottage, Southwoods Lodge, and go on to a metalled lane.

5 Turn left, following the track, signed 'Bridleway to Gormire'. At the signpost go straight ahead on the bridleway, up Thirlby Bank. This steep and often muddy track ascends the ridge; bear right at the fork part way up. Eventually you will reach a Cleveland Way sign on the ridge top.

6 Turn left and follow the Cleveland Way footpath for about a mile (1.6km) along the ridge, until you reach a bridleway sign to Boltby to the left. Descend to a gate then go straight ahead on the woodland ride, crossing a track to a gate. Continue ahead down the field, through a gate, and follow the track round to the right, along the edge of a wood.

7 At a signpost, turn right towards Boltby, to continue to a gate. Pass a tree stump with a mosaic of a toadstool and descend to a gate on to a lane. Follow the lane through another gate. Cross the stream by a footbridge and continue up the metalled lane. At the T-junction in the village, turn left back to the humpback bridge where the walk began.

Route facts

DISTANCE/TIME
5.25 miles (8.4km) 2h

MAP OS Explorer OL26 North York Moors – Western

START Boltby village. Roadside parking in the village, grid ref: SE 490866

TRACKS Mostly easy field and woodland paths; one steep, muddy climb; 4 stiles

GETTING TO THE START
At Thirsk head to the A19 heading south and then turn left onto the A170 Pickering and Scarborough road. After around 2.5 miles (4km) take the left turn signposted to Thirlby and Boltby. Boltby is about 3 miles (5km) after the turn off.

THE PUB The Carpenter's Arms, Felixkirk (located southwest of Boltby). Tel: 01845 537369; www.carpentersarmsfelixkirk.com

❶ Very steep and muddy climb up Thirlby Bank.

INFORMATION 85

■ TOURIST INFORMATION CENTRES
Helmsley
Helmsley Castle.
Tel: 01439 770173
Sutton Bank
Tel: 01845 597426

■ PLACES OF INTEREST
Byland Abbey
Coxwold.
Tel: 01347 868614;
www.english-heritage.org.uk
Duncombe Park
Helmsley. Tel: 01439 770213;
www.duncombepark.com
Helmsley Castle
Tel: 01439 770442;
www.english-heritage.org.uk
Helmsley Walled Garden
Tel: 01439 771427; www.helmsleywalledgarden.org.uk
Mount Grace Priory
Osmotherley.
Tel: 01609 883494;
www.english-heritage.org.uk
Newburgh Priory
Tel: 01347 868372;
www.newburghpriory.co.uk
Rievaulx Abbey
Rievaulx.
Tel: 01439 798228;
www.english-heritage.org.uk
Rievaulx Terrace
Rievaulx.
Tel: 01439 798340;
www.nationaltrust.org.uk
Shandy Hall
Coxwold.
Tel: 01347 868465

■ SHOPPING
MARKETS
Helmsley and Stokesley
Open-air market, Fri.
LOCAL SPECIALITIES
Furniture and Gifts
The Mouseman Visitor Centre, Kilburn.
Tel: 01347 869102;
www.robertthompsons.co.uk

■ OUTDOOR ACTIVITIES
BIKE HIRE
Oswaldkirk.
Golden Square Campsite,
Oswaldkirk.
Tel: 01439 788269
LONG-DISTANCE FOOTPATHS
The Cleveland Way
A 110-mile (176km) walk from Helmsley to Filey Brigg.
www.nationaltrail.co.uk
The Lyke Wake Walk
A 42-mile (67km) walk from Osmotherley to Ravenscar.
www.lykewake.org
HORSE-RIDING
Boltby
Boltby Trekking Centre, Johnstone Arms.
Tel: 01845 537392;
www.boltbytrekking.co.uk
Hawnby
Bilsdale Riding Centre, Shaken Bridge Farm.
Tel: 01439 798225;
www.horseholiday.co.uk

■ ANNUAL EVENTS & CUSTOMS
Bilsdale
Bilsdale Show, Chop Gate, Aug.
Coxwold
Coxwold Fair, Jun.
Helmsley
Ryedale Festival, Jul/Aug.
Kilburn
Kilburn Feast, early to mid-Jul.
Osmotherley
Summer Games, early Jul.
Osmotherley Show, early Aug.
Stokesley
Stokesley Show, Sep.

WESTERN MOORS

TEA ROOMS & PUBS

Tea Rooms

Lord Stone's Café
Carlton Bank Car Park,
Chop Gate TS9 7LQ.
Tel: 01642 778227
This one of Britain's very few underground cafés. Inside you'll find that the rock-hewn room behind the conventional café façade offers a warm welcome and some good food, from delicious home-made soups and corned-beef pie to cakes and pastries. You can also get draught beer, too – or try the spring water; it's cool, clear and free!

Coxwold Tearooms
School House,
Coxwold YO61 4AD.
Tel: 01347 868077; www.coxwoldtearooms.co.uk
You can eat in either of the two rooms, one very cosy and the other airy, or outside in the tea garden. Why not treat yourself to afternoon tea with home-baking, or sample the delights of Yorkshire ham-and-eggs.

The Castlegate Bakery and Café
12 Castlegate,
Helmsley YO6 5AB.
Tel: 01439 770304
Two of the specialities here are Yorkshire Curd Tarts and traditional Yorkshire Parkin, both made in the bakery alongside. The traditional café serves a generous cream tea with its home-made scones, or try the celebrated steak pie.

The Angel Café Tearoom
22 High Street, Stokesley
TS9 5QD. Tel: 01642 713622
A traditional town-centre tea room set on the handsome main street. There's a small area with sofas at the front of the premises, with tables behind. All the cakes and scones are home-made; locals make a bee-line for the coffee cake. The Angel also serves a range of full meals and snacks.

Pubs

The Black Swan Inn
Oldstead, Coxwold YO61 4BL.
Tel: 01347 868387; www.blackswanoldstead.co.uk
This is a proper country pub with a relaxed and welcoming atmosphere. As you'd expect there is real ale available in the Drovers Bar, with its flagged floor, comfy chairs and a bar made by Robert Thompson's craftsmen in nearby Kilburn. There's a pretty garden, and views of woodland and hills. The food is freshly prepared from local ingredients and includes a particularly impressive choice for vegetarian diners.

The Golden Lion
6 West End, Osmotherley
DL6 3AA. Tel: 01609 883526;
www.goldenlionosmotherley.co.uk
Furnished with wooden flooring and benches, this charming pub offers a wide range of ales. There is a superb menu, from excellent pub food through to top-notch cuisine. The home-made burgers are delicious, and there's a good selection of fish, as well as a tasty steak and kidney pie.

The Hare Inn
Scawton YO7 2HG.
Tel: 01845 597769;
www.thehareinn.co.uk
This is a great place to relax, with a drink in the charming low-beamed bar (real ales, including guest beers) or a meal in the adjoining dining area. Make sure you leave room for a pudding – the lemon posset is excellent.

The Wombwell Arms
Wass YO61 4BE.
Tel: 01347 868280
There are two bistro-style restaurants, serving a menu that includes steak and Guinness pie, as well as plenty of local produce and fish. The bars stock Yorkshire ales, including Black Sheep and Timothy Taylor's.

WESTERN MOORS

ROSEDALE

89

Central Moors

Cropton Forest	94
Farndale	95
Hovingham	96
Hutton-le-Hole	96
Kirkbymoorside	98
Lastingham	99
■ WALK 5 Lastingham	100
Nunnington	102
Rosedale	102
Standing Stones	105
Wheeldale	107
■ WALK 6 Rosedale	108

INTRODUCTION

The central moors include high moorland, beautiful valleys and delectable villages. The North Yorkshire Moors Railway runs through the wooded Newtondale Gorge on the edge of Cropton Forest, which offers a host of leisure possibilities, from energetic cycling and riding through to easy strolls and quiet picnics. To the north of the forest is Wade's Causeway on Wheeldale, a well-preserved section of road thought to be of Roman origin.

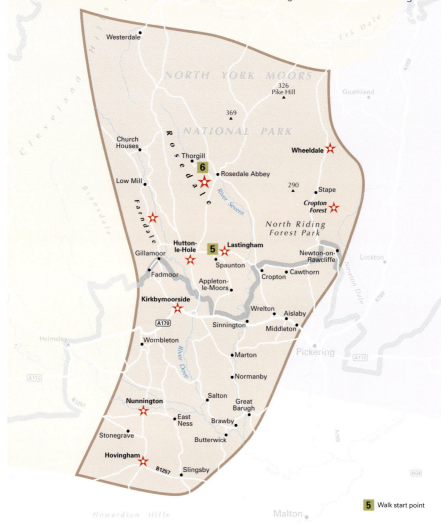

CENTRAL MOORS 91

CHURCH HOUSES, FARNDALE

HOT SPOTS

Unmissable attractions

Discover the remains of the Roman road on Wheeldale Moor...visit Nunnington Hall to see the miniature rooms...walk across the moors to Lilla Cross, the oldest on the moors...climb the one-in-two hill called Rosedale Chimney out of Rosedale Abbey...sit quietly in the crypt at Lastingham church for an experience of early history...hire a bike and follow the track of the former Rosedale Railway...have lunch at the Spa Tea rooms of Hovingham Bakery...visit Farndale in spring for the superb display of wild daffodils...take the road across the moors from Rosedale Abbey to Egton Bridge when the heather is blooming...have dinner in the garden at the famed Star Inn at Harome...travel through Newtondale Gorge on the North Yorkshire Moors Railway.

1. Nunnington Hall
The lovely old manor house of Nunnington Hall dates mainly from the 17th century. It is set in beautiful gardens on the banks of the River Rye.

2. Chimney Bank
Wonderful scenery unfolds from the top of snow-capped Chimney Bank, between the villages of Rosedale Abbey and Hutton-le-Hole.

3. Cyclists at snow-covered Rosedale
Cycling the quiet back roads over the central moors is a popular way to explore the National Park, whatever the season.

4. Ryedale Folk Museum
An amazing collection of rural buildings rescued from all around the North York Moors has been reconstructed in a hamlet setting behind the modest entrance to this museum of local life.

5. Rosedale Abbey Sundial
As the name of the village suggests, Rosedale Abbey was once the site of a small Cistercian priory founded in 1158. Little remains of the original building (the stone was reclaimed for building houses in the village and the new church) except a turret staircase and a sundial.

CROPTON FOREST

The moors are continually evolving, and one of the most dramatic changes of the 20th century was the creation of large-scale conifer plantations. The Forestry Commission began the process in the 1920s; now the area comprises one of the most extensive man-made forests in the country. Cropton Forest occupies a large area of the North Riding Forest Park between Rosedale in the west and Newtondale to the east.

■ Activity

BACK TO NATURE
The recreational possibilities of Cropton Forest are now being realised. On any summer weekend you will see mountain bikers tackling the forest trails, walkers following well-waymarked footpaths and families enjoying themselves at the many picnic sites and adventure playgrounds. Those who prefer their nature 'red in tooth and claw' will head for the solitude of the breezy moor-tops. The Newtondale Horse Trail, offers 37.5 miles (60km) of bracing, traffic-free riding. Local riding stables hire out horses by the hour or day.

■ Insight

MAULEY CROSS
Moorland crosses are generally reliable indicators that an old thoroughfare, or crossroads, is near at hand. Mauley Cross stands on the route of one of the oldest known roads across the moors to have survived, which may date from Roman times. The cross stands where the track meets the medieval Brown Howe Road. It is named after the de Mauley family of Mulgrave Castle near Whitby and probably marked the limits of grazing rights. The cross once stood on open moorland.

Conifer planting on this scale has not met with universal approval; many feel that well-loved views have been unfairly smothered beneath the starkly dark geometric shapes of these plantations. Nevertheless, the afforestation of what had mostly been moorland and poor-quality farmland brought much-needed employment to many rural areas.

The woodlands are now reaching maturity, and upwards of 120,000 tonnes of timber are felled every year to meet consumer demand for softwoods. More recently, greater care has been taken to ensure that plantings harmonise with their surroundings. Areas of broadleaved and mixed woods provide a more varied habitat for wildlife, and are easier on the eye than vast conifer plantations.

Cropton Forest provides plenty of outdoor activities – there is a campsite, forest cabins and educational outdoor activity centres set out amid the trees, and plenty of opportunities for walking and biking. The North Yorkshire Moors Railway, from Pickering to Grosmont, passes through the eastern edge of the forest, and stations at Levisham and Newtondale provide easy access for visitors to the woodland.

Roman roads are not hard to find, on the map at least. The Roman road, commonly known as Wade's Causeway, across Wheeldale Moor, immediately to the north of Cropton Forest, is still that rare thing – a Roman road which is still visible on the ground.

There are Roman remains to be seen at Cawthorn Camp, which is believed to have been as a training camp, which is signposted from the minor road between

CROPTON FOREST – FARNDALE

the villages of Cropton and Newton-on-Rawcliffe. From the purpose-built car park the waymarked path, no more than a mile (1.6km) long, guides you around them. The well-preserved earthworks reveal a camp, two forts and an annexe wedged side by side on a plateau, which enjoys panoramic views to the north across Cropton Forest to the moors beyond. By the year AD 122, when the Emperor Hadrian was constructing his famous wall to the north, the Cawthorn camps had been abandoned.

FARNDALE

Farndale is a delightful valley at any time of the year, but every Easter it blooms with a profusion of golden wild daffodils. The daffodil walk accompanies the River Dove between Low Mill and Church Houses. This is an undeniably pleasant stroll, and suitable for wheelchairs, but try to pick a weekday, if possible, to make your visit; or venture a little further afield, for wild daffodils can be found throughout the valley. The traffic has become so heavy in recent years that a field in the village of Low Mill becomes a car park while the daffodils are in bloom. There is a park- and-ride bus service operating from Kirkbymoorside and Hutton-le-Hole.

But why Farndale? And why in such profusion? Farndale's blooms are wild, short-stemmed daffodils; stories variously attribute their planting to the monks of Rievaulx, and to Father Postgate, a Catholic priest who was persecuted for his faith. We merely know that wild daffodils have flourished in these dales for centuries.

■ Insight

SARKLESS KITTY
The dales are rich in folklore; one story tells of Kitty Garthwaite, 'Sarkless Kitty', from the village of Lowna Bridge, who, more than 200 years ago, was 'walking out' with Willie Dixon of Hutton-le-Hole. A rumour came to Kitty that Willie was seeing another lass. A lovers' tiff by the River Dove was followed, tragically, by Kitty being found drowned in a pool, wearing only her 'sark', or petticoat. After their argument, Willie had ridden to York to get a marriage licence. On his return his horse stumbled and Willie drowned in the same pool where Kitty had earlier been found. The ghost of Kitty, naked but carrying her sark over her arm, began to haunt the riverside spot where the lovers had kept their trysts.

The greatest threat to the daffodils has been the ever-increasing numbers of visitors, who were once unable to admire the spectacular springtime displays without gathering armfuls of the flowers. Once market traders found this free source of daffodils the flowers were in danger, and in 1953 about 2,000 acres (810ha) of Farndale were designated as a nature reserve; the daffodils are safe for us all to enjoy. Resist the temptation to pick any.

At other times of the year Farndale reverts to being a peaceful farming community. Both sides of the valley are accessible; from either Kirkbymoorside and Hutton-le-Hole on the A170 to the south, or, most dramatically, from the north down a steep road which descends from Blakey Ridge just to the south of the Lion Inn.

CENTRAL MOORS

HOVINGHAM MAP REF SE6675

One of North Yorkshire's prettiest villages, Hovingham, lies on the route of an old Roman road from Malton to Boroughbridge. When the foundations of Hovingham Hall were being laid, in 1745, Roman remains were unearthed, including part of a bathhouse. The Hall's first owner, Sir Thomas Worseley, was a descendant of Oliver Cromwell. His passion for horses led him to build the stable block facing on to the village green. In a rather unusual arrangement, visitors have to pass through the stable block to reach the Hall's main entrance. The Hall opens to the public in June for guided tours.

The attractive architectural unity of the surrounding houses, the neat layout with broad grass verges and an air of gentility all mark Hovingham out as an estate village. One of the Hall's lawns is today the village's cricket pitch; surely one of the loveliest grounds on which to watch or play the summer game. The houses at the northern end of the village are clustered either side of a pretty little beck, with a ford, where ducks swim and await visitors who may have stale bread to feed to them.

HUTTON-LE-HOLE

MAP REF SE7090

It is to Hutton-le-Hole's benefit that it lies just off the main A170 between Thirsk and Scarborough, for it, unlike its larger neighbours, has managed to maintain its distinct personality instead of selling its soul to the tourist trade. One of Yorkshire's 'picture postcard' villages, its houses are set back from Hutton Beck, a little watercourse spanned by a succession of pretty little bridges. The village green is the size of a meadow, but the grass is cropped short by grazing sheep, which wander wherever they choose – as likely as not in the middle of the road.

The houses of discreet grey stone, with the red-tiled roofs so typical of the moors, lend a timeless air to the village. The tiny church has some very fine oak furniture made by Robert Thompson of Kilburn; a close examination will reveal the trademark carved mouse that can be found on his work.

Once you have seen the village, don't neglect to visit Ryedale Folk Museum. This open-air collection is based on the displays of bygones built up by two local collectors. From its beginnings in a single old farm building, the museum has expanded far beyond its walls, to include many other vernacular buildings – brought stone by stone to the museum and painstakingly re-erected.

For nearly 500 years a thatched, cruck-framed cottage has stood here in Danby village. In 1967 this typical farmer's house was moved to the museum's 2.5-acre (1ha) site. The tall, 16th-century manor house, also thatched and cruck-framed, is a huge hall open to the roof beams. This was once the meeting place of the Manor Court, where disputes were settled and common rights safeguarded. Other museum buildings house a primitive 16th-century glass furnace, a photographer's studio, and a row of shops recreated as they would have looked more than a hundred years ago.

Insight

RYEDALE'S WITCH POST

The cruck-framed house at the Ryedale Folk Museum contains one of the rare examples of a witch post to have survived – most of which are found in the north of England. This post, of mountain ash, is elaborately carved with a cross and other, more ambiguous, symbols. It stands by the fireplace, so it would be passed by anyone who came into the living area, and also had the practical purpose of supporting the beam across the inglenook. It was designed, of course, to ward off evil spirits and protect those who sat here enjoying the fire's warmth.

Insight

ST GREGORY'S SUNDIAL

The engraved inscription on the sundial at St Gregory's Minster is in Old English. Translated it reads 'Orm, the son of Gamal, bought St Gregory's Church when it was utterly broken down and fallen, and he rebuilt it from ground level, to Christ and St Gregory, in the days of King Edward and Earl Tostig. Howarth made me and Brand the priest. This is sun's marker at all times'. The Edward of the inscription is King Edward the Confessor, who ruled between 1042 and 1066; Tostig became Earl of Northumberland in 1055; Howarth made the sundial; Brand was the name of the parish priest. This brief inscription is the longest example of Anglo-Saxon carving to have survived.

Insight

CRUCK-FRAMED HOUSES

The crucks and their cross-beams made a shape like the letter 'A'; these heavy timbers supported the entire weight of the building's roof, allowing the walls to be infilled. Since the walls were not load bearing, it was an easy matter to alter the position of doors, or create extra windows.

Throughout these buildings, exhibits in their own right, are informal displays showing what life was like in such moorland villages in bygone days. The site is also the venue for various events which are held through the year.

KIRKBYMOORSIDE

MAP REF SE6986

The market town of Kirkbymoorside lies on the edge of the moors just outside the National Park, on the A170 between Helmsley and Pickering. Don't judge the place by first appearances; you should leave the main road to investigate the old heart of the town. The broad main street is lined with inns, a reminder that Kirkbymoorside was an important halt in the days of stage coaches. The oldest inn is the Black Swan, whose elaborately carved entrance porch bears the date 1632. The market cross, mounted on a stepped base, can be found in a side street near by. Market day is Wednesday, as it has been since medieval times.

Kirkbymoorside has a road called Castlegate. Once it had a castle too, on a hill behind the parish church, but stones salvaged from its ruins were used to build the 17th-century tollbooth in the market place. Another fortified building was once a hunting lodge built by the Neville family. The church, though old, was largely rebuilt last century.

Lovers of beautiful old churches should rejoin the A170 and travel westwards in the direction of Helmsley for just a few hundred yards, before following the sign for St Gregory's Minster. If the word 'minster' conjures up some grand edifice, you will be surprised to find a tiny, dignified church built of grey stone, almost hidden away in beautiful, secluded Kirkdale.

This ancient building was dedicated to St Gregory – the pope who dispatched St Augustine to preach Christianity to the pagan English in AD 597. There has long been a church here, certainly before Anglo-Saxon times, as it had to be rebuilt in c1060, perhaps as a result of Viking destruction. Recent excavations have revealed a prehistoric standing stone by the west tower, evidence of Christians reusing a pagan site. Many visitors ask: why a minster? And why here, in such an isolated spot? The term 'minster' is derived from the Latin *monasterium*, which denoted a community of priests or monks who used the church as a base from which to serve the surrounding countryside before the parish system evolved. This status has remained with churches; some like this one are small, some like York Minster are large and important.

We can be more certain about the dates of the rebuilding because ancient – yet tantalisingly brief – details are carved on a sundial mounted over the south door. The sun doesn't reach it any more; to protect the sundial, the best Anglo-Saxon example known, a porch was added in the 19th century.

LASTINGHAM MAP REF SE7290

The casual visitor to the small village of Lastingham will see a collection of good-looking houses, a few wellheads and a welcoming inn, but Lastingham has something more to offer – a unique place in the history of Christianity.

St Cedd left the island of Lindisfarne (Holy Island) in AD 655 and chose this site on which to build a monastery. It was an area which, according to the Venerable Bede, was 'the lurking place of robbers and wild beasts'. St Cedd was buried in his monastery, close to the altar. This early building was later sacked by invading Danes.

In 1078 Abbot Stephen of Whitby moved his own community to Lastingham. He built a crypt dedicated to St Cedd, in which the saint's remains were re-interred. Apart from cosmetic changes (and the stairs leading down into it from the nave of the church above) the crypt looks the way it did almost a thousand years ago.

Itself a church in miniature, the crypt has a chancel, aisles, an eastern apse, stout Norman pillars, a low vaulted roof and a stone slab for an altar. Here, too, are fragments of ancient crosses. It was to have been part of a large abbey, but Abbot Stephen's plans were thwarted and the community moved to the larger site of St Mary's Abbey, York.

The present church, planned merely as the abbey's chancel, was eventually consolidated to meet local needs; the congregation was derived from those who lived in many of the surrounding villages. Today, visitors to Lastingham's church come from further afield to see a building that has happily survived years of neglect and clumsy 'restorations'. A closer examination of two of the village's wellheads reveal that one is dedicated to St Cedd, the other to his more famous brother, St Chad, who succeeded him as Abbot of Lastingham.

CENTRAL MOORS

Lastingham and Hutton-le-Hole

From Lastingham and St Cedd's monastery the walk reaches Spaunton before leading on to Hutton-le-Hole clustered around an irregular green and along the banks of a beck. The route passes through fields and woodland on the return leg.

Route Directions

1 Begin the walk by The Green and follow signs to Cropton, Pickering and Rosedale, past the red telephone box. Where the road swings left, go right to wind over a small bridge and beside a stream. Ascend to a footpath sign, and go right, uphill, through a gate and through woodland to

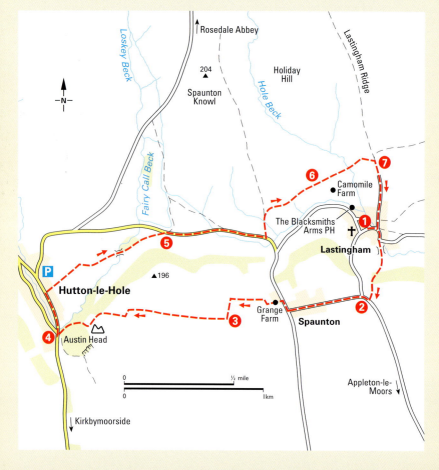

WALK 5

a handgate on to a road. Turn right, signed 'Spaunton'.

2 Follow the road through Spaunton, and bend right at the end of the village, then turn left by the public footpath sign over the cattle grid into the farmyard. The waymarked track curves through the farm to reach another footpath signpost, where the track bends left. After 100yds (91m), at a barn, the track bends left again.

3 After about 200yds (183m), follow a public footpath sign right and walk on to follow another sign as the track bends left. After 100yds (91m), take a footpath to the right, down the hill into woodland. Follow the track as it bends left, then go right, following the waymarks, down a steep grassy path into the valley. Descend to a gate beside a stream, and on to the road through Hutton-le-Hole.

4 Turn right up the main street and then right again at a footpath signpost opposite the Village Hall. Follow the waymarked route along the field-edges and through five waymarked gates to a kissing gate before a footbridge. Follow the path through woodland to a gate and follow the grassy track to the road.

5 Turn right and follow the road for 0.5 mile (800m). Turn left at a footpath sign just before the road descends to a stone bridge. Continue on the grassy path, going over a stile, and follow the track towards a farm.

6 Follow the waymarked posts, bending left alongside the wall beside a clump of trees and descending into a valley. Cross over the stream and follow the wall on your right-hand side uphill. You will reach a bench and then a carved stone with a cross and a three-pointed sign near by.

7 Take none of the directions indicated by the sign, but turn right, downhill through a gate and on to the metalled road. Follow the road downhill back into the village of Lastingham.

Route facts

DISTANCE/TIME
4.5 miles (7.2km) 2h

MAP OS Explorer OL26 North York Moors – Western

START Village street in Lastingham, grid ref: SE 729905

TRACKS Farm tracks and field paths, 2 stiles

GETTING TO THE START
Lastingham is reached by turning north from the A170 Thirsk to Scarborough road between Kirkby Mills and Sinnington. Park on the village street. Turn left by the church to visit The Blacksmith Arms.

THE PUB The Blacksmiths Arms, Lastingham.
Tel: 01751 417247

❶ Route finding could be difficult when the mists come down over the moors – save this route for settled weather.

CENTRAL MOORS

NUNNINGTON MAP REF SE6679

At Nunnington a delightful 17th-century three-arched bridge spans the River Rye. From one of its embrasures (the V-shaped spaces constructed to shield pedestrians from the traffic) you can gaze down into the water and try to spot basking trout, superbly camouflaged against the sandy river bed. Set in beautiful gardens across the river is honey-coloured Nunnington Hall. This tranquil setting offers no clue to the Hall's turbulent past; this isn't one of those stately homes that cruised serenely through the centuries, while leaving barely a ripple.

Nunnington Hall's early history is sketchy; it is thought to have been built on the site of a nunnery – hence its name. It passed through many hands, including the Abbot of St Mary's, York. Another later owner, Viscount Preston, served James II as Secretary of State for Scotland; charged later with treason, he escaped the gallows only by implicating his fellow conspirators.

While the Hall's west wing can be dated to 1580, most of the building, a concoction of Tudor and Stuart styles, was built during the 17th century. The Hall, housing the entrancing Carlisle collection of miniature rooms and regular art and photography exhibitions, is now cared for by the National Trust.

Nunnington's handsome houses in grey stone are hidden from sight to those who drive straight through the village; it's better to explore on foot. Nunnington's church, with its double dedication to St James and All Saints, dates largely from the 13th century. Here, in an alcove, is the effigy of a knight in chain mail. This recumbent figure commemorates Sir Walter de Teyes, Lord of the Manor of Nunnington and Stonegrave until his death in 1325.

ROSEDALE

Rosedale is a lovely tranquil valley today, echoing with the bubbling cry of the curlew and the distant barking of farm dogs. City visitors will feel themselves to be a long way from the noise and grime of Yorkshire's industrial heartlands. But appearances can be deceptive. Just one hundred years ago the scene was very different: Rosedale was a veritable moorland 'Klondike'.

Ironstone had been mined here, sporadically, since the Iron Age. During the 13th century mining added to the wealth of the monks of Byland Abbey; but it was only in the middle of the 19th century that the extent of Rosedale's subterranean wealth was realised, with the discovery of massive quantities of top-grade iron ore. The Industrial Revolution brought a huge demand for iron; the blast furnaces on the Rivers Tees and Tyne needed a constant supply for building ships, railways and general engineering. Other mines were driven – at Glaisdale, Beck Hole and on the coast, for example – but the mines at Rosedale proved to be the most productive.

The transport of ore was difficult from isolated Rosedale. In 1861 the North Eastern Railway Company built a line from Battersby Junction on the Stockton–Whitby line, over the bleak moorland to Rosedale West. In 1865 a branch was built around the head of

Rosedale to the east mines, joining the original line at Blakey Junction, just below the Lion Inn on Blakey Ridge. To reach Teesside the wagons, now laden with ore, were winched down the steep descent of the Ingleby Incline. The engines that plied the high-level line between the Rosedale mines and the incline never came down from their moorland heights, except when they had to be repaired.

The Rosedale railway was closed in 1929, by which time the valley's mining boom was over. Though the demand for iron was as buoyant as ever, ore could be mined more cheaply elsewhere. The route of this fascinating line is used today by walkers, cyclists and horse riders. The valley is quietly 'going back to nature', but the massive calcining kilns (where ironstone was roasted to reduce its weight) are being preserved, so that Rosedale's mining past will not be forgotten.

You will search in vain for the abbey that gave the village of Rosedale Abbey its name. The ladies who serve in the tea shops answer the question with a weary resignation that suggests this is not the first time they've been asked. The truth is that you can see the remains of the abbey (it was actually a priory) wherever you look: the population explosion of the mid-19th century meant that the priory was plundered for its building stone to build homes for the ironstone miners. Whether this is seen as the desecration of a religious site, or the sensible recycling of a valuable resource, depends on your own reading of history. The priory was founded in 1158 as a Cistercian nunnery by William of Rosedale. It was never a large establishment: there were probably only nine nuns and a prioress living here.

St Lawrence's Church stands on the site of the priory's chapel. To find a couple of relics from the earlier building, walk up to the altar rail. One of the stones set into the floor here bears a carved cross and, faintly, the name Maria, in memory of one of the nuns. Beyond the altar rail is an ancient stone seat from the nunnery; it is carved from a single block of stone.

■ Insight

YORKSHIRE'S 'KLONDIKE'
Between 1850 and 1870 the population of Rosedale quadrupled, as the mines were driven deep into the valley sides. A system of underground passages was dug, consolidated by wooden supports. The miners excavated to either side of these tunnels, with pick and shovel, to win the ore-bearing rock. The news soon spread, with experienced miners converging on Rosedale from all over the country – and particularly from Cornwall and Wales. At the height of production, more than 5,000 men found work here.

■ Activity

CYCLING IN ROSEDALE
The old Rosedale railway is ideal for cycling for much of its length, as it is relatively level and surfaced with ash ballast. The best section is from Rosedale Bank Top to Blakey Junction, near the Lion Inn (4 miles/6.4km) and then across the moors to Ingleby Bank Top, another 7 miles (11.3km). You could even cycle down the incline – but remember what goes down must come up again.

ROSEDALE – STANDING STONES

STANDING STONES

It is appropriate that Ralph Cross should have been chosen as the emblem of the National Park, for standing stones and wayside crosses are one of the most intriguing features of the moors. No other area of the country can boast so many examples.

Within the National Park boundary there are more than a thousand stones raised by man, standing witness to many centuries of settlement on the moors. The moorland stones are known as 'crosses', even though only a small proportion of them are actually carved into the shape of a cross. Some are simple monoliths fitted with side-pieces to make a cruciform shape. One particular design, repeated in many moorland crosses, is known as the wheelhead. It consisted of a widening of the top of a stone, which is pierced with four holes to create the shape of a cross. Other stones simply have the design of a cross carved into their surface.

The moorland crosses weren't erected at random; they were put up for a variety of reasons. A number of them were preaching crosses, marking the spot where itinerant monks would attempt to bring the gospel to the pagan Anglo-Saxon communities. If the monks were successful and their words fell on willing ears, a church might be built on, or near, the site of the preaching cross.

In the Middle Ages other crosses were put up as waymarkers, to guide travellers across the largely featureless expanses of 'Blackamore'. Moorland roads were established by usage; they weren't 'built' like the Roman roads; at best, the routes might be delineated by a line of causeway stones. The moorland crosses would help to mark the route, and offer weary travellers further targets in the distance to aim for. Other crosses were erected to mark the boundaries of the monastic sheep-grazing land.

During these times the building of bridges and wayside crosses was seen as an act of piety. Many rich men would attempt to improve their chances of getting into heaven by providing money for such good works. So, here too, a stone shaped as a cross would reflect both the donor's good intentions and the travellers' gratitude to find another waymark. It's hard for us, in our cars,

Visit

EARLY SIGNPOSTS
Stone signposts were erected at all the crossroads on the moors in 1711 by order of the Justices at Northallerton, to prevent travellers from getting hopelessly lost. They sign the direction of each road to the nearest main town, and sometimes the distances. The spelling is distinctly idiosyncratic, and some have primitive hands carved on them. There is a good example about 2 miles (3.2km) north out of Hutton-le-Hole on the road to Ralph Cross at map reference SE 693926.

Activity

THE CROSSES WALK
The Crosses Walk is a challenge walk of about 53 miles (85km), created to be undertaken in a single day. Starting and finishing at the village of Goathland, it uses thirteen prominent crosses for their original purpose, as waymarkers.

MILLENNIUM CROSS, ROSEDALE HEAD

to imagine how reassuring it would have been to see a moorland cross appear through the mist. The spiritual aspect of these moorland crosses was further emphasised by the custom of leaving coins on them – many had an indentation on the top – for needy travellers.

Many stone crosses on the moorland now exist only as empty 'sockets' or just names on old maps. However, at least 30 of the moorland crosses still stand to their full height. Ralph Cross, at 9 feet (2.75m) high on the top of Blakey Ridge, is also known as Young Ralph. It has been a familiar landmark for centuries, since it marks a meeting of important tracks. Now it can be seen by motorists driving between Castleton and Hutton-le-Hole. Close by are two more crosses: 'Old Ralph' is a mere 4 feet (1.2m) high, while 'Fat Betty' comprises a rounded stone 'head' on a square stone 'body'.

The oldest cross still standing on the moors is reckoned to be Lilla Cross, off the Whitby–Pickering road at Ellerbeck Bridge. Possibly of 10th-century origin, it is said to mark the final resting place of Lilla, a minister to King Edwin, whose kingdom encompassed the Yorkshire Wolds. Lilla saved the life of his king by falling on to the sword of an assassin, but inevitably died in the process. King Edwin commemorated this selfless act with the cross you can still see today.

WHEELDALE

The Romans made few incursions into what we now know as the North York Moors. The inescapable conclusion is that the wastes of what for centuries was known as 'Blackamore' held few attractions for the colonists. However, they may have built a road across the moors to link a settlement at Malton with the signal stations on the coast near Goldsborough and Whitby.

A section of road on Wheeldale Moor, just over a mile (1.6km) in length and known as Wade's Causeway, is reckoned to be the best-preserved Roman road in the country, though doubts have been expressed in recent years about its Roman origins. The road gradually fell into disuse, eventually disappearing beneath the encroaching heather and bracken. It was rediscovered in 1914. It can be reached by driving north from Pickering on an unclassified road. Once past the village of Stape, follow the Wheeldale Road with Cropton Forest on the right and the expanse of Wheeldale Moor to the left. Park your car near to the watersplash at Wheeldale Bridge, and the old Roman road is immediately ahead. The Roman road over Wheeldale is also signposted from the village of Goathland, west of the A169.

We all learned about the Romans' innovative road-making skills at school, yet this particular road looks a rather rocky thoroughfare. That's because what you can see today is merely the road's foundations, made up of large stones set into gravel. The original road surface would have been much smoother, overlaid with finer aggregate. The road is cambered so that water would drain off to the edges and be carried away in culverts. You can follow the route and decide for yourself whether or not you are walking in the footsteps of those Roman legions.

The Iron Valley of Rosedale

Rosedale is a peaceful valley that pushes northwest into the heart of the North York Moors. Yet little more than a hundred years ago the village of Rosedale Abbey had a population ten times its present size. The reason was the discovery of ironstone in the hills in the mid 1850s. The dramatic remains of the Rosedale East Mines, which opened in 1865, can be seen during much of the walk. The long range of huge arches is the remains of the calcining kilns, where the ironstone was roasted to eliminate the impurities and reduce its weight.

Route Directions

1 From the parking place take the lane downhill by the Sycamore Farm sign. It bends right. Follow the waymarkers to turn right through Low Bell End Farm gateway. Follow the track through two gates and continue downhill. Near a gate on the left the track bends right, following the stream. After going through another gateway, bend left towards the stream to cross a footbridge with stiles at each end. Follow the waymarked

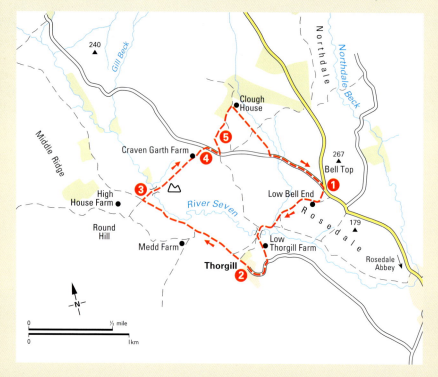

WALK 6

footpath half left, uphill, towards the farm buildings. The route passes through the buildings and on to a farm track. Follow the track uphill, forking right to reach a lane. Turn right.

2 Continue up the metalled lane, which takes you through the hamlet of Thorgill. Just beyond the buildings the metalled lane soon becomes a track. Follow the track for 0.75 mile (1.2 km), going through a wooden gate near Medd Farm and continuing downhill. Pass a small caravan site called Seven Side and begin to rise again. Almost opposite another farmhouse – High House Farm – on the left, go right over a waymarked wooden stile beside a gate.

3 Walk down the slope beside the fence and pass over the River Seven on a gated footbridge. At the end, turn left to go uphill – a short but steep slope. At the top, the path goes above the stream, generally parallel with it. Continue through a gate into the field and walk ahead. Go through another gate and continue up the field with a fence on your left. Go through a metal gate into the yard of Craven Garth Farm. Go through another gateway and pass between the cluster of buildings to reach a metalled country lane at a T-junction.

4 Turn right and follow the lane; just before reaching the row of former ironworkers' cottages, look for the Rosedale parish notice board on the left. Turn up the track beside it. A little way up the track, before reaching the farm, look for a gate across a track to Clough House.

5 Go over the stile beside the gate and follow the track downhill towards the wood. The track bends right just before Clough House, then bends left to pass the front of the house. Opposite the building, go through a waymarked gate on the right and walk down the field towards houses. Leave the field by a gate, and follow the track to the road. Turn left and follow the road back to the car parking place.

Route facts

DISTANCE/TIME
3.5 miles (5.7km) 1h30

MAP OS Explorer OL26 North York Moors – Western

START Road junction northwest of Rosedale Abbey, near Sycamore Farm sign, grid ref: 717970. Roadside parking near junction.

TRACKS Mostly field paths and tracks, 7 stiles

GETTING TO THE START
From the A170 between Pickering and Wombleton, head north to Rosedale Abbey. The junction at the start of the walk is a short distance northwest.

THE PUB The White Horse Farm Inn, Rosedale Abbey. Tel: 01751 417595; www.whitehorserosedale.co.uk

CENTRAL MOORS

■ TOURIST INFORMATION CENTRE
Hutton-le-Hole
Ryedale Folk Museum.
Tel: 01751 417367

■ PLACES OF INTEREST
Cawthorne
Remains of Roman camp on road between Cropton and Newton-on-Rawcliffe. Free.
Hovingham Hall
Hovingham.
Tel: 01653 628771;
www.hovingham.co.uk
Nunnington Hall
Nunnington.
Tel: 01439 748283;
www.nationaltrust.org.uk
Ryedale Folk Museum
Hutton-le-Hole.
Tel: 01751 417367; www.ryedalefolkmuseum.co.uk

■ SHOPPING
MARKET
Kirkbymoorside
Open-air market, Wed.
LOCAL SPECIALITIES
Ceramics
James Brooke, The Pottery, Appleton-le-Moors.
Tel: 01751 417514
Glass
Gillies Jones Glass Design, The Old Forge, Rosedale Abbey.
Tel: 01751 417550;
www.gilliesjonesglass.co.uk

■ SPORTS & ACTIVITIES
HORSE-RIDING
Newtondale Horse Trail
35 traffic-free miles (56km). Guidebook from North York Moors National Park Authority.
www.northyorkmoors.org.uk
Sinnington
Friars Hill Riding Stables.
Tel: 01751 432758; www.friarshillstables.co.uk
MOUNTAIN BIKING AND CYCLE HIRE
Cropton
Keldy Cycle Hire, Keldy Forest Cabins, Cropton Forest.
Tel: 01751 417510.
North York Moors Mountain Bike Routes.
www.muddybums.org.uk
www.mtb-routes.co.uk/northyorkmoors

■ ANNUAL EVENTS & CUSTOMS
Farndale
Farndale Show, Aug.
Rosedale
Rosedale Show, Aug.
Ryedale
Ryedale Show, Kirkbymoorside, Jul.

TEA ROOMS & PUBS

Tea Rooms

Hovingham Bakery Spa Tearoom
Brookside, Hovingham
YO62 4LG. Tel: 01653 628898
The Bakery provides delicious fresh bread and cakes to locals and visitors, and serves them in its little tea room by the beck – you can sit outside on summer days. The hearty sandwiches are a meal in themselves, and there are excellent cream teas – the fruit scones are a particular favourite.

Nunnington Hall
Nunnington YO62 5UY
Tel: 01439 748283;
www.nationaltrust.org.uk
As you'd expect from the National Trust, the food is top-notch. Cream teas, cakes (try the special Nunnington Fruit Loaf) and light lunches will tempt you. If you're there later in the season, you'll find old apple varieties from the orchard used in pies, flans, crumbles, soups and chutneys – worth making a special autumn journey for!

Abbey Tea Room and Store
Rosedale Abbey YO18 8SA
Tel: 01751 417475;
www.abbeytearoom.co.uk
As well as plain, fruit and cheese scones, you can find cherry scones, scones made with treacle, scones made with blueberries and ginger... and you can spread them with blueberry and lavender jam. If you're more peckish, try the Yorkshire Ham afternoon tea.

Lastingham Grange
Lastingham YO62 6TH
Tel: 01751 417345;
www.lastinghamgrange.com
Take tea in this elegant hotel on the hillside on the edge of Lastingham. The traditional afternoon teas are served in the drawing room, where you can loll on comfy chintz sofas in front of the fire – it's almost like visiting the gracious home of a wealthy great aunt.

Pubs

The Lion Inn
Blakey Ridge,
Kirkbymoorside YO62 7LQ
Tel: 01751 417320;
www.lionblakey.co.uk
The Lion is set on the high moors at the heart of the National Park. Expect to rub shoulders with walkers and mountain-bikers, as well as lovers of real ale and those who enjoy good, well-cooked and substantial meals, eaten either in the restaurant or the bar. You're sure of a warm welcome, whatever the weather at this exposed spot.

The New Inn
Cropton, Nr Pickering
YO18 8HH. Tel: 01751 417330;
www.newinncropton.co.uk
The Cropton micro-brewery produces fine ales that you can sample in its own pub, the New Inn. There is good food available, too, using local ingredients, including fish from Whitby. You can eat either in the cosy bar or in the elegant restaurant.

The Star Inn
Harome, Nr Helmsley
YO62 5JE. Tel: 01439 770397;
www.thestaratharome.co.uk
While you're welcome to drop in for a drink (hand-pulled beers, a good selection of wines) it's the Michelin-rated food that is the draw. It is superb, though not cheap. There's a shop selling home-made delicacies.

The George and Dragon
Market Place,
Kirkbymoorside YO62 6AA
Tel: 01751 433334;
www.georgeanddragon.net
The George caters for visitors and locals, who enjoy its historic atmosphere. There's real ale on tap and more than 50 types of whisky. The good food is available either in the restaurant or bistro, or by the fire in the bar. The menu is strong on seafood and fish.

Eastern Moors & Coast

Brompton	120
Goathland	121
■ WALK 7 Goathland	122
Hackness	124
Hole of Horcum	125
Levisham and Lockton	127
North Yorkshire Moors Railway	127
Pickering	128
Ravenscar	129
Robin Hood's Bay	130
■ WALK 8 Cleveland Way	132
■ WALK 9 Raincliffe Woods	134
■ WALK 10 Fylingdales and Lilla Cross	136
Scarborough	138
Sleights	140
Thornton-le-Dale	141
■ CYCLE RIDE 2 Dalby Forest	142
■ CYCLE RIDE 3 From Ravenscar to Robin Hood's Bay	144

INTRODUCTION

The eastern moors is the triangle formed between Whitby, Scarborough and Pickering. The coastline provides spectacular cliffs, hidden coves, sandy beaches and fascinating rock formations. To preserve the area's unique character, many miles have been declared designated Heritage Coast. Robin Hood's Bay is one of the loveliest fishing villages in the country, while Scarborough is Yorkshire's premier seaside resort.

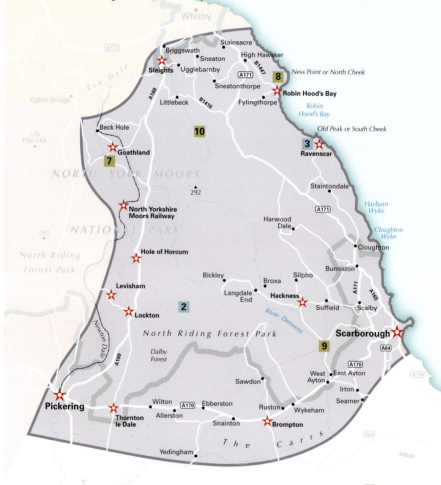

7 Walk start point
2 Cycle start point

EASTERN MOORS & COAST 117

ROBIN HOOD'S BAY

HOT SPOTS

Unmissable attractions

Explore Levisham and Lockton, a pair of delectable moorland villages and discover one of the earliest sites for Iron Age smelting on the nearby moors...explore the beautiful Forge Valley, which is a haven for wildlife...negotiate around the Hole of Horcum, sometimes known as the Devil's Punchbowl, a huge natural amphitheatre scooped out of Levisham Moor...ride high on the restored North Yorkshire Moors Railway, steam-hauled trains taking you deep into the moors...explore the charming resort of Robin Hood's Bay...treat yourself to a day out at Scarborough, one of Britain's oldest medicinal spas and bucket-and-spade seaside resorts.

1 Hole of Horcum
Otherwise known as the Devil's Punchbowl, this deep-sided, natural hollow offers plenty of good opportunities for walks.

2 Robin Hood's Bay
With its cobbled streets and tiny cottages, Robin Hood's Bay is one of the loveliest fishing villages.

3 Scarborough rock pools
These young holidaymakers are well equipped to explore the fascinating rock pools exposed at low tide in Scarborough.

4 Quoits in Goathland
The game of quoits is played in many moorland villages. The object is to throw a heavy iron quoit over the peg, a metal pin, but there's much more to it than that, as you'll discover if you watch seasoned players, like these in Goathland.

5 North Yorkshire Moors Railway
During the summer months steam trains haul their passengers through some of the finest scenery of the North York Moors.

EASTERN MOORS & COAST

BROMPTON MAP REF SE9482

Motorists on the A170 tend to drive straight through Brompton in their haste to get to the Yorkshire coast. The pretty little village is set around a small lake, into which the church doors were thrown during the Civil War; they were later recovered and re-hung. The poet William Wordsworth took the time to get to know the village, for he courted Mary Hutchinson, a local girl who lived at Gallows Hill Farm. When they married, in 1802, it was in Brompton's 14th-century church. The wedding ceremony was recorded in her diary by his sister Dorothy; she even joined the happy couple on their honeymoon in Grasmere, in the Lake District.

The village has a unique (though sadly little-known) place in the history of aeronautics. Everybody knows it was Wilbur and Orville Wright who made the first manned flight, in their flimsy craft, *Kittyhawk*. Yet a remarkable 50 years before that memorable occasion, an unsung squire of Brompton Hall quietly set about building a flying machine.

Brompton Hall (now a school and not open to the public) had been the home of the Cayley family since Stuart times, and Sir George Cayley (1771–1857) developed an unquenchable scientific curiosity. This was an age when enthusiastic amateurs, especially those blessed with private incomes, could indulge their whims in the arts and sciences. Sir George, however, was no mere dabbler; his inventions included caterpillar tracks and a new form of artificial limb, prompted by an accident to one of his estate workers. Seeing how the River Derwent regularly flooded the flat countryside, to the chagrin of local farmers, he designed and constructed a sea cut to divert flood waters straight into the North Sea near Scarborough.

But the prospect of flight remained Sir George's passion. Even before the 18th century was out he was designing gliders – continuing to refine the craft's aerodynamics until he had a controllable machine that could carry a man. He had already experimented with propellers, abandoning them merely because the internal combustion engine was not even on the horizon. His various experiments proved that a contoured wing could provide much greater lift than a wing with a flat profile.

Though an inscription in the porch of All Saints Church acknowledges Sir George as the 'Father of Aeronautics', his pioneering efforts are largely overlooked. Facing the main road through the village is the six-sided building, the summerhouse, now boarded up, unfortunately, where Sir George worked on his flying machines.

■ Insight

A RELUCTANT VOLUNTEER

Taking to heart the notion 'Why have a dog and bark yourself?', Sir George Cayley volunteered his understandably reluctant coachman to make the first manned flight. On a still day in 1853 the glider made a short 55-yard (50m) hop across Brompton Dale. The coachman, relieved to have survived unscathed, but unwilling to entertain thoughts of another death-defying flight, resigned on the spot, telling Sir George that he was paid to drive, not to fly.

GOATHLAND MAP REF NZ8301

This pleasant village has achieved fame by proxy as the location for the popular television series *Heartbeat*. On the small screen Goathland was transformed into fictional Aidensfield, where the local police constable trod his rural beat. Episodes were filmed throughout the moors, but the village of Goathland will be especially familiar to viewers; there is no need to search for locations the cameras have blessed.

Goathland was a popular destination for visitors long before the television series began, and though by no means the prettiest village on the moors, it is certainly well worth visiting in its own right. The broad grass verges, closely cropped by sheep, lead directly on to the heather and bracken of the moors. The village also makes an excellent centre for exploring the surrounding moorland and the stretch of Roman road known as Wade's Causeway. Fame brings its own problems, however, and Goathland does get very busy on Bank Holidays.

Black-faced moorland sheep are everywhere, local farmers enjoy grazing rights throughout the village, so the sheep roam where they will. They keep the grass closely cropped, but have only the most rudimentary road sense.

A brief investigation of the village and its surroundings will reveal a number of delightful waterfalls. The best known is the 70-foot (21m) Mallyan Spout, easily reached via a footpath adjacent to the Mallyan Spout Hotel. The hotel's Victorian architecture is a reminder that the first influx of visitors came with the building of the railway in the 1830s.

■ Visit

THE COLOURFUL MOORS
Leave Goathland in any direction and you will soon find yourself on expansive heather moorland. Though blackened in winter (hence the old name for the moors: 'Blackamore') the heather bursts into life during July, August and September, when miles of tiny flowers paint the uplands in glorious purple. The bell heather has deep purple flowers, while those of the cross-leaved heather have a pinker hue. The scene is made even more colourful during late summer by the blue-black bilberries and the rich brown bracken.

Before that, the village's moorland setting kept it in relative isolation. Goathland's church, just a century old, but on a site of Christian worship for a thousand years, was furnished by Robert Thompson of Kilburn. Look for the little carved mice that were the craftsman's trademark. Near the church is a pinfold, a small, square paddock enclosed by stone walls, where stray beasts could be corralled until claimed by their owners.

Goathland was one of the stations on the main Whitby–Pickering line, a status it retains now that the once-defunct line has a new lease of life as the North Yorkshire Moors Railway. The steepest section of the line was known as the Beck Hole Incline, and it was so steep that the earliest carriages had to be hauled up and down by using a system of counter-balanced weights: a very hazardous procedure. Though tiny and unspoiled today, Beck Hole was briefly, during the middle of the last century, a busy centre of ironstone mining.

EASTERN MOORS & COAST

Moorland around Goathland and Mallyan Spout

A walk from the popular moorland village of Goathland, also used as the fictitious village of Aidensfield for the television series *Heartbeat*, through shady woodland and over the moors. The walk begins with a visit to the impressive 70-foot (21m) Mallyan Spout waterfall. In dry weather only a trickle of water may fall into the stream below, but after rain it can become an impressive torrent. After you have crossed the ford and turned on to the moorland by Hunt House you might find yourself accompanied by the sudden flutter of red grouse rising from their nest sites on the heather moorland.

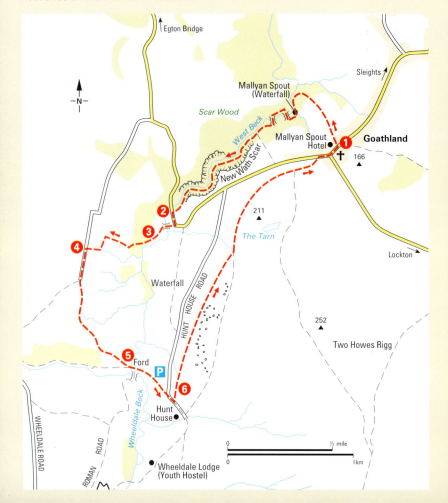

WALK 7

Route Directions

1 Opposite the church go through the kissing gate beside the Mallyan Spout Hotel, signed 'Mallyan Spout'. Follow the path to a streamside signpost and turn left. Continue past the waterfall (take care after heavy rain). Follow the sometimes-difficult footpath over two footbridges, over a stile and up steps, then for another mile (1.6km) to a stile on to a road beside a bridge.

2 Turn left along the road and climb the hill. Where the road bends left, go right along a bridleway through a gate. Turn left down a path to go over a bridge, then ahead beside the buildings, through a gate and across the field.

3 Part-way across the field, go through a waymarked gate to the right into woodland. Ascend a stony track and go through a gate, eventually turning right up the field, alongside the wall, just before you reach a facing gate as you leave the wood. Go left at the field top, through a gateway. Continue with a wall on your right and go through a waymarked gateway in the wall and up the next field, to emerge through a gate on to a metalled lane.

4 Turn left along the lane, go through a gate and follow the Roman Road sign. Go through two more gates by the farm, still following the public bridleway signs as you join a green lane. Continue through two handgates to descend to another gate and over a stile, then on until you reach a ford.

5 Cross the ford and go straight ahead along the gated track, eventually to reach a road by farm buildings. Turn right up the road and, just before a wooden garage, turn left on a green track up the hillside.

6 Bend right towards a small cairn on the ridge, then bend left, keeping below and parallel to the rocky ridge. Take a left fork by another cairn, to go slightly downhill to join a clear track. Goathland soon comes into sight. Pass a bridleway sign and descend to the road near the church, to return to the start.

Route facts

DISTANCE/TIME
4.5 miles (7.2km) 2h30

MAP OS Explorer OL27 North York Moors – Eastern

START The easiest parking is at the west end of Goathland village, near the church, grid ref: NZ 827007

TRACKS Rocky streamside tracks, field and moorland paths, 3 stiles

GETTING TO THE START
Goathland is 8 miles (12.9km) southwest of Whitby. It lies just 2 miles (3.2km) west of the A169 Whitby to Malton road and can also be reached using the North Yorkshire Moors Railway from Grosmont or Pickering.

THE PUB The Goathland Hotel, Goathland. Tel: 01947 896203; www.goathlandhotel.co.uk

❶ The initial riverside path to Mallyan Spout is slippery.

EASTERN MOORS & COAST

HACKNESS MAP REF SE9790

Steep-sided, wooded valleys fan out from the lovely village of Hackness, which was established at the point where Lowdale Beck meets the River Derwent. It's hard to believe that this secluded spot is only 3 miles (4.8km) from the outskirts of Scarborough. St Hilda, Abbess of Whitby Abbey, established a nunnery here in AD 680, with Abbess Œdilburga; two centuries later Danish invaders razed it to the ground. The community rose again in the 11th century, finally to disappear in 1539 on the orders of Henry VIII.

Hackness Hall (not open to the public), a handsome Georgian house built in 1791 by lord of the manor Sir John Vanden Bempole Johnstone, occupies the site where the nunnery once stood. The only major evidence of that community is the lake, which may have served as a fishery. A more tangible relic, a fragment of an Anglo-Saxon cross, is displayed inside St Peter's Church. Inscriptions, in English, Latin and runic characters, offer up praise to Abbess Œdilburga and prayers for the nuns' own safety. When the cross was carved, possibly in the ninth century, the nuns may have been aware of the cruel fate that awaited them at the hands of marauding Danes.

While Hackness hides in its valley, you can enjoy panoramic views by taking the minor roads to the hilltop villages of Broxa and Silpho. Immediately to the south of Hackness is the Forge Valley, a beautiful, wooded dale created at the end of the Ice Age by glacial meltwater. The River Derwent was diverted from its original direct route, east to the sea at Scalby, to flow south into the Humber.

Forge Valley takes its name from the iron forges, thought to have been worked by the monks of Rievaulx Abbey in the 14th century, which were fuelled by timber felled from this ancient woodland. Today the Forge Valley is a beauty spot and a haven for wildlife. The woods on either side of the river feature native species, including oak, ash, elm and willow, a pleasant contrast to the regimented conifer plantations elsewhere. Woodpeckers drum insistently; wagtails search for food along the riverbank; tiny warblers fill the woods with song each summer. The walking is excellent during any season. A wheelchair-friendly boardwalk follows the river for a mile (1.6km) and there are car parks and picnic sites.

■ Insight

THE GHOST OF HACKNESS

The ghost of Hackness was the invention of an 18th-century vicar's daughter when she found herself a little short of money. She reported seeing a spectral figure that intimated a sum of £50 would allow his soul to be put at rest!

■ Insight

SALT

Since Anglo-Saxon times salt had been valued for its use in curing meat and fish; it was so valuable that a special tax was levied on it. The River Tees, to the north of the National Park, was the site of important salt pans. Tidal waters were evaporated to leave their salt solution, and salt roads – known as saltersgates – led towards Rievaulx, Old Byland and other monastic communities in the north.

HACKNESS – HOLE OF HORCUM

Follow the road southwards through woodlands to emerge at the villages of West and East Ayton, sitting astride both the River Derwent and the main A170. At this point the River Derwent is a mere 4 miles (6.4km) from the seaside resort of Scarborough, yet it still has many miles to flow before it reaches the sea at the mouth of the Humber. The river bridge was constructed in 1775, from stone salvaged from the 14th-century castle that once stood near by. Built as a pele tower, a design more commonly found further north, Ayton Castle survives as a ruin.

HOLE OF HORCUM
MAP REF SE8594

This remarkable landform, sometimes known as the Devil's Punchbowl, is a huge natural amphitheatre seemingly scooped out of Levisham Moor. The valley bottom is primarily pastureland, while the steep slopes support woods and moorland. Motorists on the A169 Pickering–Whitby road skirt the rim of the Hole of Horcum, and so many stop to gaze in wonderment, and follow some of the good paths in the area, that a large car park has been provided.

Many stories account for the origin of the Hole of Horcum; take your pick between the factual and the fanciful. Legend tells that Wade, a local giant, scooped up a handful of earth to throw at his wife, Bell, thus creating the huge landform. Apparently, he missed her and the clod of earth landed to form Blakey Topping, little more than a mile (1.6km) away. To judge from the plethora of folk tales, Wade and his wife spent much of their time tossing missiles at one another. But the origin of the Hole of Horcum is more prosaic, scoured over millennia by glacial meltwater.

Just beyond a steep hairpin bend is the Saltersgate Inn, one of the many solitary inns in the National Park. They were generally sited on junctions of well-used tracks, catering to people on the move, as, indeed, many still do today. The people who stood at the bar of the now-closed Saltersgate Inn in its heyday were most likely to have been hauliers leading trains of heavily laden packhorses across the moors, as the inn lay on an old salt road linking the port of Whitby with the market town of Pickering. Later it catered to stagecoach traffic, and was the site of a tollbooth when the road became a turnpike. Its exposed location meant that it was regularly cut off by snow and buried in deep drifts. After centuries of serving beer and providing shelter to all-comers, the Saltersgate Inn finally closed its doors in 2006.

■ Visit

A SMUGGLERS' TALE
The smuggling of untaxed salt led to a tragedy. An excise man arrived incognito at the Saltersgate Inn, hoping to catch the smugglers 'red-handed'. When his motives were discovered he was quickly murdered and his body hidden behind the fireplace. From that day, almost 200 years ago, until the inn closed, the turf fire was said never to have been allowed to go out. Now the hearth is dead, and the excise man's ghost is said to be free to haunt whoever takes on the building in the future.

LEVISHAM & LOCKTON
MAP REFS SE8390/SE8489

Levisham and Lockton are a pair of delectable villages lying off the A169, about 5 miles (8km) north of Pickering. Until 1938 the most prominent feature of Lockton's squat church was an ash tree growing out of the top of the square tower. It was removed and replanted in the churchyard, but it failed to thrive. Apart from that, the village has a youth hostel, a duck pond (sadly, few other village ponds in the National Park have survived intact) and limestone cottages set back from wide grass verges.

Neighbouring Levisham is just a mile (1.6km) away, but it is a long mile if you happen to be walking – the villages are divided by a deep gorge. At the bottom, close to Levisham Beck, is a converted watermill and the ruins of St Mary's Church. Though it was built in this isolated spot to be equidistant from both villages, the church can hardly be said to be convenient for either.

Houses, and the Horseshoe Inn, surround a large village green. Pass the pub to join a single track road, with long views along well-wooded Newton Dale. Keep ahead down the road to arrive at Levisham Station, one of the stops for steam trains on the preserved line between Grosmont and Pickering, where the public road ends.

THE NORTH YORKSHIRE MOORS RAILWAY

The North Yorkshire Moors Railway is a remarkable success story. No visit to the moors would be complete without a trip along this most scenic of lines.

Today the line is purely recreational, but it was commerce and industry that provided the original spur for the line to be built. Two centuries ago Whitby was one of the most important ports in the country. By the early 1800s, however, the town's traditional industries – whaling, ship building and alum mining – were in decline and Whitby's traders decided that the town needed to improve the communications over land.

In 1831, George Stephenson arrived fresh from his engineering triumphs on the Stockton and Darlington Railway and surveyed the terrain between Whitby and Pickering. His recommendation was for a railway line on which the carriages would be horse-drawn.

A veritable army of navvies was hired in 1833 to drive the line over the moors. Armed only with pick and shovel they tackled the rough terrain. The line from Whitby to Pickering was opened, with the usual fanfare, in 1836, when a trainload of dignitaries was pulled along the track at a sedate 10 miles per hour.

The line revitalised the area; a variety of industries, such as ironstone mining, sprang up once a regular train service had been established. A few years later it was converted to carry steam engines; the first one chugged noisily into Whitby in 1847. The rather troublesome Beck Hole Incline was bypassed by blasting a new route between Beck Hole and Goathland. By the time a new century dawned the moors and coast were well served with rail links; the trains not only transported goods, they also began to bring visitors from the crowded cities to enjoy the moorland landscape.

EASTERN MOORS & COAST

■ Insight

THE BECK HOLE INCLINE
The section of the original line of the North Yorkshire Railway between Beck Hole and Goathland (bypassed in 1865) consisted of a 1-in-10 incline. Coaches had to be winched up and down with an imaginative arrangement of counter-balanced weights. Primitive though it was, the moorland railway was immediately hailed as a wonder of engineering.

■ Insight

DETERMINED ENTHUSIASTS
When Beeching closed the railway line between Pickering and Grosmont in 1965, the story might have ended there, except that a group of enthusiasts, convinced that the line still had a viable future, formed themselves into the North Yorkshire Moors Railway Preservation Society. They raised enough money to buy the trackbed from British Rail and then restored the line and the stations along it. After plenty of hard work, the line was partially reopened in 1969 and from end to end in 1973. Today, it is a popular attraction with tourists and railway enthusiasts.

In 1965, as a result of the Beeching Reports, nearly 130 years of rail services came to a halt. The Esk Valley line was reprieved, but the section of railway line between Pickering and Grosmont was unceremoniously closed. Eight years of careful restoration and hard work later the line was reopened by the North Yorkshire Moors Railway Preservation Society. More than just another line run by enthusiasts, the North Yorkshire Moors Railway operates a full timetable from March to October.

The 18-mile (29km) rail journey takes visitors into the very heart of the moors. Today, more than 300,000 passenger journeys are taken every year, making the railway the biggest single attraction within the North York Moors National Park. Many travellers board the train at Pickering Station, which dates from 1845 and the advent of steam-hauled trains. Railway enthusiasts will be happy to know that, a century and a half later, the age of steam hasn't disappeared. The line climbs into the spectacular, steep-sided, wooded gorge of Newton Dale, before arriving at Levisham Station. Trains also call at Newtondale Halt, the starting point for a number of waymarked walks.

The next stop is Goathland, which is a favourite destination for visitors, whether travelling by car or rail. With its waterfalls, Rail Trail and delightful moorland setting, the village is well worth exploring. The northern terminus of the North Yorkshire Moors Railway is Grosmont, where travellers can join the main Northern Rail line between Middlesbrough and Whitby.

PICKERING MAP REF SE7984

The market town of Pickering lies just to the south of the National Park. Overlooking the market place is the large parish church dedicated to Saints Peter and Paul. Hemmed in by houses and shops, the building is approached by gates (streets) and ginnels (alleys). Inside are fine 15th-century frescoes, illustrating scenes from the lives of saints and martyrs. St George slays a dragon; Thomas Becket expires in the cathedral; St Edmund raises his eyes towards heaven as arrows fired by Vikings pierce his flesh.

After the Norman Conquest, King William created outposts in the north to establish order and quell uprisings; Pickering was one of these strategic sites. The first castle was built to a basic motte-and-bailey design; by the 12th century the wooden keep and outer palisade had been rebuilt in stone. It was besieged by Robert the Bruce on one of his incursions south of the border. When the Scots inflicted a heavy defeat on the army led by Edward II in 1322, the king found shelter here.

The castle saw no further military action, and was used by a succession of monarchs as a hunting lodge. Some parts of the old forest are still royal properties, but Pickering Castle is now in the hands of English Heritage.

Beck Isle Museum, housed in a fine Regency building close to Pickering Beck, offers fascinating glimpses into the more recent past. Successive rooms are devoted to different aspects of bygone life in town and country; you can visit the cobblers, gents' outfitters, kitchen, barber's shop and even the bar of a public house. Outbuildings house a blacksmith's forge, wheelwright and a collection of old farming implements.

RAVENSCAR   MAP REF NZ9801

Great things were planned for Ravenscar. A developer called John Septimus Bland decided to build a holiday resort that he thought would rival Whitby and Scarborough. A station was built, Bland laid out the town's network of roads and began to build shops and houses. But Bland's company went bankrupt, and work stopped. Despite the panoramic sea views, this exposed site was clearly unsuitable for such a development. It is geologically unstable, and visitors would have been faced with an awkward descent to the stony beach far below.

■ Visit

MEDIEVAL FRESCOES

The wall paintings in Pickering's church have had a chequered history. They were probably first hidden from view during a bout of puritanical zeal after the Reformation, when such images were considered idolatrous. Rediscovered in 1851, they were almost immediately concealed once again beneath layers of whitewash on the directions of a vicar who shared this puritanical outlook. However, the frescoes were revealed once again in 1878, and are now recognised as some of the best medieval church paintings to be seen in the country.

■ Visit/Activity

RAVENSCAR'S COASTLINE

The fault-line that runs along the coast between Boulby and Scarborough is most clearly visible at Ravenscar. At low tide the rocky shoreline is revealed as a series of concentric curves, formed from layers of hard and soft rock, eroded by the waves over millions of years. This is excellent walking country, on either the beach or cliff-top. The Cleveland Way and the trackbed of the old Whitby–Scarborough railway, open to walkers and cyclists, are near by. Ravenscar is also the finish to the 42-mile (68km) hike across the moors from Osmotherley known as the Lyke Wake Walk.

You can see Ravenscar's street layout today, though grass is growing where the buildings ought to have been. When the Raven Hall Hotel was built in 1774, it was simply Raven Hall. The hotel was to have been the centrepiece of the resort; now it stands alone, its mock battlements a landmark for miles around.

The Romans built a signal station here; its foundations and an inscribed stone (on display in Whitby's Pannett Park Museum) were found when Raven Hall's own foundations were being laid. The signal station relayed warnings of Anglo-Saxon invaders to military bases.

This part of the coastline (in the care of the National Trust, visit their Coastal Centre in Ravenscar) was exploited in the 17th century for alum, used in dyeing to fix colours permanently. Remains of the quarries and buildings can be found near Ravenscar.

ROBIN HOOD'S BAY
MAP REF NZ9505

Robin Hood's Bay vies with Staithes for the title of the prettiest fishing village on Yorkshire's coastline. Both communities have to juggle the conflicting demands of tourism with the needs of local people. To visit Robin Hood's Bay be sure to leave your car at the top of the hill, where there are two large car parks. The road down to the beach is a cul-de-sac and visitors' cars are barred.

Apart from the access road, the houses – which cling precariously to the side of the cliff – are reached by narrow alleyways and steps. The result is a jumble of whitewashed cottages and red-tiled roofs leading down the main street and almost into the sea. An old story tells of a ship which at high tide came so close to shore that its bowsprit knocked out the window of a pub!

There is no harbour. Where once there were more than a hundred fishing boats, there are now just a handful, and they are launched down a slipway. Many of the old fishermen's cottages are now holiday homes. There is a good stretch of sandy beach and a rocky foreshore; children love to investigate the little rock pools left in these scars by the receding tide. Take care; it is easy to get cut off by the tide when it starts coming in again.

Robin Hood's Bay has had its share of storms, their effects exacerbated by the softness of the rock that forms the cliffs. A sea wall helps to blunt the worst of the buffeting, though every winter still brings memorable storms.

The only community of any size between Whitby and Scarborough, the relative isolation of Robin Hood's Bay helped to make it a haunt of smugglers. It used to be said that a boat-load of contraband could be beached, and the load transferred to the top of the village through a maze of secret passages between the tightly packed houses, all without seeing the light of day.

You can walk at low tide along the beach (keep an eye out for the incoming tide) to Ravenscar, high on its cliff-top to the south, or along a fascinating section of the Cleveland Way. On your way, about a mile (1.6km) from Robin Hood's Bay, is Boggle Hole, a little wooded cove. An old water mill, once powered by Mill Beck, is now a youth hostel conveniently situated for Cleveland Wayfarers.

ROBIN HOOD'S BAY

Cleveland Way and Robin Hood's Bay

A walk through fields and along the coastal Cleveland Way from Robin Hood's Bay and back. On the coastal path you will notice how the sea is encroaching on the land: the loss here is said to be 6 inches (15cm) every two years.

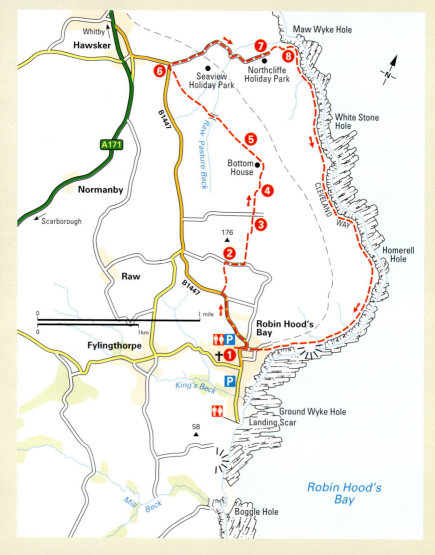

WALK 8

Route Directions

1 From the car park, return via the entry road to the main road. Turn left up the hill out of the village. Just after the road bends round to the left, take a signed footpath to the right over a stile. Walk up the fields over three stiles to a metalled lane.

2 Turn right. Go left through a signed metal gate. At the end of the field the path bends right to a waymarked gate in the hedge on your left. Continue down the next field with a stone wall on your left. Again, go right at the end of the field and over a stile into a green lane.

3 Cross to a waymarked stile and continue along the field-edge with a wall on your right. At the field end, cross over a stile on your right, then make for a waymarked gate diagonally left.

4 Walk towards the farm, pass through a gate and take the waymarked track through the farmyard. Continue with a stone wall on your right, go through another gate and on to a track that eventually bends left to reach a waymarked stile.

5 Continue to another stile before a footbridge over a beck. Cross the bridge, then bear right across the hedge line, following the waymarker, then diagonally right towards the next waymarker and a signpost for Hawsker. Cross the stream and bear right. As the hedge to your right curves left, go through a gap on the right and over a signed stile, walking straight ahead through the field to another stile on to the main road.

6 Go right and right again, following the footpath sign, up the metalled lane towards the holiday parks. Pass Seaview Holiday Park, cross the former railway track and continue along the metalled lane, which bends right, goes downhill, crosses a stream and ascends to Northcliffe Holiday Park.

7 Follow the Robin Hood's Bay sign right, and follow the metalled road, bending left beside a gate and down through the caravans. Just beyond them, leave the track to bear left to a waymarked path. Follow the path towards the coastline, and continue to a signpost.

8 Turn right along the Cleveland Way for 2.5 miles (4km). The footpath goes through a kissing gate and over three stiles, then through two more kissing gates. It passes through the Rocket Post Field by two more gates. Continue to follow the path as it goes past houses and ahead along a road to reach the main road. The car park is directly opposite.

Route facts

DISTANCE/TIME
5.5 miles (8.8km) 2h30

MAP OS Explorer OL27 North York Moors – Eastern

START There are two main car parks, both off to the right of the B road in the upper part of the village. The lower streets are access only. Car park at top of hill by the old railway station, Robin Hood's Bay, grid ref: NZ 950055

TRACKS Field and coastal paths, a little road walking, 12 stiles

GETTING TO THE START The old smugglers' village at Robin Hood's Bay huddles in a coastal hollow at the end of the B1447. It can be accessed from High Hawsker on the A171 Whitby to Scarborough road.

THE PUB The Victoria Hotel, Station Road, Robin Hood's Bay. Tel: 01947 880205; www.victoriarhb.com

❶ Take care on the road at the beginning of the walk. Keep well away from the friable cliff edges.

EASTERN MOORS & COAST

Through Scarborough's Raincliffe Woods

Just outside Scarborough, a walk through woodland to the rare remains of a glacial lake. The steep hillside of Raincliffe Woods overlooks a deep valley carved out in the ice ages. Although mostly replanted in the 1950s and 60s, the woods in places retain remnants of ancient oak and heather woodland – look out for the heather and bilberry bushes beneath oak trees that will show you where. Throughout the walk you will come upon humps and banks, depressions and pits that show that this hillside has been a hive of human activity in the past. As the path approaches Throxenby Mere it crosses part of a Bronze Age dyke system, while elsewhere are medieval banks and the remains of pits for charcoal burning.

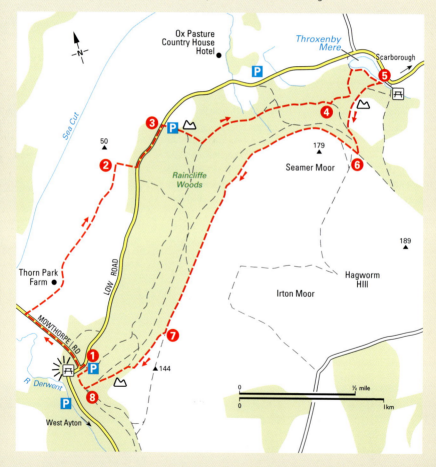

WALK 9

Route Directions

1 From the car park, turn left on the road, then right at the junction. Go downhill, and after the woodland ends, pass houses on the right. Opposite a bungalow, No 5, turn right down a track to Thorn Park Farm. Follow the track as it bends left by the farm buildings, then right past a cottage to a metal gate. Continue to follow the track, which bends left then right, then through two gateways.

2 Just before the next gateway, turn right and walk up the field side to go through a gateway, which takes you on a short path to the road. Turn left, follow the road and continue ahead to the next car park on the right.

3 Go up through the car park, bearing left towards a signboard, then go uphill on the path ahead. Where the main path bends right, go straight ahead, more steeply, to reach a crossing, grassy track. Turn left and follow the path. Where it forks, take the right-hand path.

4 After 500yds (457m) look out for a faint path on the left, which immediately bends right over a drainage runnel. The path goes down into a small valley. Turn left, downhill, then follow the now-obvious path as it bends right again, past an old quarry. The path descends to reach Throxenby Mere. Turn right along the edge of the Mere – this part of the path is on boardwalks.

5 Just before you reach a picnic place, go through a gate and immediately turn right. Follow the path which goes up steeply, ignoring all joining paths until it reaches a track at the top of the hill.

6 Turn right and go beside a metal gate, then follow the path for a mile (1.6km), parallel with first a fence and then a wall. It passes through a gateway with a stile by it and eventually reaches a gate with a public bridleway sign.

7 Do not go through this gate out into fields, but turn right and continue beside the wire fence on the edge of the woodland. Where the main path swings left and another goes right, go straight ahead, steeply downhill. When the path joins another go left, down steps and along a boardwalk to meet a crossing path.

8 Turn right and follow the path, which soon descends to the car park at the start of the walk.

Route facts

DISTANCE/TIME
5 miles (8km) 2h

MAP OS Explorer OL27 North York Moors – Eastern

START Hazelhead picnic site on Mowthorpe Road, near road junction, grid ref: SE 984875

TRACKS Field tracks, woodland paths, some steep, 2 stiles

GETTING TO THE START
West Ayton is on the A170 around 3 miles (5km) west of Scarborough. Hazelhead picnic site on Mowthorpe Road, near road junction. Car park on Low Road

THE PUB Ox Pasture Hall Country Hotel, Throxenby. Tel: 01723 365295

EASTERN MOORS & COAST

Early warnings at Fylingdales and Lilla Cross

The past and the future come together on this walk on the North Yorkshire coast. Unlike in most of upland Britain, the most important roads and tracks in the North York Moors follow the ridges between the valleys. The tracks are often marked by standing stones or crosses, many of them of great antiquity. The most impressive and most ancient of the Moor's crosses is Lilla, which commemorates a selfless deed of bravery in AD 626, when Lilla died protecting King Edward of Northumbria from assassination. Dominating the middle section of the walk is the improbably large sandcastle that houses the Fylingdales early warning system. It's heavily fenced and there are forbidding notices, but from a distance it's impressive.

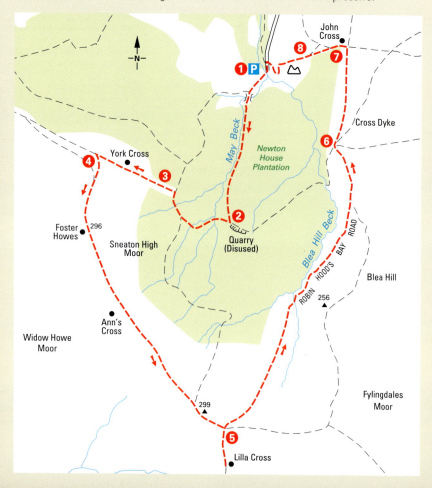

WALK 10

Route Directions

1 Walk up the wide track opposite the approach road. Where the track bends round to the right, go left down a signed footpath and descend to go over a bridge and bear right to continue along the green track. Go through a kissing gate and up the valley, eventually swinging away from the stream and into the forest.

2 On reaching a forest road turn right, passing a flooded quarry on your right. At the next junction of forest roads bear right. After about 0.25 mile (400m), turn up a track to the left.

3 Go up the track, leaving forest for moorland. Continue past the base and shaft of York Cross. At a track going left, near a waymarked post, turn sharp left.

4 Walk along the track, bearing left at the Foster Howes tumuli, and continue with the fence on your right. Pass Ann's Cross to your right and 0.5 mile (800m) beyond you'll reach a T-junction. Turn right through a gate and take the track to the left.

5 When you reach a crossroads with a signpost, turn right along the track to visit Lilla Cross. Return to the crossroads, and go straight ahead, following the Robin Hood's Bay sign. Follow the path, which goes parallel with the forest edge, for 2.5 miles (4km), eventually heading for a lone tree to the right of the wood's end.

6 Bear right when you reach a post with the number 9 on it. Pass posts 8 and 7, going left when you reach a trail sign.

7 Pass post 6, (by the remains of John Cross) and go through a gate, to continue walking downhill on a track. After 50yds (46m), go left off the track and walk parallel with the woodland to a waymarked stile near the ruins of a building.

8 Go to the left of the building and ahead to another stile. Follow the obvious footpath downhill through the bracken, passing two public footpath signs, down to the road. Turn left to return to the start.

Route facts

DISTANCE/TIME
6.75 miles (10.9km) 3h

MAP OS Explorer OL27 North York Moors – Eastern

START May Beck car park, beside stream, grid ref: SX 106836

TRACKS Forest tracks and moorland paths, 3 stiles

GETTING TO THE START From Whitby take the A171 south, passing the turn off to Robin Hood's Bay. Turn right at the junction with the B1416. Take the 1st left, a minor road, to May Beck car park.

THE PUB The Birch Hall Inn, Beck Hole, Goathland. Tel: 01947 896245

EASTERN MOORS & COAST

SCARBOROUGH MAP REF TA0488

The resort of Scarborough can claim to be one of the oldest in the country. Its prosperity can be traced back to the occasion in the year 1620, when a visitor, Mrs Elizabeth Farrow, was drinking a glass of spring water. Finding the water acidic in taste, she came to the natural conclusion that something that tasted so unpleasant must surely have medicinal qualities too.

Promises of miraculous cures have always had willing ears, the more outlandish the better. Scarborough's spring water was said to cure many ills, even hypochondria: surely a rather self-defeating exercise, since hypochondriacs were precisely the sort of people to whom the town extended the warmest welcome. Scarborough's spring water certainly contains Epsom salts and a cocktail of minerals. It was definitely good for one thing – giving the town's economy a much-needed shot in the arm. The taking of the waters was soon put on a more commercial footing. Scarborough became known as a spa town; a name borrowed from the Belgian resort. Scarborough was put firmly on the map as a place where the well-heeled might come to recuperate at leisure. Emboldened by this success, a local doctor started to extol the health-giving properties of sea bathing. One way or another Scarborough's waters were responsible for its success.

The first spa house was built over the original spa well in 1700. However, it was to suffer the fate shared by many other Scarborough buildings, by falling into the sea. Ever more elaborate spa houses were built, each one getting the royal stamp of approval for the water's efficacy. By the time Queen Victoria ascended to the throne, Scarborough was arguably the North's finest resort; many of the town's most distinguished buildings date from Victoria's reign. The Grand Hotel, overlooking the South Bay, seems to sum up the prosperity of Scarborough during the busiest time in its long history.

Scarborough Castle has dominated the town with an air of fortress-like impregnability for the best part of a millennium. Standing proudly on its headland, between the North and South Bays, it enjoys an uninterrupted view over the town and out to sea. Remains of even earlier defences have been unearthed, including an Iron Age settlement and a Roman signal station.

The Norman edifice we see today can be dated to the year 1136, when William de Gros decided to rebuild in stone an earlier wooden fort. Henry II, concerned that many of his noblemen were growing too powerful, set about destroying their castles. He spared Scarborough Castle, however. Impressed by its air of impregnability, he requisitioned the castle and kept it for himself.

Besieged on a number of occasions, Scarborough Castle was never taken by force, but attacking forces managed to starve the defenders into surrendering. On one occasion, in 1645, Hugh Chomley's Royalist troops were besieged by John Meldrum's Scottish army and the Great Keep was badly damaged by the Scottish artillery. Unable to hold out any longer, they were allowed to

surrender with honour intact; those men who could still stand were allowed to march out of the castle. The castle was heavily besieged again in 1648 when the Parliamentary garrison, discontented because they had not been paid, went over to the King's side; they too were starved into submission.

St Mary's Church also suffered artillery damage, which is still visible, at the hands of the Royalists defending the castle. Anne Brontë was visiting Scarborough in 1849 when she succumbed to tuberculosis and died. The author of *The Tenant of Wildfell Hall* is buried in the churchyard.

While many of British resorts have lost out to the ease of foreign travel, Scarborough has enough attractions to keep the most fastidious visitors coming back for more. Cricket lovers eagerly anticipate the Scarborough Festival, traditionally held towards the end of the season. Playwright Sir Alan Ayckbourn keeps faith with local theatregoers by premiering most of his plays here in his Stephen Joseph Theatre before they are transferred to London's West End. The miniature North Bay Railway runs for just under a mile (1.6km) between Peasholme Park and the Sealife Centre at Scalby Mills where you can see a colourful Caribbean-style coral reef, hundreds of fish, turtles and sharks.

SLEIGHTS   MAP REF NZ8607

Sleights straddles the River Esk in a sheltered dip in the landscape, just outside the boundary of the National Park. There are few buildings here to attract the eye, but it is a convenient spot from which to explore the surrounding countryside – whether you head for open moorland, or the more intimate environs of the Esk.

Ruswarp, inside the National Park, between Sleights and the sea, marks the tidal limit of the River Esk. Here, on a quiet stretch of the river, you can hire a dinghy for a leisurely row.

A minor road from Sleights leads to a hamlet that glories in the name of Ugglebarnby. The meaning is 'the farm of old owl beard'; the explanation is less easy to fathom. Continue past Ugglebarnby to arrive in Littlebeck, on a road that snakes through this delightful village. Here you can enjoy fine walks, one along May Beck and the other to the south to see Falling Foss, an exquisite waterfall in a woodland setting.

■ Insight

AN IMPREGNABLE FORTRESS

Scarborough Castle has never been taken by force. When the castle was besieged by the Roundheads in 1645 a deep well provided a good supply of fresh water for the Royalist inhabitants. However, the beleaguered soldiers inside the castle eventually ran out of food, and were reduced to eating rats and deriving what little sustenance was available by boiling up their leather belts and boots.

■ Insight

A MIRACULOUS CURE

Elaborate claims were made for the many ailments which Scarborough's spring waters might cure. Once stomach ache, consumption, rheumatism and fever had been taken care of, the waters would sort out palsy, madness and leprosy.

SCARBOROUGH – THORNTON-LE-DALE

THORNTON-LE-DALE
MAP REF SE8383

Despite being split in two by the busy A170, Thornton-le-Dale is still said to be one of the prettiest villages in Yorkshire. The thatched cottage beside Dalby Beck must be one of the most photographed buildings in the county, making regular appearances on calendars and biscuit tin lids. The boundary of the National Park makes a little detour to include the village – a good indication that it is worth making a stop here. Try to time your visit outside the busier holiday periods, for Thornton-le-Dale is best explored when the crowds are gone.

The tone is established by the beck; its meandering course through the village is punctuated by a succession of tiny bridges. At the crossroads, in the centre of the village, is a small green where the slender, stepped market cross and a set of wooden stocks still stand. On the opposite side of the road are Lady Lumley's Almshouses, a block of 12 dwellings, built in 1670 and still retaining their original use.

The churchyard is the burial place of Matthew Grimes, who died in 1875 at the grand old age of 96. His claim to fame is that he guarded Napoleon during the emperor's exile on the island of St Helena, and helped to carry his body to the grave. Thornton-le-Dale's churchyard is also the last resting place of Sir Richard Chomley, known as The Great Black Knight of the North. He served at the court of Elizabeth I; his home, Roxby Castle, once stood just to the west of Thornton-le-Dale. His effigy can be seen inside the church.

■ Insight
'FLINT JACK'
Sleights was the birthplace, in 1815, of 'Flint Jack', who delighted in fooling those experts who came to the moors in search of antiquities. He established a lucrative sideline by manufacturing his own relics, and offering them to collectors and museums as genuine archaeological finds. His fakes and forgeries were so convincing that even the British Museum was fooled into parting with money.

■ Insight
SUPERSTITIONS
Superstitions were rife in rural areas. Charms considered to be lucky included a horseshoe (or stone with a natural hole in it), hung from the door of the house. Picking up a pin, or other piece of metal, would prevent a witch from using it in her spells. The rowan tree was also known as witchwood; carrying a crucifix made of rowan wood was a common way to guard against the 'evil eye'. Of course, those who scoff at such unsophistication should examine their own habits: crossing the fingers, playing 'lucky' lottery numbers…

In Ellerburn, just to the north, is the tiny Church of St Hilda, where you'll find many examples of Viking stone work, including several cross heads and a serpent sculpture.

To explore further afield take the Forest Drive (toll payable) through Dalby Forest, which is easily accessible by driving north from Thornton-le-Dale, where there are numerous walking trails, mountain-bike routes, fishing areas and picnic places, a useful visitor centre and shop.

Dalby Forest

This is a short ride through the forest to seek the wildlife – if you stay quiet and look hard enough, you'll see it in abundance. In quieter corners you may stumble upon the Bambi-like roe deer, but it's bird life you're more likely to spot. Besides the common blue tits, you're quite likely to see a wading heron, or a tiny warbler such as that summer visitor, the chiffchaff, so called because of its birdsong.

Route Directions

1 The green cycle route begins beyond the trees at the southeast end of the large Adderstone Field (the furthest from the visitor centre). Here you turn left along a narrow slightly downhill track. Though still easy, it's the most difficult section of the route – use gentle braking if you're a little unsure. Ignore the two lesser, unsigned left fork tracks.

2 Turn right along a much wider forestry track which takes a winding course round the afforested valley of Worry Gill. Where the more demanding red route goes off on a rough track to the right, your green route goes straight on, still using a well-graded track.

3 Where a track doubles back, go straight on up a

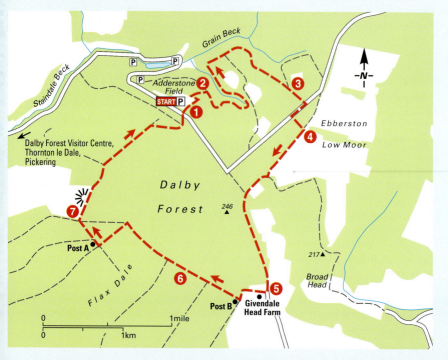

CYCLE RIDE 2

steady hill before meeting up with the forest drive again. Cross this with care – it can be quite busy on summer weekends – before turning right along it for 200yds (183m). Turn left along a narrow path signed with red and green waymarkers and just before a 30 mile per hour speed limit sign (hope you were not speeding!). If you're early and it's summer, you may be able to dally and eat some of the bilberries that grow beside the path.

4 The path reaches a flinted road at the southeast edge of the forest. Turn right along this, then turn left at the next junction. Looking to your left, you'll see the rougher high pastures of Ebberston Low Moor decline to the greener, more fertile fields of the Vale of Pickering.

5 Turn right just before reaching Givendale Head Farm along a rutted farm track with a grassy island in the middle. Turn right at the next junction (Post B) on a downhill section, followed by an uphill one where you're joined by a farm track coming in from the left.

6 A long hill follows to a wide junction where you go straight on along a tarred lane. A sign tells you that you're now at the head of Flax Dale. Stay with the tarred lane at the next bend and junction. Turn right at the crossroads along a long sandy track (Post A), then turn right again at the next junction. Note the linear earthwork to both left and right – nobody seems to know the exact origins of these.

7 After going straight on at the next junction past a fine stand of Scots pines, you get fine views over the farm pastures of High Rigg to reach Levisham Moor. Here, there's another downhill section followed by an uphill one. Take a right fork at Newclose Rigg. Where the red route goes straight on, your green route veers right along the main track. There's a downhill left curve beyond which you take the upper right fork, which brings the route back to the forest drive opposite Adderstone Field.

Route facts

DISTANCE/TIME 6 miles (9.7km) 2h

MAP OS Explorer OL27 North York Moors Eastern

START Car park at Adderstone Field, Dalby Forest, grid ref: SE 883897

TRACKS Forestry roads and a few narrow paths, mostly well graded

GETTING TO THE START From the A170 at Thornton le Dale head north on a minor road signed the Dalby Forest, then turn off right on the Dalby Forest Drive, where you'll come to the tollbooths. Adderstone Field, the start of the ride, lies about 5 miles (8km) beyond the visitor centre.

CYCLE HIRE Cycle Hire Kiosk next to Visitor Centre, Low Dalby. Tel: 01751 460400

THE PUB New Inn, Maltongate, Thornton le Dale. Tel: 01751 474226.

❶ There's a short, rough and slightly downhill section of track at the start. The forest drive road needs to be crossed with care twice.

EASTERN MOORS & COAST

From Ravenscar to Robin Hood's Bay

The former railway line between Whitby and Scarborough can now be followed, in its entirety, on two wheels. The full distance is 20 miles (32.2km) one way, so this ride picks out probably the finest section, looping around Robin Hood's Bay. It is a little confusing that the name of the bay and the much-photographed village are exactly the same, but the ride gives great views of the former and a chance to visit the latter.

Route Directions

1 Descend the road until it bends sharply right. Turn left, past the National Trust Coastal Centre, and continue on an obvious descending concrete track. A rougher section needs more care, but lasts for less than 100yds (91m). Now swing left and go through a gate on to the old railway trackbed and a much easier surface.

2 The track now runs below the scarred face of the alum workings, with some ups and downs that clearly don't match the original rail contours exactly. After this section, take care crossing a steep concrete track that runs down to a farm.

3 Pass under an arched bridge. Note more quarried cliffs up on the left, while

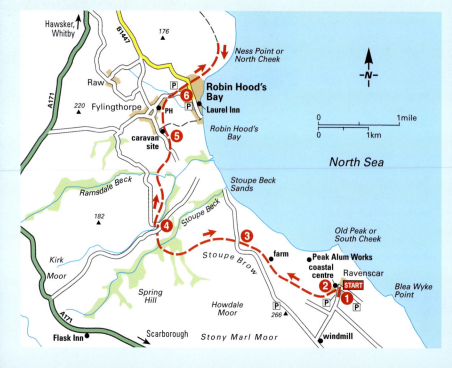

CYCLE RIDE 3

looking down to the right – if the tide is not too high – there are extensive rocky platforms in the bay, with conspicuous parallel strata. There's a short cutting and the sea views are hidden by tall gorse and broom, then it becomes more open again as the track swings gradually inland. A tall embankment crosses a steep wooded valley. Go under a bridge and then make a sharp left turn on to a lane.

4 Go up 20yds (18m), then sharp right to continue on the track. Keep right at a fork and the track resumes its steady gentle descent, then starts to turn uphill for the first time on the ride. As you come out into the open after a tunnel of trees, the direct way ahead is again blocked (unless you're Evel Knievel!). Here slant down left, cross a lane, and then climb back up on to the continuing trackbed.

5 Pass a cricket ground, the back of a caravan site, then a farm. Cross the rough farm track and keep straight on ahead, through a gate where the surface changes to tarmac, on the outskirts of Robin Hood's Bay. Go through another gate and drop down to a road. Turn right down this road for 100yds (91m) then go left on a lane signposted to Station Workshops. At the top of the rise is the old station building and just beyond it a large car park. (It is, of course, possible to descend the road all the way into the village of Robin Hood's Bay, but it's a very steep climb back. An alternative is to lock the bikes at the car park and go down on foot.)

6 Continue alongside the car park, drop down to a road, turn left and almost instantly right (very nearly straight across) on to Mount Pleasant. Follow this to its end then bear left up a short gravelled ride to regain the railway path. Continue for about 0.5 mile (800m). There are good views back now over Robin Hood's Bay to the cliffs near Ravenscar. Look for a National Trust sign for Ness Bay. There is open access on foot so you could leave your bikes and walk down to the headland, a great picnic spot. This makes as good a turn-round point as any, though the track continues into Hawsker and on to Whitby.

Route facts

DISTANCE/TIME 11.25 miles (18.1km) 2h

MAP OS Explorer OL27 North York Moors – Eastern

START Roadside parking on way into Ravenscar, grid ref: NZ 980015

TRACKS Almost entirely on well-surfaced old railway track; short street sections at Ravenscar and Robin Hood's Bay

GETTING TO THE START Turn off the A171, midway between Whitby and Scarborough – signed for Ravenscar. Turn left at a T-junction, then right near an old windmill. The road descends into Ravenscar and there is extensive roadside parking as the descent gets steeper.

THE PUB The Laurel Inn, Robin Hood's Bay. Tel: 01947 880400

● Busy roads and car park in Robin Hood's Bay village (possible to turn round before this).

ROBIN HOOD'S BAY

EASTERN MOORS & COAST

■ TOURIST INFORMATION CENTRES

Pickering
The Ropery.
Tel: 01751 473791

Scarborough
Brunswick Shopping Centre, Westborough.
Tel: 01723 383636
Harbourside, Sandside.
Tel: 01723 341000 (seasonal)

■ PLACES OF INTEREST

Beck Isle Museum
Bridge Street, Pickering.
Tel: 01751 473653;
www.beckislemuseum.co.uk

Crescent Arts Workshop
The Crescent, Scarborough.
Tel: 01723 351461;
www.crescentarts.co.uk
Free.

National Trust Centre
Ravenscar.
Tel: 01723 870423;
www.nationaltrust.org.uk

North Yorkshire Moors Railway
Pickering Station, Pickering. Tel: 01751 472508;
www.nymr.co.uk

The Old Coastguard Station Visitor Centre
Robin Hood's Bay.
Tel: 01947 885900

Pickering Castle
Tel: 01751 474989; www.english-heritage.org.uk

Robin Hood's Bay Museum
Fisherhead.

The Rotunda Museum
Vernon Road, Scarborough.
Tel: 01723 353665:
www.rotundamuseum.org.uk

Scarborough Art Gallery
The Crescent.
Tel: 01723 374753; www.scarboroughartgallery.co.uk

Scarborough Castle
Tel: 01723 372451; www.english-heritage.org.uk

Sea Life & Marine Sanctuary
Scalby Mills, Scarborough.
Tel: 0871 423 2110;
www.sealifeeurope.com

Staintondale Shire Horse Farm
Staintondale.
Tel: 01723 870458;
www.shirehorsefarm.co.uk

Woodend Creative Workspace
The Crescent, Scarborough.
Tel: 01723 367326; www.woodendcreative.co.uk

■ FOR CHILDREN

Staintondale Shire Horse Farm
Staintondale.
Tel: 01723 870458;
www.shirehorsefarm.co.uk

■ SHOPPING

MARKET
Open-air market, Pickering, Mon.

LOCAL SPECIALITIES
Ceramics
Green Man Gallery,
8 Park Street, Pickering.
Tel: 01751 472361

Honey
The Honey Farm, East Ayton.
Tel: 01723 865198

Ice-Cream
Beacon Farm, Beacon Way, Sneaton.
Tel: 01947 605212;
www.beacon-farm.co.uk

Trout
Moorland Trout Farm, Pickering.
Tel: 01751 473101

■ PERFORMING ARTS

Futurist Theatre and Cinema
Foreshore Road, Scarborough.
Tel: 01723 365789;
www.futuristtheatre.co.uk

Spa Entertainment Complex
South Bay, Scarborough.
Tel: 01723 376774;
www.scarboroughspa.co.uk

Spa Theatre
South Bay, Scarborough.
Tel: 01723 357869

Stephen Joseph Theatre
Westborough, Scarborough.
Tel: 01723 370541;
www.sjt.uk.com

■ SPORTS & ACTIVITIES

ANGLING
Sea
Boats for hire at the harbour in South Bay, Scarborough.

Fly
Pickering Trout Lake.
Tel: 01751 474219; www.

INFORMATION 149

pickeringtroutlake.co.uk
The Mere, Scarborough.
Day tickets on site.
Tel: 01723 507588
Wykeham Trout Lakes
(coarse and trout).
Tel: 01723 863148;
www.dawnay.co.uk

BEACHES
There are sandy beaches with easy access at Robin Hood's Bay and Scarborough (North Bay and South Bay).

CRICKET
Scarborough
North Marine Road,
Tel: 01723 365625; www.scarboroughcricket.co.uk

GOLF COURSES
Kirkbymoorside
Kirkbymoorside Golf Club,
Manor Vale.
Tel: 01751 431525
Scarborough
North Cliff Golf Club,
North Cliff Avenue.
Tel: 01723 360786;
www.ncgc.co.uk
South Cliff Golf Club,
Deepdale Avenue.
Tel: 01723 365150;
www.southcliffgolfclub.com

CYCLE HIRE
Dalby
Purple Mountain Bike Hire,
The Courtyard, Low Dalby.
Tel 01751 460011;
www.purplemountain.co.uk

HORSE-RIDING
Robin Hood's Bay
Farsyde Stud and Riding Centre. Tel: 01947 880249; www.farsydefarmcottages.co.uk
Snainton
Snainton Riding Centre.
Tel: 01723 859218; www.snaintonridingcentre.co.uk
Staintondale
Pony Trekking Centre.
Tel: 01723 871846

LONG-DISTANCE ROUTES
Moor to Sea
80-mile (129km) cycle route linking Pickering, Scarborough and Whitby. www.moortoseacycle.net
The Rail Trail
A 3.5-mile (5.6km) walk from Goathland to Grosmont following the track bed of George Stephenson's original railway line.
Scarborough to Whitby Railway Trail
Route for walkers and cyclists follows the old railway line. (Cycle hire at Hawsker.) Tel: 01947 820207; www.trailways.info

FORESTS
Dalby Forest Drive. Free for pedestrians, cyclists and Moorsbus passengers. Dalby Forest Visitor Centre and shop. Tel: 01751 472771

■ ANNUAL EVENTS & CUSTOMS
Littlebeck
Littlebeck Rose Queen Ceremony, Aug.
Pickering
Jazz Festival, Jul.
Traction Engine Rally, Aug.
Robin Hood's Bay
Folk Festival, Jun.
Scalby
Scalby Fair, early Jun.
Scarborough
Scarborough Fayre, Jun/Jul.
International Music Festival, Jun/Jul.
Scarborough Cricket Festival, end Aug/Sep.
Thornton-le-Dale
Thornton-le-Dale Show, Aug.

TEA ROOMS & PUBS

Tea Rooms

The Mallyan Spout Hotel
The Common, Goathland
YO22 5AN. Tel. 01947 896486;
www.mallyanspout.co.uk
You can relive the highlights of television's *Heartbeat* while you have afternoon tea at the Mallyan Spout. Choose from scones, delicious cakes and sandwiches, or a more substantial meal from the selection that's served all day. Relax in the lounge or enjoy the garden and patio.

Ravenscar Tea Rooms
1 Station Square, Ravenscar
YO13 0LU. Tel: 01723 870444
With 12 sorts of tea and six coffees, the Foxcliffe offers a wide choice. Based in one of the few buildings – part of the station – that were erected in what was planned to be a coastal resort to rival Scarborough, the café offers home-baked cakes and hot food – and spectacular cliff-top and sea views.

The Old Bakery Tea Rooms
Chapel Street,
Robin Hood's Bay YO22 4SQ
Tel: 01947 880709
A lovely, traditional tea room, situated in the heart of the village, that serves hot food all day. The bread and cakes are produced in the attached bakery. Scones with home-made preserves are a favourite, along with the chocolate and coffee cakes. There's an enclosed balcony overlooking the stream – a good place to rest and watch the world go by.

Warrington House
Whitbygate, Thornton-le-Dale
YO18 7RY. Tel: 01751 475028;
www.warringtonhouse.co.uk
Just a few yards from the bustling centre of Thornton-le-Dale, this tea room is the place to enjoy afternoon tea with a selection of home-made cakes and scones, or ploughman's lunch. There's a delicious array of puddings on offer, too,

Pubs

Birch Hall Inn
Beckhole, Goathland
YO22 5LE
Tel: 01947 896245
The Birch Hall is a bit off the beaten track, though near the North Yorkshire Moors Railway line. But it's worth persevering to find it, as it's a real gem. There's nothing flashy about it, but if you like real local ales properly kept and served, wholesome food like tasty pies, substantial sandwiches and their own delicious beer cake, this is the place to come.

Moorcock Inn
Langdale End Scarborough.
YO13 0BN. Tel: 01723 882268
This remote Moors pub has a tiled floor and a rather odd assortment of benches in two small rooms. However, you're guaranteed a decent drink, with a changing selection of beer from local regional and micro-breweries. Home-cooked food is always available, and you can sit outside in good weather.

Laurel Inn
New Road, Robin Hood's Bay
YO22 4SE
Tel: 01947 880400
Near to the bottom of the winding main street, this pub has a cosy, traditional atmosphere, with an open fire. It offers real ales.

The New Inn
Moorgate, Thornton-le-Dale
YO28 7LF
Tel: 01751 474226;
www.the-new-inn.com
This fine Georgian building at the heart of the village retains its traditional atmosphere, with log fires and hand-pulled beer. There is a flower-filled patio on which to enjoy a drink on a warm day, while the restaurant offers a wide range of meals using fresh, locally sourced ingredients.

BOULBY CLIFFS

USEFUL INFORMATION

■ NORTH YORK MOORS NATIONAL PARK INFORMATION POINTS

North York Moors National Park
The Old Vicarage, Bondgate, Helmsley. Tel: 01439 770657; www.northyorkmoors.org.uk

The Moors National Park Centre
Lodge Lane, Danby.
Tel: 01439 772737

Sutton Bank National Park Centre
Sutton Bank, Thirsk.
Tel: 01845 597426

Useful Websites
www.north-york-moors.com;
www.visityorkshire.co.uk;
www.yorkshire.com

■ OTHER INFORMATION

Angling
Numerous opportunities for fishing on farms, lakes and rivers. Permits and licences are available from local tackle shops and TICs.

Coastguard
Dial 999 and ask for the Coastguard Service, which co-ordinates rescue services.

English Heritage (Yorkshire)
37 Tanner Row, York.
Tel: 01904 601901;
www.english-heritage.org.uk

Environment Agency
Yorkshire and Humber Office, Phoenix House, Global Avenue, Millshaw, Beeston Ring Road, Leeds.
Tel: 08708 506506; www.environment-agency.gov.uk

Forest Enterprise
Outgang Road, Pickering.
Tel: 01751 472771

Health
Information on health problems is available from NHS Direct. Tel: 0845 4647; www.nhsdirect.nhs.uk
Dental Helpline
Tel: 0845 063 1188

Moorsbus Summer Coach and Minibus
Tel 01439 770657;
www.moorsbus.net

The National Trust (Yorkshire)
Goddards,
27 Tadcaster Road, York.
Tel: 01904 702021;
www.nationaltrust.org.uk

Parking
Information on parking permits and car parks in the area is available from local TICs.

Places of Interest
There will be an admission charge unless otherwise stated. We give details of just some of the facilities within the area covered by this guide. Further information can be obtained from local TICs or the web.

Yorkshire Tourist Board
Wecome to Yorkshire, Dry Sand Foundry, Foundry Square, Holbeck, Leeds.
Tel: 0113 322 3500;
www.yorkshire.com

Yorkshire Wildlife Trust
10 Toft Green, York.
Tel: 01904 659570;
www.yorkshire-wildlife-trust.org.uk

■ ORDNANCE SURVEY MAPS

ESK DALE & NORTH
Explorer 1:25,000 Outdoor Leisure; sheets 26, 27
Landranger 1:50,000;
Sheets 93, 94

WESTERN MOORS
Explorer 1:25,000 Outdoor Leisure; sheet 26, 27
Landranger 1:50,000;
Sheets 93, 100

CENTRAL MOORS
Explorer 1:25,000 Outdoor Leisure; sheet 26
Landranger 1:50,000;
Sheets 93, 94,100

EASTERN MOORS & COAST
Explorer 1:25,000 Outdoor Leisure; sheet 27
Landranger 1:50,000;
Sheets 94, 100, 101

ATLAS LEGEND 155

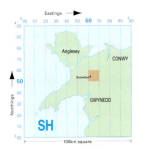

The National Grid system covers Great Britain with an imaginary network of grid squares. Each is 100km square in area and is given a unique alphabetic reference, as shown in the diagram above.

These squares are sub-divided into one hundred 10km squares, identified by vertical lines (eastings) and horizontal lines (northings). The reference for the square a feature is located within is made by adding the numbers of the two lines which cross in the bottom left corner of that square to the alphabetic reference (ignoring the small figures). The easting is quoted first. For example, SH6050.

For a 2-figure reference, the zeros are omitted, giving just SH65. In this book, we use 4-figure references, which allow us to pinpoint the feature more accurately by dividing the 10km square into one hundred 1km squares. These squares are not actually printed on the road atlas but are estimated by eye. The same process is carried out as before, giving an enhanced reference of SH6154.

Key to Atlas

M4	Motorway with number
S Fleet	Motorway service area
	Motorway toll
11	Motorway junction with and without number
3	Restricted motorway junctions
	Motorway and junction under construction
A3	Primary route single/dual carriageway
BATH	Primary route destinations
	Roundabout
5	Distance in miles between symbols
A1123	Other A Road single/dual carriageway
B2070	B road single/dual carriageway
	Unclassified road single/dual carriageway
	Road tunnel
Toll	Toll
	Road underconstruction
	Narrow Primary route with passing places
→	Steep gradient
—○—×—	Railway station and level crossing
	Tourist railway
- - - - -	National trail
....	Forest drive
	Heritage coast
	Ferry route
6	Walk start point
1	Cycle start point
3	Tour start point
	Abbey, cathedral or priory
	Aquarium
	Castle
	Cave
	Country park
	County cricket ground
	Farm or animal centre
	Garden
	Golf course
	Historic house
	Horse racing
	Motor racing
	Museum
	Airport
	Heliport
	Windmill
NT	National Trust property
NTS	National Trust for Scotland property
	Nature reserve
★	Other place of interest
P•R	Park and Ride location
	Picnic site
	Steam centre
	Ski slope natural
	Ski slope artifical
i	Tourist Information Centre
	Viewpoint
V	Visitor or heritage centre
	Zoological or wildlife collection
	Forest Park
	National Park (England & Wales)
	National Scenic Area (Scotland)

INDEX

The page numbers in bold refer to main entries.

A
Aelred, St 6, 62
Aidan, St 76
Albert, Prince Consort 46
Ampleforth **58**
Arden Hall 64
Atkinson, Canon John 24, 33
Ayckbourn, Sir Alan 140
Ayton Castle 125

B
Baysdale Beck 33
Beck Hole Incline 121, 127, 128
Beck Isle Museum, Pickering 129
Bede, Venerable 76, 99
Beggar's Bridge 27, 28
Bellasis, Anthony 64
Bilsdale **58–59**, 74
'Blackamore' 121
Bland, John Septimus 129
Boggle Hole 130
Boltby 56, 82–83
Boulby Cliffs 42
Boulby Potash Mine 42
Bransdale 6, **59–60**
Bransdale Mill 60
Bridestones 58
Brompton **120**
Brontë, Anne 140
Broxa 124
Bruce, Robert 29, 129
Bruno of Reims, St 71
Byland Abbey 6, 54, 64, 72–73, 74, 102

C
Caedmon 47
Carlton 59
Carroll, Lewis 41
Castleton 20, **24**
Cawthorn Camp 94–95
Cayley, Sir George 120
Cedd, St 62, 99
Central Moors 88–113

Chad, St 99
Challoner, Sir Thomas 29
Chimney Bank 93
Chomley, Hugh 138
Chomley, Sir Richard 141
Chop Gate 56, 58, 74
Civil War 68–69, 140
Cleveland Hills 6, 34–35, 36, 54, 63, 74, 79
Cleveland Way 33, 56, 62, **63**, 68, 71, 129, 130, 132–133
Cockayne 56
Colman, Bishop of Lindisfarne 24
Columba, St 76
Commondale 24
Cook, Captain James 6, 28, 33, 38–39, 41–42, 47
Coxwold 56, **63–64**, 74
Cropton Forest 90, **94–95**
crosses, stone 11, **60–62**, 94, 105–107
Crosses Walk 105
Crossland, Colonel Jordan 68
Crunkly Gill 33
cycling 17

D
Dalby Forest 141, 142–143
Danby 24–25
Danby Castle **25**
Danby Dale 24
Derwent, River 120, 124, 125
Devil's Punchbowl 119, 125
Dickens, Charles 41
Domesday Book 25
Dove, River 60, 95
Dracula 47
Duck Bridge 25
Duncombe, Sir Charles 68
Duncombe Park 69, 78

E
Easby Moor 33
East Ayton 125
Eastern Moors and Coast 114–151

Edward II, King 129
Edward the Confessor, King 98
Edwin, King of Northumbria 60, 107
Egton Bridge 10, **25–27**
Ellerburn 141
Esk, River 20, 24, 25, 27, 33, 43, 140
Esk Dale and the North 18–51
Esk Valley 10, 15, 25
Esk Valley Railway 24, 33
Esk Valley Walk 20

F
Fadmoor 60
Fairfax, Sir Thomas 68
Falling Foss 140
Farndale 6, 10, 60, **95**
Farrow, Elizabeth 138
Ferris, Tom 27
Feversham, Lord 68
Filey Brigg 63
'Flint Jack' 141
Forest Drive 141
Forge Valley 124–125
Fylingdales 136–137

G
Garthwaite, Kitty 95
Gillamoor 59, 60
Gilling East 58
Gisborough Priory 63
Glaisdale **27**, 28
Goathland 28, 33, 105, 119, **121**, 122–123, 127, 128
Goldsborough **30**
Gormire Lake 79
Gray, Charles Norris 69
Great Ayton 6, **27–28**, 33
Gregory, St 99
Grimes, Matthew 141
Gros, William de 138
Grosmont **28–29**, 33, 58, 128
Guisborough **29**

H
Hackness **124–125**
Hambleton Drove Road 71

INDEX

Hambleton Hills 54, 57, 58, 63, 74, 78, 79, 80–81
Hawnby **64**
Heartbeat 121
Helmsley 12, 54, 58, 62, 63, **68–69**, 74
Helmsley Castle 6, 56, 57, 68–69
Henry II, King 138
Henry VIII, King 25, 63, 64, 71, 78, 124
Heritage Coast 30, 116
Hilda, St 46–47, 62, 124
Hodgson, John 69, 79
Hole of Horcum 119, **125**
Holland, Thomas de 71
Hood Hill 57
Hovingham **96**
Howardian Hills 6, 58
Hutchinson, Mary 120
Hutton-le-Hole 6, 9, 33, 93, **96–98**, 100–101

I
'intakes' 24

J
jet, Whitby 46
Johnstone, Sir John Vanden Bampole 124

K
Kettleness **30**
Kilburn 56, **69–70**
Kilburn, White Horse of 54, 69, 79
Kildale **33**
Kirkbymoorside 59, 60, **98–99**
Kirkdale 62

L
Lastingham 6, 62, **99**, 100–101
Lealholm 27, **33**
l'Espec, Walter 68
Leven, River 27, 78
Levisham 94, **127**
Levisham Moor 125
Lilla Cross 107, 136–137
Limber Hill 27
Little Fryup Dale 25

Lockton **127**
Lyke Wake Walk 70, 71, 129

M
Mallyan Spout 121, 122–123
Malton 30
Mary, Queen of Scots 64
Mauley Cross 94
Meldrum, John 138
Middlesbrough 20, 27, 36
Missing Link 62
monks and monasteries 60–63
Moors Centre, Danby 25
Mosaic Trail 56
Mount Grace Priory 56, 63, 70–71
'Mouseman' (Robert Thompson) 58, 69–70, 96, 121
Mouseman Visitor Centre, Kilburn 56
Mulgrave Castle 41

N
Nab End Moor 58
Nevill, Father Paul 58
Newburgh Priory 64
Newgate Bank 58
Newtondale 94, 128
Newtondale Gorge 90
North Yorkshire Moors Railway 28–29, 90, 94, 119, 121, **127–128**
Nunnington **102**
Nunnington Hall 93, 102

O
Œdilburga, Abbess 124
Olstead Observatory 72–73
Osmotherley 64, **70–71**
Oswald, St 76
Oswaldkirk **76**
Oswy, King of Northumbria 46

P
Parr, Catherine 25
Paulinus 60
Percy family 33
Pickering 116, 127, **128–129**
Pickering-Whitby Railway 28–29

Postgate, Father Nicholas 25–27, 95
Postgate School, Great Ayton 28

R
Rail Trail 28, 128
Raincliffe Woods 134–135
Ralph Cross 11, 24, 105, 107
Ravenscar 70, 71, **129–130**, 144–145
Riccal Bank 58
Richard II, King 71
Rievaulx Abbey 6, 9, 54, 56, 57, 58, 62–63, 64, 68, 74, **76–78**, 124
Robert the Bruce 29, 129
Robin Hood's Bay 11, 116, 119, **130**, 132–133, 144–145
Roos, Robert de 57, 68
Roseberry Topping 23, 27, **36**, 38–39
Rosedale 6, 24, 93, **102–104**, 108–109
Rosedale Abbey 93, 104
Roxby Castle 141
Roulston Scar 57, 69, 79
Runswick Bay 30, **36**
Ruswarp 140
Rye, River 9, 59, 64, 102
Rye Valley 76, 78
Ryedale 62–63, 68
Ryedale Folk Museum 59, 93, 96–98

S
salt 124, 125
Saltburn 30, 63
Saltersgate Inn 125
Sandsend 23, **41**
Sarkless Kitty 95
Scalby Ness 30
Scarborough 6, 62, 63, 116, 119, 134–5, **138–140**
Scarborough Castle **138–140**
Scott, Sir Gilbert 68
Scott, Sir Giles Gilbert 58
Seph, River 59

ACKNOWLEDGEMENTS

Shandy Hall 56, 64
signposts, stone 105
Silpho 124
Sleights **140**
Staithes 6, 9, **41–42**, 130
standing stones **105–107**
Stephenson, George 28, 127
Stephenson, Tom 63
Sterne, Laurence 64
Stoker, Bram 47
Stokesley 20, 29, 58, **78–79**
stone circles 58
stone crosses 11, **60–62**, 94, 105–7
Strickland, William and Emmanuel 60
Sun Inn 59
superstitions 141
Sutcliffe, Frank Meadow 43
Sutton Bank 9, 56, 57, 74, **79**
Swainby 6, 66–67

T
Taylor, Thomas 79
Tees, River 124
Thirlby Bank 82–83
Thompson, Robert ('Mouseman') 58, 69–70, 96, 121
Thornton-le-Dale 33, **141**
Tocketts Mill 29

U
Ugglebarnby 140
Urra Moor 63

V
Vale of York 57, 79
Victoria, Queen 46, 138
Vikings 36, 47, 62, 99, 141

W
Wade's Causeway 30, 90, 94, 121
Wainstones 58
Wakefield, William 69
Walker, Captain John 47
walking 16
Wesley, John 64
West Ayton 125
Westerdale 20, 24, 33
Western Moors 52–87
Westside Track 56
Wheeldale **107**
Wheeldale Moor 94
Whitby 6, 15, 20, 28, **43–47**, 62, 116, 127
Whitby Abbey 23, 41, 62
Whitby jet 46
White Horse of Kilburn 54, 69, 79
Whorlton 66–67
William the Conqueror, King 129
William of Orange, King 25
Wordsworth, Dorothy 120
Wordsworth, William 41, 120

The Automobile Association would like to thank the following photographers and companies for their assistance in the preparation of this book. Abbreviations for the picture credits are as follows – (t) top; (b) bottom; (c) centre; (l) left; (r) right; (AA) AA World Travel Library

1 AA/Mike Kipling; 4/5 AA/Mike Kipling; 8t AA/Mike Kipling; 8b AA/Mike Kipling; 9 AA/Mike Kipling; 10t AA/Mike Kipling; 10b AA/Mike Kipling; 11t AA/Mike Kipling; 11b AA/Mike Kipling; 13 AA/Mike Kipling; 14tl AA/Mike Kipling; 14tr Stephen Gregory; 14b AA/Mike Kipling; 18/19 © Mike Kipling Photography/Alamy; 18r AA/Mike Kipling; 19 AA/Mike Kipling; 21t AA/Mike Kipling; 21b AA/Mike Kipling; 22 AA/Mike Kipling; 23t AA/Mike Kipling; 23b AA/Mike Kipling; 26 AA/Mike Kipling; 31 AA/Mike Kipling; 32 AA/Mike Kipling; 37 AA/Mike Kipling; 40 © Jon Arnold Images Ltd/Alamy; 44/5 AA/Mike Kipling; 50 AA/Mike Kipling; 52/53 AA/Mike Kipling; 55tl AA/Mike Kipling; 55tr AA/Mike Kipling; 55b AA/Mike Kipling; 56 AA/Mike Kipling; 57t AA/Linda Whitwam; 57b AA; 61 © Les Gibbon/Alamy; 65 AA/Mike Kipling; 77 AA/Mike Kipling; 84 AA/Mike Kipling; 86 AA/Richard Newton; 88/89 AA/John Morrison; 88r AA/Mike Kipling; 89 AA/John Morrison; 91tl AA/Chris Coe; 91tr AA/Mike Kipling; 91b AA/Mike Kipling; 92c AA/Mike Kipling; 92b AA/Linda Whitwam; 93t AA/Linda Whitwam; 93c AA/Mike Kipling; 93b AA/Linda Whitwam; 97 AA/Mike Kipling; 103 AA/Mike Kipling; 106 AA/Mike Kipling; 111 AA/Mike Kipling; 112 © Christine Whitehead/Alamy; 114/115 AA/Mike Kipling; 117tl AA; 117tr AA/Mike Kipling; 117b AA/Linda Whitwam; 118c AA/Mike Kipling; 118bl AA/Mike Kipling; 118br AA/John Morrison; 119t AA/Mike Kipling; 119b AA/Mike Kipling; 126 AA/Richard Newton; 131 AA/Mike Kipling; 139 AA/Peter Wilson; 146/7 AA/Mike Kipling; 151 AA/Mike Kipling; 152/3 AA/Mike Kipling.

Every effort has been made to trace the copyright holders, and we apologise in advance for any accidental errors. We would be happy to apply the corrections in the following edition of this publication.